WRIGLEY
BLUES

WRIGLEY BLUES

The Year the Cubs Played Hardball with the Curse (but Lost Anyway)

WILLIAM J. WAGNER

TAYLOR TRADE PUBLISHING

Dallas ❖ *Lanham* ❖ *Boulder* ❖ *New York* ❖ *Toronto* ❖ *Oxford*

Published by Taylor Trade Publishing
An imprint of The Rowman & Littlefield Publishing Group, Inc.
4501 Forbes Boulevard, Suite 200
Lanham, MD 20706

Distributed by NATIONAL BOOK NETWORK

Library of Congress Cataloging-in-Publication Data

Wagner, William J., 1964–
    Wrigley blues : the year the Cubs played hardball with the curse
(but lost anyway) / William J. Wagner.—1st Taylor Trade Pub. ed.
        p.   cm.
    Includes index.
    ISBN 1-58979-212-2 (pbk. : alk. paper)
    1. Chicago Cubs (Baseball team)—History—20th century.   I. Title.
GV875.C6W34   2005   2004020694

⊚ ™ The paper used in this publication meets the minimum requirements of American National Standard for Information Sciences—Permanence of Paper for Printed Library Materials, ANSI/NISO Z39.48-1992.

Manufactured in the United States of America.

*To Cassie, Cole, and Olivia. Unlike the Cubbies,
you're always winners at the end of a long day.*

CONTENTS

PREFACE

I'm one of you. Over the years, I've dreamed hundreds of dreams and died hundreds of deaths with the Lovable Losers. The 2004 season was no different. Unbridled optimism eventually turned into yet another layer of scar tissue.

So goes the cycle of Cubdom.

I've been a sports journalist for nearly two decades. As such, I'm supposed to be surly, jaded, and curmudgeonly—and for the most part, I am. When the games become a job, they lose some of their luster. The Cubs, however, always have been the exception. Through it all, I've maintained a soft spot for these bumbling fools from Chicago's North Side.

I'm sure it goes back to my childhood, as these things usually do. My friends and I would pedal our bicycles to the El station in the northern suburb of Wilmette, then ride the rails to Wrigley Field. Once at the shrine, I would pitter-patter up the stairs of the concourse and catch my first glimpse of the outfield grass, the ivy, and the scoreboard. Without fail, I would get goose bumps. No other feeling compared to it. And the fact that the Cubs rarely won? It didn't seem to matter. I was just a kid, and I didn't know anything different. I figured the Cubs were *supposed* to lose. In hindsight, I guess I was wise beyond my years.

My first taste of what it means to be a Cubs fan came in 1969. I was only five, so the details of the team's epic collapse were lost on me. But I knew something was amiss. I sensed it in the dark cloud that seemed to hang over everyone around me for weeks after the season ended.

By 1984, I was in college . . . and in uncharted territory. For the first time in my life, the Cubs weren't losers. They were in the playoffs, and I wasn't quite sure how to deal with this sudden turn of good fortune. In the first two games of the National League Championship Series, it was easy. I skipped class, commandeered a choice seat in front of the TV at my fraternity house, and watched the Cubs throttle the San Diego Padres.

"This winning thing is awesome," I said to my friends.

Then the Cubs stopped winning. I watched in horror as they lost Game 3. I watched in even more horror as they lost Game 4, washing this one down with a few beers. By the decisive Game 5, I was slumped in front of the TV with a bottle of Jim Beam in my hand, taking monstrous swigs out of it as the final scenes of unspeakable horror unfolded. It took awhile to recover from 1984—from the hangover and the epic collapse. In fact, that term at school, I wound up getting my worst grades ever. Within five months or so, though, I had taped myself back together and was moving on with my life.

I dealt with things much better in 1989. The Cubs didn't even turn me into a candidate for the Betty Ford Clinic. I was in the working world now—I had responsibilities—and I couldn't afford to let the Cubs crush me. I cut out of work to watch their playoff games against the San Francisco Giants, of course, but I stayed relatively sober. When Chicago folded this time, I lapsed into only a mild depression. I figured this edition of the Cubs—which was long on heart but didn't have an abundance of talent—went about as far as it deserved to go, anyway. Within a month or so, I was back to normal.

In 1998, I was courageous again in the face of defeat. I had a wife and a kid now—people were depending on me—and I had to be strong. These Cubs eked out a berth in the playoffs as a wild card, then were promptly launched into oblivion by the Atlanta Braves.

But again, this was a team that went about as far as it deserved to go. Within a few weeks or so, I was changing diapers again and performing my other duties around the household.

The 2003 season? Well, this one was brutal. The Cubs were within five outs of the World Series when the inevitable collapse occurred. I had two kids now, and the mood in the Wagner household was decidedly gloomy. It was a week before I even could talk to anybody. My kids feared for me, I think—but how could I possibly explain to these two angels that the curse had just delivered a sucker punch? I couldn't, not in a way their little minds would comprehend. So somehow, I stoically taped myself back together—for their sake. Within three months or so, I had a bounce in my step again.

Then came 2004. This time, I really jumped into the blue abyss—I decided to write a year-in-the-life type of book about Cubdom. I'd write about the players, the fans, the neighborhood, the ballpark, the strange history of the team—the whole ball of wax. I'd capture the essence of this quirky culture. I figured this was the perfect year to do it. The Cubs actually were expected to contend for the World Series title in 2004, and this unique hook would make the freakishness that accompanied every season even more exaggerated and plentiful.

I was right. In fact, I got more than I bargained for—much more. From weird injuries to clubhouse implosions to fans sitting on pins and needles to a ballpark that began falling apart, it was among the most fascinating and morbidly funny Cubs seasons ever, complete with the requisite collapse at the end.

So goes the cycle of Cubdom.

The years keep passing, and the Cubs keep losing. But amid all of the scar tissue in my heart, a soft spot remains. I'm 40 now, and I still get those same goose bumps every time I catch my first glimpse of the outfield grass, the ivy, and the scoreboard.

Better times are ahead for the Cubbies. That's what keeps us going. Next year is only four or five years away.

ACKNOWLEDGMENTS

The refrain is always the same for anyone who writes a book: "This was a lot more work than I thought it would be." How true it is. Writing a book is a monumental undertaking—but when all is said and done, it also is extremely fulfilling.

This book was particularly difficult, given that I wrote it as the season progressed, with no real idea of what the ending would bring. Sure, I figured the Cubs would lose, but I didn't know exactly how it would happen. Despite the tricky logistics, I'm glad I wrote it in this manner. Had I waited until the season ended to put a pen to paper, the book would have lacked the emotional punch I was able to give it.

Of course, this unique approach wouldn't have worked as well as it did without the able efforts of the people at Taylor Trade, including Rick Rinehart, Jehanne Schweitzer, Nancy Rothschild, and Tracy Miracle. I also owe a debt of gratitude to Jill Langford, who helped get the project off the ground.

A special thanks goes to my baseball buddy Bob Kuenster. Without him, the road would have been a lot rockier. Not only did he spend endless hours talking with me about all things stick and ball, he did some valuable legwork on my behalf. A tip of the cap also goes to another baseball buddy, Jim McArdle. Actually, Jim is much more than a baseball buddy. We've known each other for so long now, our friendship transcends baseball, journalism, and all of the other work-related stuff.

Thanks to Ann Cole for hatching a few great ideas for the book. Ann is the best at brainstorming, but more important, she's a dear friend.

The splendid photography comes from David Durochik and Chris Dolack. I've been working with these two pros for several years, and I'm sure future endeavors will continue to draw us together.

I would be remiss if I didn't acknowledge my ne'er-do-well buddies from the e-mail party line: Dirt, Stench, Dick, Stink, and Scratch. We created the party line to maintain our sanity way back in the Bullpen days, and it always has been a fertile breeding ground for ideas. I also want to thank my lifelong pal, Bill Bennett. We've watched more Cubs games together than I can remember, and he takes losing as hard as I do.

Of course, nothing I accomplish in life would be possible without my family. It all starts with my wife, Cassie, and my kids, Cole and Olivia. Thanks, thanks, and thanks again for being so understanding while I was at the ballpark or spending nights and weekends writing this beast.

I owe a ton of thanks to my parents for steadfastly supporting everything I've ever done. My mother exposed me to the beauty of baseball; my father exposed me to the beauty of the written word. Somehow it all came together here.

And where would I be without my sister, Suzanne, who is my most trusted confidant? Suzanne is the rock of the family. Meanwhile, my brother, Clark, is my best friend. I learned all about the national pastime playing Strat-O-Matic Baseball with Clark when we were kids. And I forgive him for locking me out of the house on the many occasions I beat him.

Finally, thanks to the countless Cubs fans out there. Without their passion, there would have been no reason to write this book.

PROLOGUE

At the end of the movie *Apocalypse Now*, the renegade soldier Kurtz, wasted and twisted up inside from the atrocities he has witnessed, is down to his final breath. Kurtz whispers the words, "the horror . . . the horror," then he expires.

Many onlookers at Wrigley Field felt the same way on the night of October 14, 2003. Even by the epic standards of futility the Chicago Cubs had established over the past century or so, this was beyond compare. It was the mother of all meltdowns.

Earlier in the evening, the mood among the 39,577 people in attendance gave no indication of what was to come. The stadium, a sea of blue, was swelling with eager anticipation—and why not? History was in the offing. The Cubs were on the verge of going to their first World Series since 1945. The pesky Florida Marlins had put up a noble fight in the National League Championship Series, but now they were down three games to two and were facing elimination at the hands of Cubs pitcher Mark Prior. The same Mark Prior who was 2-0 with a 1.69 earned run average in the playoffs and had lost only once since July 11.

The script in that Game 6 couldn't have unfolded any better: The Cubs scored one run in the first inning, one in the second, and another in the sixth. All the while, Florida was powerless against Prior's dazzling array of fastballs and breaking balls. With "Mighty" Mark Prior on the bump, a 3-0 lead may as well have been a 12-0 lead.

Then fate intervened.

With one out and a man on second base in the top of the eighth inning, Florida's Luis Castillo lifted a pop fly into the chilly autumn air. It looked harmless enough as it drifted to the edge of the left field stands by the bullpen. Left fielder Moises Alou homed in on the ball, planted, and timed his jump perfectly.

But that ball never did make it into Alou's glove. In the final millisecond, some guy characterized by earphones, glasses, and a Cubs cap—a twentysomething named Steve Bartman, who had the grave misfortune of being in the wrong place at the wrong time— instinctively reached for the ball and knocked it away from Alou. For an instant, time seemed to stand still. The moment ended, however, when Alou went ballistic, slamming his glove to the ground and yelling toward the stands. And just like that, a sort of cosmic chain of events was loosed upon Wrigley Field.

Prior, whose control had been typically outstanding all night, walked Castillo. Then he threw a wild pitch. Then a run came in on a single by Ivan Rodriguez. Then Chicago's Alex Gonzalez, who had the best fielding percentage of any shortstop in the National League, booted a possible inning-ending double-play ball. Then two more runs scored on a double by Derrek Lee. Then, with the vanquished Prior now on the bench, another run crossed the plate on a sacrifice fly by Jeff Conine. Then three more on a double by Mike Mordecai. And then a final one on a single by Juan Pierre.

The score was 8-3. In a span of mere minutes, Chicago's seemingly impenetrable lead had been blown to bits—and so had its dreams of October glory.

The shell-shocked masses turned ugly, chanting "asshole . . . asshole" at Bartman. Decades of pent-up frustration, in the form of ice-cold beer, rained down from the upper deck and onto his section. Finally, for his own safety, security personnel escorted Bartman out of the stadium . . . and into Cubs mythology.

After the game, dozens of fans milled around the Bartman section, looking like zombies from the movie *Night of the Living Dead*. One woman was clad in a Cubs jersey, a Cubs hat, and Cubs mittens. She had come to Wrigley Field that evening for a coronation, but now she found herself at a wake. Looking solemnly at the offending seat, she pointed her blue mitten and said, "They need to tear it out and get rid of it, as sort of an exorcism."

Meanwhile, in a cramped and musty interview room in the bowels of Wrigley Field, Chicago manager Dusty Baker addressed the media horde. He quickly discovered, however, that not everyone there was interested in discussing baseball. Curses were the order of the day: goats, black cats, Bartman. You name it. Baker insisted the talk of a Cubs curse was nonsense, saying, "This isn't over by a long ways." He spoke in the gurgling tone of a drowning man.

This was Baker's first season with the Cubs. Upon arriving at the team's spring training site in Mesa, Arizona, in February, he had coined a battle cry for his troops: WHY NOT US? It seemed a little far-fetched, considering Chicago was coming off a 95-loss season. But there was no denying he was the perfect man for a franchise that, to put it mildly, had an inferiority complex. Not only was Baker a proven winner—just the season before, he had taken the San Francisco Giants to the World Series—but he also exuded a backslapping optimism that was contagious.

From day one, Baker accomplished what so many Cubs managers before him had failed to do: He got his players to believe in themselves. The Cubs exceeded all expectations by eking out the National League Central Division title on the final weekend of the season, and they raised the bar even higher when they beat the heavily favored Atlanta Braves in the National League Division Series. Suddenly, anything and everything seemed possible.

Until Game 6 against the Marlins, anyway.

Now Baker sat in that cramped and musty interview room. He looked worn, like he was shouldering the weight of the world. He was, in fact, only shouldering the weight of Cubdom, but that was heavy enough. Welcome to Chicago, Dusty.

Mathematically, of course, the Cubs weren't dead yet. They still had Game 7, and logic dictated that Chicago had a great chance of winning it. Why? Kerry Wood was pitching. The same Kerry Wood who had outdueled the Braves in the decisive Game 5 of the National League Division Series and had led the major leagues in strikeouts in the regular season with 266.

But logic was a dicey proposition when it came to the Cubbies. An unusually subdued crowd gathered at Wrigley Field for Game 7, hoping for the best but bracing for the worst. The worst occurred before some fans even could find their seats. Struggling with his control, Wood allowed three runs in the first inning. An air of grim resignation settled over the stadium.

In the second inning, however, a miracle occurred: Wood—the pitcher, for crying out loud—sent a three-run blast into the left field bleachers. Tie score. Wrigley Field exploded. The next inning, the Cubs struck again: Alou hit a two-run homer to give his team a 5-3 lead. The place was really rocking now.

Then fate intervened.

Those never-say-die Marlins reclaimed the lead in the fifth inning with three runs. They then knocked the reeling Wood out of the game in the sixth with another run and scored two more in the seventh to go up 9-5. The Cubs countered with one last run in the bottom of the seventh—but it was too little too late.

Game over. Season over.

In the clubhouse, a spent and teary-eyed Wood said he had choked, let the team down. But he was being way too hard on himself. Wood hadn't choked—there simply hadn't been enough strength in that powerful right arm of his to turn the tide of history. This time, the Cubs had brushed right up against the World Series—they had come within five outs of getting there in that calamitous Game 6—but in the end, it remained the stuff of fantasies.

Why not the Cubs? Because they were, well, the Cubs.

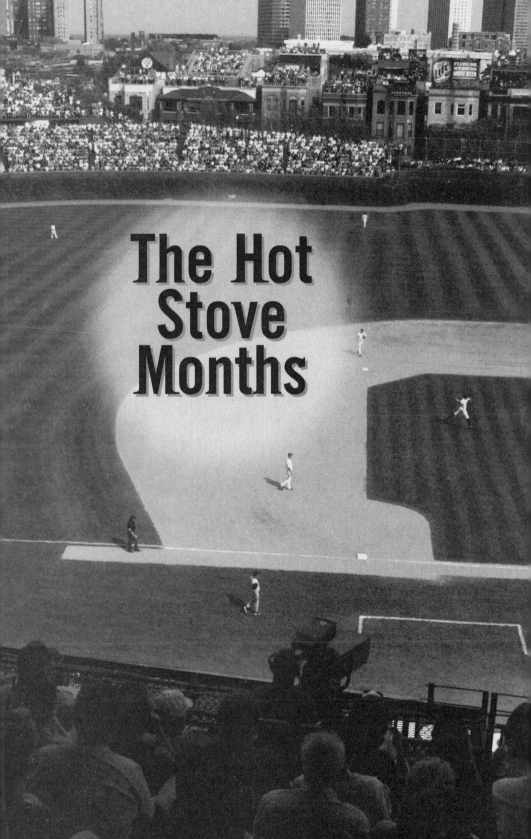

The Hot
Stove
Months

WRIGLEY FIELD
HOME OF
CHICAGO CUBS

**THESE ARE NOT
YOUR GRANDFATHER'S CUBS**

O N E

Cubs fans were a resilient bunch. They had to be. The Cubs had been a baseball power in the first decade of the 20th century, but the team's faithful followers couldn't exactly tout that accomplishment anymore during bar-stool debates. Besides, anyone still alive who had witnessed that golden era probably wouldn't add much to the conversation. Those select few had come full circle: They were in diapers then, they were in diapers now.

The Cubs hadn't won a World Series since 1908 and hadn't been to one since the end of World War II. In the 58 seasons since their last World Series appearance, they had posted a winning record only 15 times. Their overall record in that span was 4,250-4,874 for a winning percentage of .466. In other words, the Cubs would have to go undefeated for nearly four consecutive seasons just to get up to .500. Recent history was equally bleak. Since 1972, they never had put together back-to-back winning seasons.

Watching the Flubs often was excruciating. Therefore, the fans had learned how to find pleasure in the little things. They exhibited their hardy Midwest pride by knocking back a refreshing Budweiser or two as the cold April winds swirled off Lake Michigan and through Wrigley Field. They roared with glee when Sammy Sosa hit a tape-measure home run during another blistering defeat. They bathed in the inviting June sunlight while knocking back a refreshing Special

Export or two. They marveled at the perfectly manicured infield and the lush ivy on the outfield wall.

They made new friends while knocking back a refreshing Old Style or two. They gazed wistfully at the manually operated scoreboard out in center field, which harked back to a simpler, more innocent time. They enjoyed leisurely conversations on cell phones with loved ones. They gawked at the endless parade of beautiful women, who were dressed appropriately in the stifling August heat (meaning they were dressed in almost nothing at all), while knocking back a refreshing Bud Light or two.

Amazingly, in the midst of so much pitiful losing, the stands brimmed with smiling faces.

As the 2003 season receded into history, they even seemed able to swallow the bitter pill that had been Chicago's collapse against the Marlins in the National League Championship Series. The players were getting over it, too. And that was a good thing, since psychologically damaged players equaled piss-poor baseball. By late November, reliever Mike Remlinger had been afforded ample time to ponder the dizzying events of the season. Few ballplayers were more adept at the fine art of pondering than Remlinger, who graduated from Dartmouth College with a degree in economics.

"There's still some healing going on," Remlinger said. "It was at least a couple weeks before I felt like I could really talk about it with anybody. You feel like you were cheated in that you were so close and had such a great opportunity. Knowing how hard it is to come by those opportunities, it's definitely very frustrating. But the key to overcoming that is to look at the expectations coming in and what we were able to accomplish, instead of what we failed at.

"You always go into a season saying you're capable of winning the World Series and all that, but if you look at a team that had the record it did the year before and a lot of younger and unproven players, to end up finishing the way we did was really spectacular," he continued. "We'll take that into next season. I don't think there will be any series we go into where we'll feel like we can't win. The opposite side is that everyone in the league knows how good we are now and will be ready for us. But I think the positive far outweighs the negative in that situation."

Indeed, a new and utterly strange feeling was burrowing into Cubdom: hope. Not the usual blind, misguided hope—but legitimate hope.

This wasn't going to be a repeat of 1985, when the Cubs plummeted to 77-84 following their sudden rise to the National League East Division title. Or 1990, when they went 77-85 after capturing another division title. Or 1999, when they fell off the map altogether with a 67-95 mark after earning a wild-card berth in the playoffs. The teams from those seasons were pathetic. They turned the three shining moments from the post-World War II era—1984 and 1989 and 1998, years etched in the minds of everyone who loved the Cubs—into flukes, teases of the cruelest kind.

But these Cubbies? They seemed different. They had *players*. The roll call started—literally—with two of the best young arms in the business: the 23-year-old Prior and the 26-year-old Wood. Prior was a cool technician, able to work every part of the strike zone with a savvy that belied his two seasons of major league experience; Wood was a bucking bronco, a hard-throwing Texan who was capable of reducing hitters to buckled-kneed pretenders.

Furthermore, Prior and Wood seemed undaunted by their failures in Games 6 and 7 of the National League Championship Series. "They got a taste of it. Because of that, they'll be more hungry," Cubs pitching coach Larry Rothschild surmised. "They were so close, they want to put the final few pieces of the puzzle together. They saw how crazy it can get around here and what a wild ride it was. I think they want to take that ride again. It'll make them better."

The starting rotation didn't begin and end with Prior and Wood, though. Not by a long shot. Chicago had yet another young gun, 22-year-old Carlos Zambrano, who was known as much for his emotional gyrations between pitches as for the wicked sliders he threw. Baker once said that Zambrano had the potential to be the best Cubs starter of them all. It was a bold statement, but not one without merit. In only his first full season in the big leagues in 2003, Zambrano showed the type of feistiness managers love. When the Cubs were hanging on for dear life in August, he stepped to the forefront, going 3-1 that month with a 1.18 earned run average.

And was there a better fourth starter in baseball than Matt Clement, he of the Abraham Lincoln goatee? Clement was hobbled by a sore groin for most of the 2003 season, so his earned run average ballooned to 4.11. But when he was on, his slider was close to unhittable.

The anchor of the bullpen was "Sweaty" Joe Borowski, who looked as if he had just stepped out of the shower by the end of each of his outings, no matter how frigid the day. As recently as 2000, the 225-pound lug had been pitching in the Mexican League. The Cubs gave him a shot, and he stuck in 2002 as a middle reliever. Then when the Cubs thrust him into the closer's role early in 2003 following an injury to incumbent Antonio Alfonseca, he came through with 33 saves. A couple months after the season, management rewarded him with a two-year, $4.5 million contract. Sweaty Joe, age 32, had made it big. "It hasn't fully sunk in yet," he said after inking his new deal. "Knowing that I finally made it here and succeeded takes a load off of me."

These 2004 Cubbies had players, all right. They had Aramis Ramirez, who had the potential to be the team's first third baseman since Ron Santo in the 1960s and early '70s to exhibit any staying power. And young and able center fielder Corey Patterson, who was on his way back from a knee injury that cost him the second half of the 2003 season. And second baseman Mark Grudzielanek, the type of gritty little player who drove opposing teams nuts. And Gonzalez, whose critical error against the Marlins stood in stark contrast to the consistency he brought to his position. And Alou, who had an uncanny ability to deliver hits in the clutch. And, of course, "Slammin'" Sammy Sosa, the team's resident rock star . . . and right fielder.

But there was another, more important reason why the gloom of late October was turning into unbridled optimism: Unlike in the wake of 1984, 1989, and 1998, the team's ownership, the notoriously bottom-line-oriented Tribune Company, was showing a genuine interest in making the roster even better. "They saw last year that they're not necessarily building for something that is still out there—it's here," said Jim McArdle, editor of the Cubs' official publication, *Vine Line.* "Everybody knows that if the Cubs win the World Series, it's a huge story. But all the excitement last year also kind of reminded them of how successful financially they can be if they win." Cubs general manager Jim Hendry was given the OK to unsheathe his ever-present cell phone, and he dialed . . . and dialed . . . and dialed . . . and dialed.

Hendry focused his initial efforts on first base, which had been shared with moderate success in 2003 by Hee Seop Choi, Eric Karros, and Randall Simon. By Thanksgiving, he had traded Choi to the Marlins for Derrek Lee. Later, Hendry tethered Lee to Chicago for the foreseeable future with a three-year, $22.5 million contract extension. Lee was coming off a breakthrough season in which he hit 31 home runs, drove in 92 runs, stole 21 bases, and earned a Gold Glove award. His presence in the batting order would ensure that the Cubs' offense would be a lot more consistent than it had been the past season, when seemingly every game was a heart attack in the making. Score one for the Cubbies.

Then Hendry addressed the team's main shortcoming: middle relief. Throughout most of 2003, the likes of Dave Veres and Mark Guthrie had been gateways to home plate. Now they were gone—and with Christmas closing in, the premier middle reliever in baseball, LaTroy Hawkins, stood before the media at Wrigley Field, wearing a Cubs hat and talking about how happy he was to have just signed a two-year, $11 million free-agent deal. Hawkins's totals from the previous two seasons, spent with the Minnesota Twins, were downright scary: a 15-3 record and a 2.00 earned run average. Score another for the Cubbies.

Finally, the GM sought to add experience and athleticism to the bench. By the end of the holidays, the Cubs had two new presents under their tree: second baseman Todd Walker and outfielder Todd Hollandsworth. That spending spree cost a few more million dollars, but these were starting-caliber players who would provide some pop from the left side of the plate. Walker was a career .290 hitter, while Hollandsworth had been the National League Rookie of the Year in 1996 with the Los Angeles Dodgers. Score one more for the Cubbies.

In two joyous months, Hendry transformed the team's weaknesses into strengths. The long trek back to October had begun.

Cubs Fever was starting to grip Chicago when the team's convention rolled around on January 16 at the downtown Chicago Hilton. This annual gathering had the geeky feel of a *Star Trek* convention. Grown men and women would position themselves strategically at various points in the hotel, communicating with their cohorts via cell phone in an attempt to locate players and then ambush them with autograph requests. The 2004 convention was even more of a circus than usual; the lobby and hallways spilled over with people who were covered from head to toe in Cubs regalia.

The weekend opened with a media social, which was the first official opportunity to talk to the team about the upcoming season. And to think, this year there was something to talk about. The players trickled into the hotel's expansive Boulevard Room, and of special interest were the new faces.

Michael Barrett, signed in December to replace Damian Miller at catcher, surveyed the crowded room with eyes that were bulging. He had the uncertain air of a country boy who'd just arrived in the big city—and with good reason. Barrett had spent the first six years of his major league career in Montreal, where the Expos drew about as many people to their games as the Cubs did to batting practice.

"I'm a little shocked, actually, to be honest with you," Barrett said, his eyes growing wider still. "Coming from a team where we didn't get a lot of coverage and the fans didn't make it out to the ballpark because of all we went through over the years, I've been really shocked by the importance the Cubs have here. It's a little bit of an overwhelming experience, but I feel like I can fit in." Barrett was Chicago's one questionable acquisition. He had hit .208 in an injury-plagued 2003 season, and if he didn't raise that average by several dozen points, his Cubs experience was destined to become even more overwhelming.

Walker, who had spent 2003 with the Boston Red Sox, didn't get rattled by much of anything. Surrounded by new teammates who were slicked up in designer clothes, he looked as if he had crashed this party the same way he might crash into a catcher. Walker, unshaven and his bushy hair askew, clutched a bottle of beer in one hand and a bottle of water in the other. His duds of choice? Faded blue jeans, sneakers, a white T-shirt, and a bomber jacket. This veteran big-leaguer was old school. He was someone who would spare none of his limbs if a game were on the line.

Walker said all the right things, too: "This game is about pitching, and the Cubs have one of the best rotations in the game. You want to be part of something special. The Cubs are as close to winning it all as they've ever been, so I feel like I'm coming in at the right time."

Hollandsworth, meanwhile, was mending fences. He had played for that hated Marlins team in 2003, and he wanted to make it clear he was one of the good guys now. "We had the opportunity last season, we tried to come in here and take care of business, and we did," he said. "We're on the flip side now. We want to make sure it happens for the Cubs the right way this year. We want to give them the opportunity to win the World Series, as well."

The "we" to whom Hollandsworth was referring was his old Marlins teammate Lee. The lanky first baseman wasn't going to captivate the masses with any pearls of wisdom—he was from *Bull Durham*'s "I'm just taking it one game at a time" school of interviewing—but no one would notice as long as he spent the summer hitting home run balls onto Waveland Avenue.

On this day, anyway, Hawkins also didn't have a keen interest in chatting with the media. That was because he was waiting for the opportunity to shake the hand of Mr. Cub himself, Ernie Banks. A native of nearby Gary, Indiana, Hawkins was weaned on Cubs baseball. He grew up idolizing players from the 1980s like Leon Durham, Jody Davis, Keith Moreland, and Ryne Sandberg. Smiling proudly, he said, "I watched most of the games on television." Not only did this LaTroy Hawkins have a killer fastball, but he also bled Cubs blue. It was a perfect match.

The ruffled man at the center of it all was Hendry. As he sipped a glass of wine and took in the moment, he had a glow about him. "We wanted to get good character guys who are winning-type players and wanted to come here," said Hendry, who had been on the job since July 2002. "We've got it going the right way as far as our makeup."

But a GM's work is never really done, is it? There was one vital ingredient still missing from Hendry's World Series brew: Greg Maddux. The great Greg Maddux. Local fans knew him well. The right-handed starter came up with the Cubs, spending the first seven years of his big-league career in Chicago. In 1992, however, the Cubs let him slip through their fingers, and he signed with the Atlanta Braves. While Chicago mostly wallowed, Maddux put together the bulk of his Hall of Fame résumé and the Braves dominated the National League.

The winds of change were kicking up, though. After the 2003 season, the Braves went into a cost-cutting mode and decided to part ways with Maddux. Suddenly, he was there for the taking, and Hendry swooped in. On January 13—after receiving permission from his bosses to boost the payroll even higher, to around $90 million—Hendry offered Maddux a reported two-year, $12 million deal. Although Maddux's prime years were behind him, he remained one of the better pitchers in baseball; he had logged 218 innings and won 16 games in 2003. Even at age 37, he still had enough left to give the Cubs the final push they needed.

Will Maddux sign with the Cubs? Everyone wanted to know. The television crews surrounded Hendry in the Boulevard Room and popped the question: "What about Greg Maddux?"

Hendry: "We'd love to have Greg. But obviously—and rightfully so—he has earned the right to play wherever he wants. If he wants to come back to Chicago, we'd love to have him. I'm sure he'll base the decision on what's best for him and his family. There's not much we can do except hope he decides to come here."

The camera crews moved over to Baker and cornered him.

TV guys: "How hopeful are you about this Maddux thing?"

Baker: "I'm hopeful—I'm very hopeful. We'd like to have him, big time. But if we don't have him, life goes on. That's how this game goes."

Then to Lee.

TV guys: "What would Maddux bring to the Cubs?"

Lee: "We already have a great pitching staff. If we can add a guy like him, it will do nothing but help. So I encourage him to come to Chicago."

And so on and so on and so on.

A player who wasn't even at the convention was hogging the spotlight from the ones who were. But this wasn't mindless media hype—the intense interest in the subject was understandable. Imagine a starting rotation featuring Prior, Wood, Zambrano, Clement, *and* Maddux. Holy cow. It would be the most feared rotation in baseball.

THE SECOND COMING

TWO

As legend had it, the Cubs curse was cast on October 6, 1945, before Game 4 of the World Series. Chicago had been to six World Series and lost them all since last raising a championship banner in 1908, but now it seemed poised to snip that string of near misses. Not only did the Cubbies lead the Detroit Tigers two games to one, but the remainder of the Series would be played on their home turf on Chicago's North Side.

On that fateful day, 42,924 people descended on Wrigley Field. Actually, 42,924 people and a goat. The goat belonged to one William Sianis, a local tavern owner. When ushers denied the dirty beast entry into the ballpark, Sianis grew livid and unleashed the curse by uttering these words: "Cubs, they not gonna win anymore."

Lose they did. The Cubs lost that game. They lost that World Series. And eventually, they lost all hope. Was the curse really to blame? The question had been argued ad nauseam, but this much was certain: Those post-goat years defied reason. They made even the most grounded, sound-minded observers gaze up at the sky in disbelief.

The 1969 season was a real head-scratcher. The Cubs had three future Hall-of-Famers on their roster that year—first baseman Ernie Banks, left fielder Billy Williams, and starting pitcher Fergie Jenkins— and they played like it through the first five months. By the end of August, Chicago was 82-52 and had a four-game lead over the New York Mets.

Only eight days later, however, that lead had dwindled to a game and a half. On the ninth day, during a critical matchup against the Mets at Shea Stadium, a fan released a black cat near the Cubs' dugout. Some players laughed as the cat danced in front of the team's bench, but no one was amused after the game. The Cubs had lost 7-1. They lost again the next night to the Philadelphia Phillies, relinquishing their 155-day hold on first place. When the season came to a merciful end on October 2, Chicago was eight games behind the Mets.

Fifteen years later, in 1984, the Cubs finally were back in business. After reaching the playoffs for the first time since 1945, they jumped out to a two-games-to-none lead against the San Diego Padres in the best-of-five National League Championship Series. Even after the Padres tied the series, the Cubs were sitting pretty in the decisive game at San Diego's Jack Murphy Stadium. The ace of the staff, Rick Sutcliffe, had been his usual splendid self for most of the evening, and he entered the bottom of the seventh inning with a 3-2 lead.

Then with one out and a man on second, San Diego's Tim Flannery hit a grounder to first baseman Leon Durham, who mysteriously morphed into a croquet wicket. The ball rolled right through his legs and into the outfield, bringing in the tying run and opening the floodgates. By the end of the inning, the Cubs were losing 6-3. Once again, they were down for the count.

And 19 years after the Durham incident, Bartman came out of the night and snatched that foul ball from Moises Alou. The curse lived.

The uninitiated scoffed at the curse. Hollandsworth, for instance, had seen nothing metaphysical in the Bartman game from his vantage point in the Marlins dugout. "You can't blame that man—you can't blame that man," Hollandsworth said of Bartman. "That poor man. You can *try* to blame Steve Bartman, but we went out there and took care of business. The Cubbies had the opportunity to put us away, and we fought back. Wherever the opportunity was, we grabbed hold of it, whether it was a fan getting in the way or an error." Hollandsworth's take on the curse wasn't surprising. After all, players can't perform to the best of their abilities if they don't believe they're acting autonomously. This year, though, Hollandsworth would be sitting in the other dugout.

More than a few good men before Hollandsworth had been pushed to the brink. Mark Grace was a fixture at first base for the Cubs for more than a decade. With matinee-idol looks to go along with a .300 career batting average and Gold Glove fielding skills, he was a fan favorite. One August day at Wrigley in 2000, when Chicago was out of contention and well on its way to another 90-plus-loss season, Grace was relaxing in the dugout after batting practice. Seated next to him was Bobby Dernier, the former Cubs center fielder who was subbing in the radio booth for an ailing Ron Santo. As the two men talked, Grace lit a cigarette and took a drag off it. He then fixed his baby blues on the cig, studied it as smoke billowed through the dugout. Finally, Grace sighed and said to Dernier, "You know, I never smoke these things in the off-season. That's what thirteen years of being on the Cubs has done to me."

The next year, Grace no longer was on the Cubs. He was the first baseman for the Arizona Diamondbacks. And at long last, he also was a winner. In one of the most exciting World Series in recent history, the Diamondbacks toppled the mighty New York Yankees in seven games.

The curse manifested itself in other ways, too—such as front-office idiocy. The most notorious move occurred in 1964, when Chicago traded an outfield prospect named Lou Brock to the arch-rival St. Louis Cardinals for veteran pitcher Ernie Broglio. Brock went on to capture two World Series titles, set the all-time record for stolen bases, and earn induction into the Hall of Fame. Broglio? He won a total of seven games in his two and a half seasons in Chicago.

In 1977, Cubs owner Philip K. Wrigley was irritated by the contract demands of young third baseman Bill Madlock, who had just won his second straight batting title. Madlock was shipped to the San Francisco Giants in exchange for Bobby Murcer, a right fielder who was a couple of years past his prime. Madlock went on to win two more batting titles, as well as a World Series with the Pittsburgh Pirates. Murcer? In his very first game with the Cubs, at Wrigley Field against those damn Mets, he and center fielder Jerry Morales got their signals crossed on a fly ball to the gap and collided. While the dazed and confused outfielders attempted to gather themselves, the ball rolled toward the ivy, sparking the winning rally for New York. Within a few years, Murcer was plying his craft elsewhere.

But those missteps were ancient history. The gaffe for a new generation of Cubs fans involved none other than Maddux. The right-hander emerged as a bona fide star in 1992, capturing the Cy Young Award after winning a National League-leading 20 games and posting a Tom Seaver-like earned run average of 2.18. Maddux also happened to be a free agent at season's end. For those cost-conscious Cubbies, it was a combination that spelled disaster. On December 9, following a round of contentious negotiations with Chicago, he signed a five-year, $28 million contract with the Braves.

Maddux publicly claimed it was all about joining a winner—and Atlanta certainly fell into that category, having played in the World Series the previous season—but there was more to the matter than that. Maddux, a player with fierce pride, also felt betrayed by the organization that had nurtured him. After the deal went down, one of his former Cubs teammates, pitcher Mike Morgan, told the *Chicago Tribune*: "It wasn't the money. I think it was just the principle of the matter, that he wanted them [the Cubs] to come up on their number—five-hundred grand or a million dollars or whatever—just to come up. So he decided to leave."

According to the *Tribune*, Maddux's agent, Scott Boras, even called Cubs general manager Larry Himes only hours before the signing with the Braves was announced in a last-ditch effort to keep his client in Chicago. The Cubs, however, already had used up the money that had been earmarked for Maddux. Said an oblivious Himes of the turn of events, "Isn't it amazing?" Nah. It was about what most longtime followers of the Cubs had been conditioned to expect.

And wouldn't it figure that the moment Maddux put on that

Braves uniform, he became Superman, going from *one of the best pitchers in the game today* to *one of the best pitchers who ever lived?* Maddux's numbers from his seven seasons in Chicago were solid: a 95-75 record and a 3.35 earned run average. In his 11 seasons in Atlanta, however, they were off the charts. He went 194-88 with a 2.63 earned run average, and won the Cy Young Award three more times. Maddux was the constant in an incredible run for the Braves. They reached the playoffs every year he was on the team, including three trips to the World Series and one championship. Worse yet—from the perspective of those twitching folks in Cubdom, anyway—Maddux was particularly dominant against his former team. He seemed hell-bent on reminding the Flubs of their grievous mistake; in 20 games against them, he was 11-3 with a 2.39 earned run average.

Over the decades, the Cubs' house of horrors had been built brick by misplaced brick. Players came and went, managers came and went, and front-office personnel came and went—but the results remained eerily the same. This current regime, however, was determined to construct something that was easier on the eyes. There was nothing Hendry and company could do about 1969 or 1984 or Brock-for-Broglio or Madlock-for-Murcer or so many of the other blunders, but it was within their power to right the wrong that had been Maddux's acrimonious departure to Atlanta. Not that atoning for the past was a central part of their thinking. For Baker, the man responsible for turning the pieces at his disposal into a contender, it was as practical as this: "This guy's a winner."

After Hendry made his initial offer in mid-January, the long wait began. At times, it felt as if the prospect of Maddux's return was a typical Cubs pipe dream. Would he sign with the Cardinals? What about the Giants? Or the Dodgers? Or the Baltimore Orioles? No one knew . . . except Maddux. And he wasn't in a hurry to show his hand. Even the Yankees, who already had collected seemingly every noteworthy player in baseball, were rumored to be interested.

On February 18, however, the word spread quickly: Maddux had agreed to a two-year, $15 million contract with Chicago, with an option for a third year. It was more money than the Cubs had planned to spend, but they had gotten their man. That day, Maddux was re-introduced to Cubdom in a press conference at HoHoKam Park in Mesa. The smooth, boyish face of years past now was weathered, with lines streaking across it. But as he slipped into a Cubs jersey—adorned with his old number 31—he sure looked good.

"I was a little bit crushed when they booted me out eleven years ago," Maddux said to the media. "Now it's a whole new regime, and I feel honored to be invited back. It's nice to be back. I know when I left Chicago, I wasn't ready to leave the first time."

Several of Maddux's admirers gathered at the entrance of HoHo-Kam Park, hoping to catch a glimpse of him as he drove off following the day's activities. One woman, grinning from ear to ear, said, "This is better than A-Rod." She was talking about shortstop-turned-third-baseman Alex Rodriguez, whom the Yankees had acquired two days earlier in a blockbuster trade with the Texas Rangers. On the surface, it was a ludicrous statement. Rodriguez, a career .308 hitter who was on pace to break the all-time home run record, was the reigning Most Valuable Player of the American League. Although Maddux still was plenty good, he no longer was in that class, and hadn't been for a couple of years. Hell, he wasn't even the best pitcher on the Cubs.

But the woman might have been onto something. Maddux's value to the Cubs wouldn't be evident solely in his stats. There also was a certain celestial symmetry to his signing. With one stroke of the pen, good karma had replaced bad karma—at least some of the weight of history pressing down on the Cubs had been relieved. Maybe, just maybe, that would be enough.

IN SEARCH OF THE
ACHILLES' HEEL

THREE

Certain doom, real or imagined, always was lurking around some corner in Cubdom. The trick was pinpointing which corner. It had been a glorious off-season, to be sure—but could disaster be more than a few paces away? After all, the Cubs were playing baseball now.

Spring training never began in earnest without Slammin' Sammy Sosa, the man who had been the face of the franchise ever since he hit 66 homers in 1998. This year, he said he was so excited about Chicago's chances that he even was planning to arrive in Mesa *on time*. Imagine that. And sure enough, on the day position players were due to report—February 24—Sosa rolled into HoHoKam Park, looking buff in a tight-fitting V-neck shirt.

A buzz followed Sosa wherever he went, as did a pack of reporters. Sosa's sound bytes were big news—and on this day, the press wanted to know how he thought he would fit in on these new-look Cubs. As he strutted through the parking lot at HoHoKam Park, the media chased him like starving dogs going after raw meat.

"Is this still your team?" asked one reporter.

"What do you think?" Sosa shot back, flashing his trademark smile.

A few years earlier, that question wouldn't have been asked. Sosa was the biggest name in the game, banging out homers with a flair that dwarfed even the Babe. And against a backdrop of second-rate talent on the Cubs, his feats seemed even more grand. Before one game at Wrigley Field in August 2001, Sosa sat in the dugout with a writer and discussed his career. He spoke quietly, almost in a whisper, his hushed tone dramatizing his point: He was a man of action, not words. "This is my house—there's no doubt about that. I'm the kind of person who doesn't like to say too much. My attitude is going to determine everything, and the way that I play. I lead through that."

But now, at 35, Sosa was getting on in years. Besides, the Cubs had plenty of other leaders. Prior and Wood had come of age in 2003, and Maddux, Hawkins, and Lee had been added to the mix in the off-season. Would Sammy be willing to share the house? Would he be "Selfless" Sammy Sosa? Or would the pieces Hendry had stacked so carefully be knocked asunder?

Chicagoans had a love-hate relationship with Sosa. Most people lauded the numbers he had put up in his career—the 539 home runs and the 1,450 runs batted in—but his detractors insisted he was more showman than ballplayer. Sosa elicited cheers from the bleachers by sprinting to his position in right field before games; he thrilled the masses by hopping in the batter's box after each home run, like he had just won Game 7 of the World Series. He often said he played the game the way he did to please his fans, but where, the critics wondered, had that gotten his team? Slammin' Sammy was a theme-park ride, Wrigley Field's equivalent of Space Mountain.

He was a hot-button topic on Chicago's sports-talk radio—the mere mention of his name often would light up the phone lines. "First and foremost, Sammy Sosa wouldn't be such a polarizing figure without the success he has had," said Dan Bernstein, co-host of a daily show on the all-sports radio station WSCR. "The issue is, what does he want? If you told him he could be the greatest slugger of all time or win a World Series, what would he want? He believes all the superhero stuff. He believes his own hype. He really thinks he's a gladiator."

The problem was, chinks had developed in Sosa's armor, particularly in 2003. After being nailed on the head by a fastball on April 20 of that season, he began approaching his at-bats with uncharacteristic skittishness. Soon after that, he was felled by an infected toe, which put him on the disabled list for three weeks. When the Cubs arrived in Tampa on June 3 for a series against the Devil Rays, Sosa was looking decidedly mortal. He had hit only one home run since his beaning and had struck out eight times in his past 15 at-bats.

That night, he took a Sammy-size hack at a pitch, but the ball didn't sail over the fence. There wasn't a hop, a skip, or even a jump—only a shower of wood and cork after his bat shattered. Sammy Sosa, gladiator *maximus*, was busted for cheating. Corkgate produced a seven-game suspension for Sosa, but more significantly, it brought the wrath of the media down on him, creating a distraction that nearly derailed the Cubs' season.

Bernstein wasn't a bit surprised by that unsavory episode, and he sensed the possibility for similar shenanigans in 2004. "It used to be enough for Sammy to hit his home runs, but once the Cubs started winning, the expectations changed," he said. "Sammy's a phony when it comes to being a team leader. If he starts to show signs of his game deteriorating, he could become a distraction. Desperate men can do desperate things."

Would Cubdom's inevitable corner of doom veer toward Sammy's locker? It was an easy spot to find. Located near the entrance of the clubhouse, his double-wide fiefdom contained an ever-blaring boombox that drowned out all the other voices in the room.

Back in Chicago, the faithful had taken matters into their own hands. Before the Cubs could build that bright and shiny future, the forlorn past had to be blown away. So on the evening of February 26, the Bartman ball was lined with explosives and sacrificed to the baseball gods.

The ball had been purchased for a whopping $113,000 by Grant DePorter, a local restaurateur who had been a friend of the late Cubs broadcasting legend Harry Caray. DePorter was using the stunt to raise money for the Juvenile Diabetes Research Foundation. Through donations and sales of commemorative T-shirts and sweatshirts, he hoped to bring in around a million dollars. Of course, the Cubs were the other charity that might benefit from the deed.

The demolition was to occur outside Harry Caray's Restaurant in downtown Chicago, and hundreds of revelrous fans flooded the streets to see this latest installment in the strange, mostly silly saga of the Cubs. Steve Bartman wasn't among the attendees. Still underground, he said through a spokesperson that he simply wanted to get on with his life.

An Oscar-winning special effects coordinator, Michael Lantieri, was commissioned to work out the tricky logistics of sending the Bartman ball into the next world. To ensure success, he blew up about 40 practice balls back in California before coming to Chicago for the main event. As for the real ball, it was given prime rib, lobster, and a refreshing Budweiser at the Amalfi Hotel Chicago on the eve of its destruction.

When the bells began to toll, ESPN and MSNBC cut in live to Harry Caray's. Their cameras zoomed in on the Bartman ball inside its death chamber, a bullet-proof case. At 7:30 p.m., Lantieri delivered the charge, and the ball exploded into a tangle of string. It was over—for the ball, at least.

A significantly larger mob of fans assembled at Wrigley Field the following morning, when tickets went on sale for the 2004 season. Were they gluttons for punishment? Or would they be witnesses to history? No one knew. The folks who gobbled up more than half a million tickets on that frenzied day simply wanted to come along for the ride. According to Cubs ticket operations director Frank Maloney, that tally nearly doubled the previous major league record for one-day ticket sales.

Derrek Lee never experienced this type of fan interest while playing for the Marlins in Miami, where a half-empty stadium was the norm. But the first baseman already had learned that things were different in Chicago. "It's exciting as a baseball player," Lee said. "These are probably the best fans in the world." Time would tell whether they were indeed the best, or the most gullible.

Maybe that demolitions whiz Lantieri shouldn't have stopped with the Bartman ball. To finish the job, maybe he should have heaved a few cruise missiles in the direction of Wrigley Field and surrounding Wrigleyville. Something had gone horribly wrong, and now it clearly was time to panic.

On March 1, before a single exhibition game was even in the books, the Cubs announced they were shutting down Prior for seven to 10 days because he had an inflamed right Achilles tendon. Everyone did their best to stress that this merely was a precautionary measure. "We're not concerned," Baker reassured. "Things happen. I'd rather have it happen now." The right-handed prodigy wouldn't make all of his spring training starts, but he'd get three or four. That would be plenty. Cubs trainer Dave Groeschner was more than confident that Prior would be ready by the beginning of the season.

The faithful had heard it all before, which was precisely why they were freaking out. In 1998, for instance, Wood arrived on the big-league scene like a bolt of lightning. "Kid" Wood was 20 years old, but his age was nothing more than a number. In just the fifth start of his career, on May 6 against Houston, he pitched one of the greatest games in baseball history. Wood manhandled the offensively loaded Astros, striking out a major league record-tying 20 batters en route to a complete-game 2-0 victory. What's more, he allowed only two base runners, a Texas League single in the third inning and a hit batsman in the sixth. Said Cubs manager Jim Riggleman of his pitching phenom, "He's got a chance to go down along the lines of the best ever."

Instead, Wood simply went down. In August, he began experiencing "arm soreness." It turned out to be a sprained ulnar collateral ligament in his pitching elbow. Not wanting to take any chances with their bonus baby, the Cubs decided to approach his return with extreme caution. Wood sat and he sat and he sat, and before anyone knew it, the season was over.

Unlike most Octobers, however, the Cubs didn't turn their attention to golf, fishing, and other leisurely pursuits. They actually had reached the playoffs as a wild card and would take on Atlanta in the best-of-five National League Division Series. If Wood were needed, said the Cubs, he would be ready. Following two defeats in as many games, he was needed. They lost again in Wood's long-awaited return, but Cubdom was heartened by the fact that he pitched five strong innings.

By late January, Wood was itching to get going again. "I had a follow-up exam about a month ago, and everything looked good," Wood said. "I've been throwing since early January. My arm feels good."

Then spring training began, and his arm fell off. OK, it didn't *technically* fall off, but it may as well have. He blew out that ulnar collateral ligament in his elbow, necessitating major surgery that put him on the shelf indefinitely. Meanwhile, the Cubs' latest rebuilding program—the one that was supposed to center on Wood—quickly fell apart. Wood didn't pitch in the major leagues again until May 2000, and he didn't begin to resemble his former self until the following year.

Now Prior—Chicago's newest phenom, the wonder boy who had gone 18-6 with a 2.43 earned run average in 2003—was experiencing "Achilles soreness." *Gulp.* Compounding matters was the ill health of the team's only two left-handed relievers, Mike Remlinger and Kent Mercker. Remlinger wouldn't be available until late April because he still was recovering from off-season shoulder surgery, while Mercker was being slowed by a touchy back. At this rate, the Cubs would be pulling people off the street in order to fill out their roster—just like in the old days. Hey, maybe Felix Heredia was available.

At least the Cubbies still had Slammin' Sammy. When he launched his first home run of the spring on March 8—a signature blast that landed well beyond the left field fence at HoHoKam Park—the capacity crowd went crazy. While Sammy hopped around like the Easter Bunny, dozens of fans risked life and limb as they tried to retrieve the ball. The dinger was played up prominently that night on the newscasts in Chicago. The talking heads even mentioned that the Cubs won the game, 8-4 over the Milwaukee Brewers. The more things changed, the more they stayed the same.

The lead headline in the sports section of the *Chicago Tribune* on March 11 was enough to make the locals spit out their morning coffee: PRIOR MAY MISS OPENING DAY. Prior was supposed to be pitching by now. He was supposed to be on the comeback trail. Now what?

For starters, I think I'll pour a shot of whiskey into my morning coffee.

Prior, a beacon of stability in this gathering storm, put on a brave face. His Achilles tendon may have been throbbing, but the even-keeled demeanor that had helped him become such an effective pitcher was intact. "I just have to take it day by day," he said.

Relax. Everything will be OK.

Prior's new rehab schedule called for him to begin throwing from the mound on March 13. That plan wound up being scrapped, but on March 16, Mighty Mark Prior was back in action. More important, he still was standing following the workout, which consisted of about 30 pitches. Two days later, he was at it again, this time heaving around 35 pitches. On March 20, Prior threw 40 more pitches from the mound. He was getting stronger every day.

The Cubs are back, baby.

The lead headline in the sports section of the *Chicago Tribune* on March 24 was another coffee-spitter: PRIOR TO BEGIN SEASON ON DL. According to this latest revision to Prior's comeback schedule, he might not pitch his first game until around April 19, two weeks into the season. Nonetheless, the team continued to find a silver lining. Said Hendry, "He's progressing the way we hoped."

Pass the whiskey. The Cubs are doomed.

While Prior sat, everyone else forged ahead. What else were they going to do? Besides, when the Cubs prepared to break camp at the end of March and head north, there were three reasons to believe the 2004 season still could become something magical: Wood, Zambrano, and Maddux. Wood and Zambrano were lights-out throughout spring training, combining for a 9-0 record, while Maddux achieved his simple goal of limbering up the old arm. Clement, on the other hand, spent most of the spring dodging line drives, but he began to cobble his game back together as Opening Day neared.

No, these new-look Cubbies weren't going to blink in the face of adversity. Hendry moved quickly to find a fill-in for the ailing Remlinger, trading pitcher Juan Cruz to the Braves on March 25 for Andy Pratt. The 24-year-old left-hander was raw material, but he had a live arm. Pitching for Triple-A Richmond in 2003, he led the International League in strikeouts with 161.

The other encouraging news centered on Corey Patterson. The center fielder had been Chicago's first pick in the 1998 draft, and he started to show why in 2003. After his first 83 games, Patterson was leading the Cubs in home runs (13), runs batted in (55), and stolen bases (16), and he also was making all the plays in the outfield. But in early July, he tore the anterior cruciate ligament in his left knee while running to first base. As the Cubs continued their improbable march toward the playoffs, Patterson dropped out of sight and into a grueling rehabilitation routine.

By the following winter, his work was done and he proclaimed himself ready to rock. "The knee is doing good. I've been working hard, and I think it will pay off by training camp. I'll definitely be ready by Opening Day. And the knee will be able to handle the wear and tear of 162 games." Baker, however, wasn't convinced. "I need to see him run and see if he has a limp or any mental effects of the injury," the manager cautioned. "You know, you have to get past the mental part of it. And you have to run, turn, jump—there are all sorts of things he has to do before we can say he's 100 percent." Patterson passed every test with flying colors. In fact, he was among the team leaders in at-bats in spring training.

Then there was Sosa, who *always* was on display. With his customary chest-thumping machismo, he declared to the world that his only goal for the season was to win the championship. Some chinks in his gladiatorial armor still were evident—such as the time a fly ball eluded his glove and bounced off his head during an exhibition against the Padres—but his work at the plate was vintage Sosa all the way. He hit at better than a .400 clip during the club's stay in Mesa.

Of course, this being the realm of the half-empty glass, the bad overshadowed the good. Prior's injury woes had taken on a life of their own, much like the curse itself. His return date was pushed back yet again, this time to mid-May or maybe even June. In the meantime, the Cubs were hopeful they could get by with Sergio Mitre. *Sergio who?* He was a homegrown product whose big-league résumé consisted of three games and an 8.31 earned run average. *Pass the whiskey.*

The plot thickened as the curtain fell on spring training. Apparently, Prior's health issues weren't limited to his Achilles tendon. On March 29 back in Chicago, he underwent an MRI and a bone scan on his pitching elbow. The exams revealed no damage to his elbow, but his Achilles tendon remained a sore spot.

Prior called the lingering injury a mystery, something he simply was going to have to wait out. For the faithful, tortured souls that they were, it was indeed a mystery. Would Prior return triumphant and carry the Cubs to their first World Series title in nearly a century? Or would his Achilles tendon, and Chicago's season, blow up like that Bartman ball?

April

WRIGLEY FIELD
HOME OF
CHICAGO CUBS

THE FORECAST IN HELL

FOUR

The Cubs had arrived at what often was the worst part of the season—the part when it actually started. This was when blustery spring training proclamations gave way to the mournful realization that the Opening Day lineup featured Moe Thacker at catcher or Pete LaCock at first base or Dave Rosello at shortstop or Brian Dayett in left field or Jaime Navarro on the mound. It was when Cubs fans came to terms with the fact that their beloved team had absolutely no chance.

But not now, not this year. As March turned to April, the odds of the Cubs winning the World Series weren't 100,000,000-to-1, 1,000-to-1, or even 100-to-1. Odds-makers installed Chicago as anywhere from a 5-to-2 to a 6-to-1 favorite to go all the way, behind only the American League's Yankees and Red Sox. Even with Prior out of commission, Las Vegas loved the Cubbies.

Sports Illustrated loved them, too. When the magazine's 2004 baseball preview issue hit the newsstands the first week of April, Wood was on the cover, accompanied by the following headline and subhead: HELL FREEZES OVER . . . THE CUBS WILL WIN THE WORLD SERIES. "We liked the fact that the Cubs seemed to upgrade themselves in all areas," said Larry Burke, a senior editor for the magazine who oversaw the baseball preview. "We looked at them as a team that was five outs away from winning the pennant last year and got even better. This is the first time I ever remember the Cubs going into a season with any real expectations. When they won in the past, they came out of nowhere. But the expectations kind of create pressure, so it will be interesting to see how they deal with it."

The first test involved how the Cubs would react to the specter of the infamous *Sports Illustrated* jinx, which dictated that something horrific might happen to the team touted on the cover. Apparently, the results of that test weren't promising. "I wasn't involved with the cover directly, but what I heard is that they were a little skittish about the jinx factor," Burke said. "So they didn't really bend over backwards as far as giving us guys for pictures and stuff. I believe this is the first time we've ever picked the Cubs to win the World Series. I haven't researched that, but I can't imagine we ever would have."

For a franchise as goat-stricken as this one, the trepidation over adding another curse to the long list was forgivable. In fact, the *Sports Illustrated* jinx wreaked its havoc before the cover even was fully conceptualized. The magazine's editors originally toyed with putting Prior on the cover, but that idea was shelved when his Achilles tendon went haywire. And who in Cubdom could forget the June 11, 1984, issue, which trumpeted the team's arrival among baseball's elite? The cover subject was Leon Durham, with a headline that screamed, HOW 'BOUT THEM CUBBIES! The jinx didn't strike immediately, but the Cubs fell victim to it that October when their World Series aspirations slipped through Durham's legs.

At any rate, these 2004 Cubs were in basic agreement with the prognosticators. They loved themselves as much as everyone else loved them. For once, they could look in the mirror without getting sick. "As far as everyone's expectations go, there's nothing we can do about that," Baker said. "We raised the bar ourselves. I expect to win, and I expect us to keep winning." EXPECT THE BEST. It sounded like a new-and-improved rallying cry for Baker's troops.

Hell didn't seem quite ready to freeze over during the opener against the Reds on the afternoon of April 5 at Cincinnati's Great American Ball Park, but there was an undeniable nip in the air. The game-time temperature was 45 degrees, with a breeze coming off the banks of the Ohio River. Indeed, as good omens went, Opening Day couldn't have turned out any better.

The most heartening aspect of Chicago's 7-4 victory was the performance of Wood. He stunk. Wood threw 95 pitches and gave up four runs in just five innings, but he was credited with the win, anyway. The snake-bitten right-hander wasn't used to such gifts. In his 11 losses in 2003, the Cubs scored an average of 2.45 runs; in six of those games, they scored two or fewer runs. Now, though, Wood didn't have to do anything except drive the team bus in order to pick up a W. For a change, the offense proved capable of bringing *him* along for the ride.

Patterson delivered the most dramatic of Chicago's 10 hits. In his very first at-bat of the season, he homered to give the Cubs a 1-0 lead and serve official notice that his knee rehabilitation was complete. In addition, the retooled bullpen shimmered with four scoreless innings, although Sweaty Joe Borowski was particularly soaked after this one. He walked two batters in the bottom of the ninth inning to bring the tying run to the plate—a heart-in-your-throat reminder that these were, after all, still the Cubs—but the final outcome set what seemed like a curse-busting tone.

Everyone was feeling as if a new day had dawned, from the thousands of Cubs fans who made the pilgrimage to Great American Ball Park to the roughly 220,000 households that tuned in to the game on Chicago's Fox Sports Net, a record for the network for a season-opening broadcast. Amid all the excitement of the afternoon, few people even noticed Prior playing catch in the bullpen, his first activity of any kind in two weeks.

While his teammates celebrated the Opening Day win, Maddux was looking ahead to the next game of the series on April 7. It would be his first start for the Cubs since September 30, 1992. Maddux Redux had created such a stir that he needed a microphone and a table that served as a podium so that he could share his thoughts about the upcoming milestone. So much for cozy locker-side chats— this had the heady feel of a White House press briefing. With dozens of ears perked, Maddux delivered his state of Cubdom address: "I hope I don't feel any different. Hopefully, I'll have the same amount of butterflies as in the past. It's a new team, but the same game."

The same game? Maybe for Rick "Wild Thing" Vaughn from the movie *Major League,* but not for the silky-smooth Maddux. After nearly two months of buildup, the Maddux Redux era arrived with a thud, literally. He beaned D'Angelo Jimenez with his very first pitch and then plunked Ken Griffey Jr. two batters later. In 576 career games, this was the first time Maddux had hit two batters in the same inning. Shortly thereafter, those *thuds* turned into *whacks*: a solo home run by Adam Dunn in the second inning and a two-run homer by Griffey in the third.

Maddux then re-emerged as the craftsman of yore, pitching three more innings without allowing a run. But unlike Wood in the opener, he received no favors from his offense. Except for a home run by Lee in the ninth inning that cut Cincinnati's lead to 3-1, these Cubs hitters looked suspiciously like the ones from Maddux's first tour of duty with the team. A dribbler off the bat of Gonzalez to shortstop Barry Larkin ended Chicago's winning streak at one. Its undefeated season was history. After the game, Maddux was back behind his makeshift podium. "Sometimes you have to win 1-0, 2-1," he said. "I didn't do that."

Neither did Clement the next afternoon in the rubber game. He got shelled en route to a 5-3 Cubs loss, lasting only four innings and yielding four runs and six hits. But for a moment, anyway, they were dancing in the streets back in Chicago. Slammin' Sammy hit his first home run of the season.

A mere three games had been played, but the Cubbies already were showing signs of cracking. After his dismal outing against Cincinnati,

Clement told *USA Today*, "We know we're expected to win. There are many examples of teams in baseball history that were loaded and didn't win." Translation: The season still was very young—the Cubs had 159 more chances to lose.

On the evening of April 9, in the first of a three-game series against the Braves in Atlanta, the Cubs seemed determined to snatch defeat from the jaws of victory once again. Not even Zambrano was capable of stopping the negative momentum Chicago was building. He picked up right where he had left off in spring training, allowing only one run and two hits in seven innings. The Cubs, however, squandered opportunity after opportunity and scored a grand total of zero runs in that same span.

By the top of the ninth inning, the score still was 1-0. Worse yet, John Smoltz, one of the most reliable closers in baseball, was on the mound for Atlanta. With two outs, no one on base, and the Cubs staring down the barrel of a 1-3 start to this season of great expectations, Hollandsworth dug in as a pinch hitter. Cubdom was on pins and needles. "Early on as a bench player, your at-bats can get spread out a little bit," Hollandsworth said. "You keep yourself ready, and you get in there and hope you get a pitch you can handle off a guy like Smoltz." He got one. Just as he had promised at the convention back in January, Hollandsworth made things right for the Lovable Losers, hitting a 422-foot homer to tie the score.

Six agonizing innings of scoreless ball later, after the clock had struck midnight in Atlanta, Tom Goodwin pushed the go-ahead run across the plate for Chicago on a sacrifice fly and then Borowski made the lead stick in the bottom of 15th. The sleep-deprived Cubs were wobbly, but they still were standing. And the man propping them up was Hollandsworth, who had come through with the biggest hit of the young season. "That was my first hit as a Cub, and it was meaningful," Hollandsworth said. "That's what you hope for. It was exhilarating. You get back in the game right there. We got our breath back, so to speak. We were down to our last gasp, but we pulled one back from the beyond. We needed that game, and we got it. I was thanking the Lord all night for the opportunity to come through like that."

About 18 hours after that marathon, the two teams were at it again. This game unfurled in the same manner the first one did, with a notable exception: Chicago lost. Hollandsworth hit another home run to tie the score at 1-1, this time in the fifth inning. The Cubs also received an outstanding effort from their starting pitcher, Mitre, who did his best impersonation of Prior. When Mitre was lifted with two outs in the bottom of the eighth inning, he had allowed only five hits and was winning 2-1. It was looking as though it might be smooth sailing for these Prior-less Cubbies after all. Then the bullpen sprung a leak, and the Braves scored four runs.

The numbers from those first two games in Atlanta hardly were befitting of a team that had opened the season as the apple of everyone's eye: Chicago was 0-for-17 with men in scoring position and had struck out 18 times. The Cubs needed a breakout game—and they needed one quick. When the hitters were hitting, the pitchers had to pitch, and vice versa. Right on cue, that's exactly what happened the next afternoon in the series finale. The pitchers pitched: Wood threw seven innings of one-run, five-hit ball, and he tied a franchise record by striking out seven consecutive batters. And the hitters hit: Alou, Gonzalez, Barrett, and Patterson all homered in the 14-hit onslaught. The final score: Cubs 10, Braves 2. *That* was more like it.

The Cubs hadn't looked like world-beaters on this season-opening road swing, but they had managed to go 3-3. They'd take it. Clement even was feeling more upbeat than he had been a few days earlier. "It's a long season, but it turned out to be a good road trip," he said. "A good start is always going to make things go smoothly, and you don't want to put yourself in a hole. We were at a point in our road trip that it could have been a bad start if we didn't win that long game in Atlanta. I think that was key."

Besides, things only would get better. The Cubs were headed back to Chicago for their home opener.

WRIGLEY FIELD
HOME OF
CHICAGO CUBS

OPENING DAY

FIVE

Around this time each year, a 24-hour virus swept through the Chicago area. It was a nasty little bug, one that depleted the rolls in offices and schools alike. Call it the Blue Flu. In 2004 it struck on April 12, and the region's educational and economic institutions ground to a halt as throngs of people flocked to Wrigleyville to see the Cubs' home opener against the Pirates.

The weather was enough to give anyone the chills. The thermometer hovered in the low 40s, and a stiff wind made it feel even colder than that. At least the sun was shining, which was more than some years offered. In 2003, for instance, the home opener was *snowed* out. To ensure that there would be baseball the following day, the team's white-collar workers were stirred from their cubicles within the front office at Wrigley Field and given shovels so that they could clear snow from the seats and aisles. And there was indeed baseball, with icicles hanging from the railings in the dugout and everyone decked out in their winter gear.

This year, the festivities began with Prior ringing the opening bell at the Chicago Board of Trade. It wasn't as if he had anything else to do. Several miles to the north, at the intersection of Clark and Addison, the rest of the players were preparing for their much-heralded Wrigley Field debut. The Cubs had survived their season-opening road trip, and now that they were back in the Friendly Confines, the World Series Express really would start rolling.

"To come home at .500 and be ready to go, that was a big thing," Clement said after limbering up in the outfield. "I love being here—I love Chicago. I love this field, this whole setup here. It's great with the fans. It's a little chilly here, but I wouldn't have it any other way. It's just exciting to get going. Your adrenaline is definitely pumping at a high level. Everybody's here for us—this stadium is filled for us. That's part of the excitement and the advantage of playing at Wrigley Field. But we know we have to stay focused."

No one was better at doing that than wily old Maddux, who had the honor of being the home-opening starter. Clement hadn't talked to Maddux that day—it was an unwritten rule that no one talked to a starter before he was due to pitch—but he wasn't the least bit worried about his teammate. "The guy's got almost 300 wins, so I think he knows how to get ready," Clement said. "You just have to take Opening Day as a regular day."

That's how Slammin' Sammy was treating it. For him, this merely was another step toward his stated goal of winning the World Series. Said Slammin', "We have a good club. We know what it takes to win, and we know every game is important. With our pitching and offense, we will win consistently and build our confidence early."

It seemed like everybody who was anybody was on hand for this historic moment. Billy Williams wouldn't have missed it for the world. The Hall of Fame outfielder made his first home-opening start for the Cubs in 1961, and he had worked for the team in various coaching and front-office roles since retiring as a player in 1976. Williams had seen it all during his long association with the Cubs . . . except the very real possibility of this: "I do think this could be the year for the Cubs because of what we did last year and the people we added to the ballclub." Standing out on the field, Williams felt magic in the cold air. "This is exciting. There's nothing like Opening Day in Chicago because people come out. They cut out of school to come see a baseball game. Everyone wants to come to Opening Day."

They all wanted to welcome home their heroes. During the pregame introductions, the noise level was deafening, particularly after

Maddux's name was called. The lovefest continued when actor Bill Murray, one of Chicago's favorite sons, threw out the ceremonial first pitch. He intentionally sent his offering over the backstop and into the box seats, much to the delight of everyone in attendance. With the game only moments away, the grandstands were nearly filled. One seat, however, was conspicuously empty, the one Bartman had occupied in that Game 6. Club Box 4, Row 9, Seat 116 was a prime piece of real estate, but apparently nobody wanted to risk riling the baseball gods.

The impact of the Blue Flu also was evident at the innumerable bars in the neighborhood around Wrigley Field. It seemed like a dozen new ones popped up every year, but there weren't enough to comfortably accommodate the revelers in Wrigleyville on this special day. Almost every tavern was packed wall to wall with people of all shapes and sizes, including Yak-zies, which was located a short walk from the ballpark on Clark Street. One patron there, 34-year-old Glen Meyer, was sitting by himself, his eyes fixed on the game on TV. Wearing yellow-tinted sunglasses reminiscent of the ones made famous by the singer Bono from the band U2, he seemed a bit exotic for this down-home place. Meyer himself wasn't exactly sure why he was at Yak-zies—he had sort of gravitated there. This was his first bout with the Blue Flu.

"I've been living in Poland for the past 12 years without visiting the States, so I'm fresh off the boat five weeks ago," said Meyer, who originally was from College Station, Texas. "I didn't even realize it was a game day. When I realized it was, I decided I was going to walk toward Wrigley Field. I really, really admire the Cubs and Wrigley Field."

Within an inning and a half, Meyer's initiation into the cult of Cubdom was under way. Chicago was losing 5-0, and that admiration was turning to stoicism. Another gentleman, clad in a winter-proof knit cap, appeared to have more experience with all things Cubs. He walked into Yak-zies, glanced at the score on TV, grimaced, and muttered to no one in particular, "Five-to-fucking-nothing?"

A couple of bars down Clark Street at the Full Shilling, hope still was alive. The Cubs had rallied with two runs in the bottom of the second inning. Mike Atwell took a swig of beer and a drag off a cigarette, then looked at the TV screen approvingly. "It's only the second inning," he said. "There's plenty of time." Atwell, a 24-year-old commissions analyst for U.S. Cellular, hadn't called in sick that day. Instead, he had issued an ultimatum to his bosses: "I told them I'd either get the day off or I'd quit."

It mattered little to Atwell that he lacked a ticket to the game. He was overcome by an urge to simply be part of the scene, so he dressed in his Opening Day best—a Cubs hat worn backward and a Cubs T-shirt—walked to the Full Shilling from his nearby abode, and commandeered a choice stool at the bar. "I'm a crazy Cubs fan. I don't think anything else compares to the atmosphere around here. I don't think you can get this anywhere else."

The atmosphere was especially crazy at Murphy's Bleachers. Positioned a stone's throw from the big green scoreboard in center field, it was a favorite game-day destination. On this afternoon, there wasn't a scrap of space to be found in the joint. Pete Frake was among those jockeying for position in front of the television sets, but he wasn't bothered by the cramped quarters. "It's the Cubs aura," he said. "Just being around the people who are Chicago Cubs fans gives you a warm feeling. Regardless of whether the Cubs win 100 games or lose 100 games, the mystique of Wrigley Field will always be there. But this year, there is that hope that they made themselves better."

Hope, however, was rapidly dissolving. In fact, other than the sloshing of beer, groaning was the defining sound at Murphy's Bleachers. It now was the top of the fourth inning, and the Cubs were losing 6-2. Not even beer goggles could make Maddux look pretty. With five walks and another hit batter, he was throwing the ball everywhere except where he wanted. At least Bill Murray had *tried* to throw the ball over the backstop. Two outs into that fourth inning, Maddux was relieved of his duties. Hope officially had dissolved.

A paddy wagon was parked outside the Sports Corner, a no-frills tavern near the ballpark's main entrance that had some obligatory Cubs memorabilia nailed to the walls. As the game lurched into the seventh inning and Chicago's deficit expanded to 8-2, the natives were growing restless, and cold. The temperature had dropped about 10 degrees since first pitch, and fans were spilling out of Wrigley Field and into the surrounding streets and bars. A number of candidates for the paddy wagon were staggering around, most notably a burly man with a red beard who was shirtless. There was nothing unusual about seeing shirtless men at a sporting event on an ice-cold day. It was a primal, ritualistic display of toughness. What set this tough guy apart was the black brassiere he was wearing.

By the eighth inning, the Cubs were losing 10-2. Only the most die-hard of the die-hards remained in the grandstands at Wrigley Field; Bill Murray even had hightailed out of there after singing "Take Me Out to the Ball Game" midway through the seventh inning. Mullen's on Clark, yet another Wrigleyville bar with a multitude of TV sets, was getting more crowded with each pitch, but few people were fixated on the game anymore. Beer was now the featured attraction. One middle-aged man bought a round for his buddies and proposed a toast: "To Opening Day, 2000 and . . . whatever. What year *is* this?" No one had an answer readily available.

Over at the Friendly Confines, the Cubs looked cold, like they wanted nothing more than to go home. Who could blame them? It was the bottom of the ninth inning, and the score was 13-2. After the Cubs went down one-two-three in their last at-bats, they dragged their frozen carcasses into the warmth of the clubhouse. Minutes later, the flag bearing the dreaded letter "L" was raised above the center field scoreboard for everyone in the neighborhood to see.

It now was close to 4:30 p.m. Around this time each Opening Day, the Blue Flu sometimes was accompanied by a severe case of vomiting, from a combination of beer and watching nine innings of Cubs baseball. In 2004, the symptoms of the virus were particularly acute. This was the worst home-opening loss the franchise ever had suffered, dating back to 1876. It was worse than 1987, when St. Louis thumped the Cubs 9-3. Worse than 1954, when Cincinnati beat them 11-5. And worse than 1936, when Cincinnati won 12-3. Many people felt like hell, and it was plenty cold outside. Why was the winning part still so elusive?

The deejay at Mullen's on Clark must have put together his playlist prior to the opener, when the neighborhood still was bubbling with promise. As soon as the TV sets were muted at game's end, he cued up the hard-charging Thin Lizzy anthem "The Boys Are Back in Town." Somewhere in Wrigleyville, Cubs fans were doubled over.

THE WINDY CITY

SIX

It was a gift from above, or at least from the schedule-makers at Major League Baseball headquarters in New York. Traditionally, the Cubs were granted a day off following their home opener. Neither Wrigley Field nor the surrounding neighborhood was bustling, and there was no possible way the Cubs could lose. In the calm after the storm, the players and the fans alike were afforded an opportunity to nurse their Opening Day hangovers.

But a day without baseball didn't always equate to a day without bad news. On April 13, 2004, it arrived in the form of a press release from the Cubs that read: "The Chicago Cubs today announced that they have placed infielder Mark Grudzielanek on the 15-day disabled list retroactive to Saturday, April 10, with a partial tear of his right Achilles tendon. He is expected to be out of action for approximately two weeks."

The Achilles curse was spreading quickly. How long before everyone associated with the team, from the pencil pushers in the front office to the stadium-maintenance crew to the guys hawking Cracker Jack in the grandstands, started falling to the ground in agony? Grudzielanek's Achilles tendon had been bothering him for a while, and now it had given out altogether. The timing was predictably troublesome. Grudzielanek had been the Cubs' only consistent offensive spark up to this point. When he was placed on the DL, he was leading the team with a .467 average (7-for-15).

Seven games into the season, it was on to Plan B: Todd Walker. As Plan Bs went, however, this was a pretty good one. In fact, many in Cubdom had felt that Walker should have been Plan A. In a Red Sox lineup in 2003 featuring heavy hitters like Manny Ramirez and Nomar Garciaparra, Walker had been the unsung hero, one of the main reasons why the team had come within a game of reaching the World Series. Walker finished with a .283 average, 13 homers, and 85 runs batted in, but those stats paled in comparison to this one: He was the hardest player in the American League to strike out, with one K every 12 plate appearances.

After becoming a free agent at season's end, Walker piqued the interest of several teams, including that of the Cleveland Indians, who offered him $2.4 million and a guarantee of being their starting second baseman. But he signed with the Cubs, even though it amounted to a demotion. Not only would he earn less money in Chicago ($1.75 million), but he would be Grudzielanek's backup.

How in the name of Ryne Sandberg did the Cubbies pull off this coup? "First of all, you can't get ahead of yourself," Walker said. "It's just an honor to be in the big leagues. That said, when I had an option to come here and play in Chicago, I couldn't pass it up. This is a team that has a great chance of winning the World Series." It actually wasn't a bad gamble on Walker's part. If the Cubs did win the World Series, he wouldn't have to pay for another meal in Chicago for the rest of his life.

After Walker signed the dotted line on December 23, speculation arose that he eventually would unseat Grudzielanek as the starting second baseman. Baker repeatedly was asked about that possibility, to the point where his patience wore thin. Grudzielanek, after all, had hit .314 in 2003. "How do you contest second base?" Baker asked rhetorically. "I don't understand people asking me that. How do you contest a guy who hit .314? How much better can you do? He also played great defense, turned a lot of double plays. It's not a contested situation. It's a complementary situation where I have both and can rest one."

Now there were no decisions for Baker to make. For the next couple of weeks, anyway, Walker would be the main man at second base. Said Walker, "If you're not playing every day, it's very difficult to get into the right mindset. Now that I'm in the starting spot, I just have to do the best I can, do what I've always done." The Cubs, in turn, had to start doing what they were supposed to do: win. "Opening Day was very disappointing because everybody gets so excited, and we got beat up pretty bad," Walker said. "It's no fun when that happens. We wanted to win that game. But we have a saying around here that *today* is the biggest game of the year." In other words, Opening Day was history. The next game of the series on the afternoon of April 14 would offer another chance to start making some.

The early returns certainly were promising: The Cubs took a 1-0 lead in the bottom of the first inning when Sosa doubled home Walker, then scored two more in the second on RBI singles from Barrett and Walker, four more in the third on back-to-back homers by Alou and Ramirez and a two-run single by Walker, and one more in the fourth on another home run by Ramirez. The weather still was on the cool side, but Chicago's offense suddenly was red-hot.

So was Clement, who had been in a funk ever since he beat the Marlins in Game 4 of the National League Championship Series. His problems had been easy to diagnose—he couldn't throw strikes, leading to an 8.82 earned run average in spring training and that confidence-eroding first start of the regular season—but trickier to fix. Before his start against the Pirates, he was asked what it would take to reverse his fortunes. "It always comes down to going out there and getting ahead of the hitters and being aggressive," he replied. In that respect, Clement could be his own worst enemy. When things were going badly for him, his Abraham Lincoln goatee sometimes would droop and he would shuffle aimlessly around the mound between pitches, as if to say: "I can't win." Against Pittsburgh, though, Clement maintained a stiff lower lip. He still struggled with his location, allowing six base runners in the first three innings. But this time, he willed himself out of those jams and produced six shutout innings.

The man of the moment, however, was Walker, who went 3-for-5 in the 8-3 victory. Mark *who?* "I just gotta keep it going, man," said Chicago's new leadoff hitter. "You look at the numbers I've had, and that's what I'm going to do. I'm not overly concerned with being off to a good or a bad start. I just have to stay consistent. I don't panic." Walker felt exactly the same way about his fledgling team. "It was very big for us to win. Opening Day was just one day, that's all it really was. As long as you stay consistent and win some games, you're not overly concerned. I know this team is going to be there in the end."

For the final game of the series the next afternoon, the sky was a pristine shade of blue and the temperature was in the 70s. The unseasonably warm weather had been delivered by powerful gusts from the south, meaning the wind was blowing straight out of the ballpark. Such meteorological events could turn Wrigley Field into the world's largest pinball machine, with home runs ricocheting all over the bleachers. Through the years, those south winds had helped create absurd scores such as 26-23, 23-22, 18-16, and 23-10.

Before this game, however, wind talk took a back seat to tendon talk, the prevailing theme of the season. Sitting in the dugout for his daily meeting with the media, Baker discussed Grudzielanek's status. The second baseman, it seemed, was raring to go, bum Achilles and all. Perhaps he had taken note of Walker's exploits and didn't want to get Wally-Pipped. "Knowing him [Grudzielanek], you're really going to have to stay on him to keep that [walking] boot on and try not to train so hard that he doesn't allow it to heal," said Baker. "Yesterday I saw him coming down the clubhouse stairs without his boot on, and I said, 'Get your boot on.' He said, 'I feel great.' I said, 'Yeah, but feeling great is not the issue right now. The issue is for you to get your boot on.' He wants to play so badly, you hope it's not counterproductive."

Baker was feeling chatty on this April morn. He used Grudzielanek's Achilles woes as a platform to pontificate on the harsh realities of baseball, saying, "As much as you hate to admit it, injuries are not in your control. They're impossible to control. You don't know when you're going to get hurt. As long as you're playing ball, something's going to happen." Baker—who had been a big-league player himself, from 1968 through 1984—took a good long look at the green grass from his perch in the dugout. "If you dig up that field out there, you're going to find ligaments, tendons, bones. If you play long enough, you will leave something out on that field."

After the official proceedings concluded, Baker traded several jokes with the media before joining his players for batting practice. The joking continued, however, as he stood by the batting cage at home plate. Baker was the ultimate ambassador for America's pastime. He glad-handed his way through life, spreading goodwill like it was some sort of magic dust. Signs with phrases such as TRUST THE DUST had popped up all over the Wrigley Field grandstands in the past year, and the same sentiment permeated the clubhouse. "He's a great guy to play for," Borowski once said of his manager. "He's always in your corner, always encouraging you." These weren't the grim-faced Cubs of Don Baylor or Lee Elia or Herman Franks, where a 4-4 record might have felt a step removed from 4-10. Baker's Cubbies were 4-4 going on 10-4. The manager's smile was as bright and warm as the sunlight at Wrigley Field.

As for the formidable wind currents, Chicago's starting pitcher that day, Zambrano, had a plan: to keep his pitches low at all costs. And he executed it brilliantly, giving up only one run over six innings. More impressive, not a single offering of Zambrano's left the ballpark. The same couldn't be said for Pittsburgh's starter, Josh Fogg, who was unable to solve the riddle that was Wrigley Field. For him, the answers were blowin' in the wind, to the tune of four home runs allowed in the Pirates' 10-5 loss.

Two of Chicago's round-trippers came off the bat of Barrett. It was the first multihomer game of his career. Barrett still was awed by Cubdom, but he was indeed beginning to fit in. He was leading the

Cubs in runs batted in (nine) and was tied with Alou and Ramirez for the team lead in homers (three). After the game, a media relations assistant led Barrett through a couple of dark tunnels, past some groundskeeping equipment, and into the team's interview room. The setting may have been dank, but it was rich in symbolism. This was where the most notable players from each game sat.

"I can't believe I'm in this room right now," Barrett said. "It's hard for me to believe right now that I'm a member of this team and that I'm off to a pretty decent start and that I have the opportunity to play at Wrigley Field. I'm a little overwhelmed right now. I definitely don't feel like I deserve to be here, but I am." When the conversation turned to his encounters with the wind, Barrett smiled and said, "I really didn't think I hit those balls well enough for either one to go out, but the ball carried. Today was another example of how we can put runs on the board."

Chicago had bounced back with 18 runs in the two games since its embarrassing home-opening loss; it had climbed above .500 for the first time; and it was only a half-game behind first-place Cincinnati and Houston in the N.L. Central standings. Hey, hey, holy mackerel—the Cubs were on their way.

The wind at Wrigley Field was nothing compared to the rumors that were swirling regarding Prior's health. They had reached a gale-force tenor, distracting one and all from the fact that the Cubs were starting to play pretty good baseball.

Prior-less Mania had been blasting through the neighborhood all week. On Opening Day, when Prior had completed his bell-ringing duties at the Board of Trade, he joined his team at Wrigley Field and did some light throwing. Afterward, Hendry continued to toe the company line. "He threw well today—throwing a little crisper, a little harder," said the trusty GM. "Everything was positive. He saw the doctor for some more treatment. I definitely think he'll be ready to go sometime in May. I can't give you an exact date, but everything is going to be fine." Fine? Grudzielanek had a partially torn Achilles tendon and was due to miss two weeks. Prior's Achilles merely was *inflamed*, yet no one could pinpoint a return date.

It was little wonder rumors were flying far and wide. The *Newark Star-Ledger* in New Jersey reported that Prior's pitching elbow actually was the source of concern. According to the newspaper, Baker had told close friends that Prior would need "Tommy John" surgery on his elbow, the same reconstructive procedure that had sidelined Wood for a year. Baker, however, shot down that report, calling it shoddy journalism.

Regardless of how many runs the Cubs scored or how many games they won, they couldn't escape the Prior watch. The *Chicago Tribune* kept the pitcher's ill health front and center with a pullout box in each day's paper called, well, "The Prior Watch." The item included a projected date for his return and a summary of what he had done the previous day. It offered golden nuggets such as "proceeding gingerly," "proceeding with caution," and "proceeding cautiously." One day, "The Prior Watch" was packaged with an article that had the following headline: BAKER PONDERS A PRIOR-LESS SEASON. Baker went back into shoot-down mode, this time saying his words had been twisted.

The uncertainty of Prior's situation had created a breeding ground for tabloid journalism. Something definitive needed to happen soon. Otherwise, the headlines might start to read, PRIOR'S ACHILLES TENDON ABDUCTED BY ALIENS or PRIOR'S ACHILLES TENDON SPOTTED ON GRASSY KNOLL or CAUGHT ON TAPE: PRIOR'S ACHILLES TENDON HIDING OUT IN MEXICO WITH ELVIS. Prior was understandably frustrated. All he wanted to do was pitch. "There are a lot of things that have been floated out there that aren't true," he said. "It's unfortunate for me and for my teammates."

Prior-less Mania was putting particular pressure on the pitcher's replacement, Mitre. And as he prepared to face the Reds on April 16 in the first of a four-game series at Wrigley Field, he already had enough on his mind. The weather still was uncharacteristically balmy, and the flags above the center field scoreboard still were starched. With so many distractions, perhaps young Mr. Mitre forgot this was a game and not batting practice. In the top of the first inning, the Reds drilled him for three hits and two runs. The Cubs rallied with a run in the bottom of the first on an RBI single by Ramirez, but Cincinnati got three more hits and two more runs off Mitre in the third inning to extend its lead to 4-1. Then the Cubs also began to take advantage of the windy conditions: In the bottom of the third, back-to-back homers by Alou and Ramirez tied the score at 4-4. The heavyweight slugfest was on. All that was missing was the theme music from *Rocky*.

By the top of the sixth inning, Mitre was out and Michael Wuertz was in. Wuertz had been the last player to make the Opening Day roster, but he probably was wishing he was back on the farm. As Mitre had learned, Wrigley Field was no place for a rookie on a day like this one. Two homers and five runs later, and with the Cubs now losing 9-4, Wuertz joined Mitre in the clubhouse.

Game over? Not by a long shot, or at least a few more of them. The Cubs narrowed the gap to 9-5 in the bottom of the sixth, then all hell broke loose. At the start of the seventh inning, Baker made a double-switch—replacing Gonzalez with Ramon Martinez and reliever Todd Wellemeyer with Mercker—so that Martinez could lead off instead of the pitcher when the Cubs batted. After Martinez hit a double, the umpires belatedly ruled that the double-switch hadn't officially been made.

Baker ran onto the field—and he wasn't wearing his customary smile. Instead, he was fighting mad. Upon being ejected, Baker threw down his lineup card and hat and kicked around some bats in the Cubs' on-deck circle. For a 54-year-old man who had left more than a few ligaments, tendons, and bones on baseball diamonds across the nation, it was quite a physical display. Baker's legions of loyal follow-ers in the bleachers supported him the best way they knew how: They threw trash on the field. When play resumed, the Cubs players also were fighting mad. They responded to their manager's ouster by cutting Cincinnati's lead to 9-7. After the Reds scored a run in the top of the eighth, Hollandsworth continued his pinch-homer parade. His two-run shot pulled the Cubs to within a run.

Borowski then held Cincinnati scoreless in the ninth, setting the stage for Slammin' Sammy, who was due to lead off the bottom of the inning. With one swing of the bat and a sky-high hop, the score was 10-10. It was Sosa's 512th home run as a Cubs player, tying him with Ernie Banks for the all-time team record. But unlike so many of Sosa's previous 511 homers, this one meant something. The next batter was Alou, and everyone in the ballpark seemed to sense what was about to occur. After it happened—after Alou hit the ball into the left field bleachers and then circled the bases—he was mobbed by his teammates at home plate.

Sosa had hit a milestone, but it was Alou who had clubbed the game-winner. When Sosa was asked about number 512, he deflected the spotlight onto his buddy Alou. Maybe Sosa really was more interested in winning a World Series than going down as the greatest Cubs slugger ever. Alou occupied the seat of honor in the interview room, where he said, "We kept battling, we kept coming back. To finally win the game was awesome." A month's worth of highlights had been packed into nine innings. It was the type of victory that could define an entire season.

Chicago's comeback for the ages was followed by an ill-timed marketing gimmick: April 17 was 1908 jersey day. One hundred random winners were given replicas of the jerseys the Cubs wore the last time they won a World Series. Talk about a buzz kill. The Cubs were on a roll, and the last thing they needed was another reminder that it had been nearly a century since they had amounted to anything truly special. There already were enough ghosts whipping around Wrigley Field.

That second game of the series featured more wind from the south, but it was no match for the overwhelming stuff Wood was throwing. The problem was, Cincinnati starter Cory Lidle also was taming the elements. After seven innings, and with his team down only 2-1, Reds manager Dave Miley turned to his bullpen. Baker, on the other hand, stuck with his ace, a decision that would come back to haunt him. Chicago entered the ninth inning still leading 2-1, but the Reds weren't ready to call it a day. Following a leadoff single by Sean Casey, Adam Dunn walked on a pitch Wood thought was a strike. The rapidly unraveling Texan motioned bitterly to home-plate umpire Eric Cooper. "It looked like a strike to me," Wood later recalled. "When you get to that point in the ninth inning and wait two and a half hours to get to that point, and you don't get a call, it's frustrating."

Before long, the Cubs were losing 3-2. When Wood finally was pulled from the game, he exploded, running toward Cooper at home plate. After being restrained by Baker, the pitcher stormed into the dugout and chucked a batting helmet onto the field. Those were the final fireworks; the Cubs went down quietly in the ninth.

Something strange undoubtedly was in the air. In addition to crazy baseball, the past 24 hours had produced temper tantrums from both Baker and Wood. Perhaps those two had taken their cues from Cubs reliever Kyle Farnsworth. Against these very same Reds on June 19, 2003, Paul Wilson charged the mound following an inside pitch from Farnsworth. The chiseled Farnsworth threw Wilson to the ground like a rag doll, which incited a bench-clearing brawl.

Farnsworth wound up being suspended for two games, but that was a small price to pay. The incident was a turning point in the history of the Cubs, serving notice that they no longer were cuddly losers. Now if you stepped too close, they might bite. Farnsworth reveled in the notoriety he gained from his body-slamming antics. On the final day of the 2003 regular season, after Chicago's N.L. Central title had been clinched, he strutted around the clubhouse in a football jersey emblazoned with his name and number.

If only some of that fighting spirit could have rubbed off on Maddux. A few days after his home-opening misadventure, he sat by himself in the dugout as his teammates stretched before batting practice.

The fiery competitor known as "Mad Dog" looked more like "Hang Dog." That was what an 0-2 record and a 7.45 earned run average could do to a guy, particularly under the weight of such immense hopes. Baker sympathized with his slumping superstar. The manager's years of experience had taught him how critical it was for a pitcher to get that first victory. "The main thing is to get number one out of the way," said Baker. "If you don't get it early, you start wondering what's going to happen or you start thinking negatively. But if you can get number one out of the way, you just go from there."

Unfortunately for Maddux, there were gusts of up to 30 miles per hour at Wrigley Field on the afternoon of April 18, the date of his next start. A second month's worth of highlights were packed into this game, but none of them involved Maddux. He didn't have a chance. The Reds hit him early and often, scoring three runs in the first inning, two in the fourth, and two more in the sixth. By then, Baker had seen enough, and he lifted Maddux.

The day wasn't going much better for Cincinnati's starter, Paul Wilson. Sosa made history in the bottom of the first inning, launching a ball into the left-center field basket to become the Cubs' home run king. The crowd demanded a tip of the cap after he returned to the dugout, and Slammin' Sammy obliged. But why stop there? In the third inning, he hit number 514 to tie the score at 3-3.

Once again, it was time to cue up the theme music from *Rocky*. The lead changed hands continually following Sosa's game-tying homer, but after nine innings and 27 hits, the teams were back to square one. The score was 9-9. In the top of the 10th inning, Slammin' Sammy's historic afternoon broke bad. He lost a fly ball in the sun and the wind, paving the way for a two-run rally for the Reds. Sosa, however, wasn't the only outfielder that day who had been flummoxed by the elements. Almost every fly ball had turned into an accident waiting to happen, so two runs hardly seemed like enough to secure the victory.

Sure enough, the Cubs came roaring back. Patterson led off with a double and eventually scored on a one-out sacrifice fly by Ramirez.

With two outs and Alou on first base, the winning run stepped to the plate in the form of Lee, who proceeded to hit the ball as hard as almost anyone had all afternoon. As the ball traveled deeper and deeper into center field, the cheering from the grandstands reached a fever pitch. Then, like a phantom darting to and fro, the jet stream suddenly shifted and the ball died in Ken Griffey Jr.'s glove.

Although Baker desperately had wanted to pull out another improbable victory, he remained optimistic, chalking up the game's outcome to that vexing wind. Maddux, in contrast, was the very picture of defeat, with deep circles under his eyes. His earned run average now was 8.62, and he seemed as perplexed by that as everyone else. "I'm not pitching good," he said in a monotone to the assembled media. "It's one of those things where I don't think I'm pitching as bad as it looks."

After three straight nail-biters, the Cubs finally made it look easy the next afternoon in the last game of the series, even as the meteorological freak show continued. Clement muscled his way through some early trouble again, and when he left the game during the top of the seventh inning, the Cubs had a 3-1 lead.

It was Lee who delivered the knockout punch, with no outs and the bases loaded in the bottom of the seventh. The wind be damned—this time, he wouldn't be denied. His first home run in Wrigley Field as a member of the Cubs was a grand slam. "It seemed like forever since I've had a hit," said Lee, who entered the game with a .244 average. "I don't think I've ever had a quick start. April's not usually a good month for me." The fans rose to their feet for the umpteenth time in the wild series as Lee rounded the bases, and they gave Chicago another ovation after it put the finishing touches on the 8-1 victory.

In the five games after the south wind gathered, there were a total of 119 hits and 71 runs. The Cubs had earned every bit of their 3-2 record in that span. Given the volatile mood swings of Mother Nature, they just as easily could have gone 1-4. All told, the Cubs were back over .500 at 7-6—it was onward and upward from here. That evening, the team boarded a plane bound for Pittsburgh and switched its focus to the upcoming three-game series against the Pirates.

As it turned out, the Cubs got out of Dodge in the nick of time. The next day, that wind turned downright evil. A series of tornadoes ripped through northern Illinois, leveling the small town of Utica and causing untold other damage to the region. Only then did equanimity finally ensue.

WRIGLEY FIELD
HOME OF
CHICAGO CUBS

PRESSURE?
WHAT PRESSURE?

SEVEN

Prior's Achilles tendon was lost in space, and Maddux's earned run average also was somewhere in the stratosphere. A couple of months earlier, when everyone was saying Chicago would live and die by its pitching, that would have seemed like a worst-case scenario. It would have spelled, well, certain doom. Yet the Cubs were surging, mostly because their offense also was out of this world.

The catalysts were Ramirez and Alou, who were batting .538 and .448, respectively, over the past six games. But they weren't the only ones with video-arcade numbers. Barrett's season average was .333, Walker's was .324, and Sosa's was .314. Gonzalez was coming on, too. A week earlier, his average had been .174; now it was up to .244. Had the Wrigley Field wind inflated everyone's stats? Barrett didn't think so. "This team is starting to get a little more comfortable and a little more relaxed playing together," he said. "Whether the wind is blowing out or in, I don't even think it matters."

In addition to being one of the team's rising stars, Barrett was a sage. The Cubs didn't need any wind in the series opener against the Pirates on April 20. The choice offerings from Pittsburgh starter Ryan Vogelsong were enough of a gift. It was a whiplash-inducing evening for Vogelsong, who spun his head around and watched hits from Patterson, Walker, and Gonzalez fly into the stands. As if to drive home the point he had made, Barrett also had a round-tripper in Chicago's 9-1 victory, off Jason Boyd.

With 30 homers in their first 14 games, the Cubs were on pace to hit 347 homers and obliterate the team record of 212. Against Jason Fogg the next night, however, they proved they could play small ball, too. Unlike his previous start against the Cubs six days earlier, when he allowed four home runs, the Pirates right-hander kept the ball inside the park. Still, there was no joy in Foggville. He was yanked during Chicago's eight-run first inning without recording a single out.

The Cubs had a total of 15 hits in this 12-1 laugher—and not one was a home run. Instead, they did things that Cubs teams through the ages rarely had done: They mustered two-out base hits with men in scoring position, they advanced runners from second to third base on ground balls to the right side of the infield, they made the pitchers work deep into counts, and they hit sacrifice flies. That "C" on their batting helmets sure didn't seem to stand for "cursed." "Catharsis" was more like it.

Of course, this type of hitting couldn't continue indefinitely. It simply wasn't possible, not even for these new-look, bad-to-the-bone Cubbies. The pitching staff eventually would have to carry the day, if not the season. And even though Prior was ailing and Maddux was slumping, it felt prepared to do just that. "We take pride in ourselves in the rotation," said Clement, who had whittled his earned run average down to 2.76. "We look forward to going out every day and doing our jobs. All of the expectations for us reinforce the fact that we have a chance to go far. We know we don't have to go out there and have the season of our life. We have a deep staff, and we feed off of each other's success."

Zambrano, then, had created a feeding *frenzy* in that first game in Pittsburgh. The Cubs gave him nine runs to work with, but two would have sufficed. In allowing a single run over eight innings, he raised his record to 2-0 and lowered his ERA to an otherworldly 1.29. Mitre's line the next evening was equally impressive: six innings, four hits, and no runs. It was his first victory as a big-leaguer, and his teammates marked the occasion by dousing him with beer and nailing him with a shaving-cream pie.

But the Cubs had more to celebrate that night than Mitre's milestone. The victory lifted them into a tie for first place with Houston. Not even the clouds that always seemed to be hanging over Steel City could dampen the team's spirits. Although the finale was rained out the next evening, the Cubs were soaring well above those storm clouds on their plane ride back to Chicago for a three-game series against the Mets.

The Cubs were greeted at home with open arms, and lots of them. As usual, Wrigley Field was bursting at the seams for the series opener versus New York on April 23. Although the Cubs hadn't won a World Series title since moving into the Friendly Confines in 1916, they at least could count on a World Series atmosphere every day. With scarcely a ticket to be had for the remaining home games, the grand old ballpark likely would draw three million fans for the first time in its history.

"The fans were fired up at the end of last year," said Clement. "And even the first year I was here [in 2002], when we didn't do very well, the fans were here and the park was close to full every game. So you know the fans are going to be here. They're excited and ready to go. They've been ready to go since the last game of last year. It's an exciting time."

In addition to quantity, Wrigley Field was attracting quality. Bill Murray, of course, was at the home opener, and actors Matt Damon and Andy Garcia were spotted in the grandstands the following day. The parade of luminaries would continue through the spring and summer, and possibly into the fall. Even the players were soaking up the vibrant scene. "I got a chance to talk to Matt Damon," said Walker. "He's a super person. I don't really get caught up in superstars, but I like to be around the people who are good people."

As unfathomable as it might have seemed in these heady times, Wrigley Field wasn't always a destination for the rich and famous. In fact, it didn't used to be a destination for much of anyone. Three million fans? In the 1960s, 1970s, and early part of the 1980s, *two* million would have seemed like an impossible dream. The high-water mark for attendance during that period was 1,674,993 in 1969, when a rarity occurred and the Cubs spent the majority of the season in first place.

However, mostly bad baseball was only part of why Wrigley Field often was half empty decades ago. The surrounding neighborhood was every bit as downcast as the action on the diamond. Beth Murphy, the owner of Murphy's Bleachers, had learned all about those dark days from her late husband, Jim. He was a Chicago cop who moved into the neighborhood in the 1970s, buying and then rehabbing a building on Sheffield across the street from the right field bleachers. "Back in the '60s and '70s, the Cubs weren't much of a business," said Beth, who was married to Jim from 1994 until he passed away in 2003. "The neighborhood was dangerous—it was gang-infested. You went to the ballpark, and you got out of there after the game. You didn't hang around. Jim said he used to take out the garbage with a gun."

Several of Murphy's police buddies followed his lead and took up residence in the neighborhood. As they moved in, the gangs moved out. "That's what started to change the neighborhood around," said Beth. In 1980, Jim bought Ray's Bleachers on Sheffield and Waveland and changed the tavern's name to Murphy's Bleachers. Murphy wasn't alone in his entrepreneurial maneuvering. Businesses began popping up all over, creating an influx of young professionals who had disposable time and money. And what better place to spend that time and money than at the Friendly Confines?

As fate would have it, WGN-TV, which broadcast all of the Cubs games to the locals, became a "superstation" around that same time. Beautiful pictures of the center field scoreboard and the lush ivy and the brick backstop behind home plate suddenly were being beamed from coast to coast. Then in 1982, Harry Caray signed on to call the games. The Budweiser-guzzling Caray was the perfect pitchman for Wrigley Field, which had the potential to be America's biggest beer garden. He was wild and unpredictable, and one of his favorite lines was, "You can't beat fun at the old ballpark."

But one key element still was lacking that would fill the old ballpark once and for all: a winning team. The Cubs' brand of baseball had failed to evolve along with the neighborhood. One day in 1983, the natives were being harder than usual on manager Lee Elia's beleaguered players. After the game, he summed up the sorry state of Cubdom in a rant that would become legendary. "I'll tell you one fucking thing," he started, "I hope we get fucking hotter than shit just to stuff it up them three thousand fucking people that show up every fucking day." Elia's tirade went on and on and on, but the same couldn't be said of his tenure in Chicago. He was fired before the season ended.

In 1984, the Cubs had a new manager, Jim Frey, who was a bit smoother around the edges than his predecessor. They also finally fielded a winner. When the Cubs captured the division title that year, it was like the Big Bang: Their fan base rapidly expanded, and they became a national phenomenon. From 1984 on, the Cubs crammed at least two million fans into their tiny ballpark nearly every season, including a record haul of 2,962,630 in 2003.

Now the franchise had three million fans in its sights, and Hendry, the man who had helped whip everyone into a such a frenzy with his off-season acquisitions, couldn't believe his eyes. "It's a testimony to the fans we have," he said. "The greatest fans in the world, the greatest ballpark in the world. You know they're looking for a little positive action, and we're looking to give it to them for 162 games."

With so much energy in the grandstands and the Cubs now finding their footing, did those weak-hitting Mets have as much as a prayer? In a word, no. This time, it was the Prior-less pitching staff that took center stage, beginning with Maddux in the opener. The Cubs spotted him two runs in the first inning on a homer by the surging Alou, which were all the right-hander needed. In allowing one run over seven innings, Maddux finally found his control. He issued only one walk and threw an economical 86 pitches. The shine was back on Maddux—that first win was out of the way. After the 3-1 victory, he looked more relieved than overjoyed, saying, "It's nice to play in a game we've actually won."

The next day brought more of the same. Wood overpowered the Mets in Chicago's 3-0 win, pitching seven shutout innings and striking out nine. As the masses assembled at the Friendly Confines for the final game of the series on the afternoon of April 25, there was no doubt about who would be pitching for the Cubs. The grandstands were dotted with people who had Abraham Lincoln goatees attached to their chins. After those masses caught their first glimpse of the sharp break on Clement's slider, there also was no doubt about which team would prevail. Clement pitched a no-hitter through six and two-thirds innings and struck out a career-high 13. It was another win for the first-place Cubs, their sixth in a row. "We're trying to build on something," Clement said following the 4-1 victory.

What Chicago was doing was wringing the suspense from the season. It had been 53 innings since the Cubs had so much as trailed in a game, and they had outscored the opposition 39-5 during their winning streak. This was shaping up to be a far cry from 2003, when 72 of the Cardiac Cubs' 162 games were decided by two runs or fewer.

The curse, it seemed, had been buried in the past, or at least in someone's stomach. During that crazy Cincinnati series, a shirtless man in the grandstands had the words I ATE BARTMAN painted on his substantial paunch. As for the goat, there was no sign of it, either. And that was good news for the folks beyond the center field scoreboard at Murphy's Bleachers. "I'm so sick of the goat," Beth Murphy said. "I hate that thing. They bring the goat around to the bar. It's not the same goat, obviously, but it's so creepy." It was creepy, all right. But if the Cubs kept playing this well, she never would have to see another one.

❖   ❖   ❖

Leave it to Randy Johnson to spoil a World Series party. The Diamondbacks pitcher had made a career out of raining on the Cubs' parade, compiling an 11-0 record against them. And even though it was bone-dry in the Arizona desert on the evening of April 26, he drenched the Cubs yet again. They knew what to expect from the hard-throwing left-hander—"He's still Randy Johnson," Baker said as his team prepared to face him in the first of a three-game series at Bank One Ballpark—but that hardly mattered. The results were all too familiar for the Cubs: no runs, two hits, 10 strikeouts, and a loss. Zambrano even seemed spooked. He didn't make it out of the fifth inning, and his earned run average for the season skyrocketed from 1.29 to 3.55. Chicago's rapturous winning streak ended with a 9-0 whimper.

The Cubs could have attributed their lethargic play to the Johnson factor, except they rolled over again the next night versus some guy named Brandon Webb. Their timely hitting? It was gone. Their dominant pitching? It, too, had disappeared. Like Zambrano's the night before, Mitre's start ended prematurely, after only three and two-thirds innings. The game was essentially over by then, anyway; Arizona was winning 5-0. The Cubs didn't score their first run of the *series* until Hollandsworth hit a solo homer in the ninth inning of the 10-1 debacle. Two days after arriving in Phoenix as the hottest team in baseball, the Cubs were facing the possibility of being swept in a three-game series for the first time in Baker's tenure with the team.

Ironically, Baker would be powerless to help sway the outcome of the series finale. On April 28, the league office issued five- and one-game suspensions to Wood and Baker, respectively, for their outbursts in the Cincinnati series. Wood could appeal his suspension, but Baker would have to serve his immediately, meaning bench coach Dick Pole would be in command of the Cubs dugout that night. "This is the first suspension of my entire life—anywhere," Baker said. The timing couldn't have been better. This was just the prod the Cubs needed to awaken from their slumber. It was a reminder that they were supposed to be the nail-spitting Cubs, not the warm, fuzzy and comatose ones of yesteryear.

Who better to put some bite back into the Cubs than the rejuvenated "Mad Dog" Maddux? When Pole pulled Maddux after six innings, the Cubs were winning 3-2. But then Hawkins, Chicago's $11 million setup man, skidded through his first rough patch of the season, giving up a game-tying home run to Steve Finley in the bottom of the eighth inning. Was broom time approaching in Phoenix? No, these were the fighting Cubs. Gonzalez—who already had five last at-bat, game-winning homers in his two-plus seasons with Chicago—did it again, and the Cubs salvaged the series with a 4-3 victory.

The season wasn't going to be the cakewalk people had started to envision a few days earlier, but the Cubs remained on a collision course with the World Series. At 13-8, they were in first place in the N.L. Central with a one-game lead over Cincinnati. Wrigleyville was buzzing. Said Beth Murphy, "I want to tell people at the bar that it isn't World Series time in April. Let the season develop. Everybody's too intense. People are actually watching the games."

Hollandsworth had a similar message for the flock: Relax. That was what he and his teammates were trying to do. Prior's Achilles tendon was MIA, Remlinger's 38-year-old shoulder still was healing, and Grudzielanek had spent part of the month lumbering around in that boot—yet the World Series Express was chugging forward.

"I don't think the expectations bother anyone around here," Hollandsworth said. "That's what the media's going to build up, and that's what they're going to talk about. You know what? So what. You've got to be who you are and go out there and dig it up. Right now, we're just trying to get healthy. We're not even at full strength."

At what point, then, might the Express start picking up steam? "There's no set date for kicking it into high gear—never," Hollandsworth continued. "There's nothing tougher than trying to win when you feel like you *gotta* win. You can't really play the game that way.

[But] there is always going to be a time when there might be a game or a series or a trip that may be more important."

One such marker arrived as April came to a close. The Cubs were bound for St. Louis, where they would resume their 112-year-old rivalry with the Cardinals. It was indeed beginning to feel a lot like October.

SEEING RED

EIGHT

Blood feud. Bitter enemies. Epic war. These were but a few of the terms that sportswriters, in their never-ending quest to create drama, had used over the decades to describe the Cubs-Cardinals rivalry. Truth be told, it had been neither bloody, bitter, nor epic. It simply had been long—interminably long, dating all the way back to 1892. This was baseball's version of *The Waltons*, the homespun TV show that ran seemingly forever and lacked compelling plot twists almost every step of the way.

The Cubs and Cardinals had played each other more than 2,100 times, which amounted to about 13 full seasons. They had played and played and played—but for what? There had been that nasty flourish in the 1920s and '30s, when the teams had battled occasionally for National League supremacy, but they hadn't finished one-two in the standings since 1945. This quaint little affair had taken place in a vacuum. Rarely had anything more than lighthearted pride been at stake.

Joe Girardi, who played catcher for Chicago from 1989 through 1992 and again from 2000 through 2002, characterized the rivalry as a civil war, with the emphasis on civil. "Both teams have a lot of respect for each other," he said. "It's not hard to get caught up in it. It's been pretty civil so far." Journeyman infielder Ron Coomer was on the Cubs for only one season, in 2001, but that was all the time he needed to get to the heart of the matter. "There's a little chirping that goes on occasionally during the games," he said, "but I don't think there's any real animosity." Chirping? That conjured images of birds nesting, not titans clashing.

The heavy-duty verbiage applied to a different rivalry, the one that was fueled by "The Curse of the Bambino." When the Red Sox sold Babe Ruth to the Yankees after the 1919 season, the fortunes of both franchises were inexorably altered. The Yankees never had captured a World Series title before the Ruth deal went down, while the Red Sox had won six. After it, however, the Yankees became the most celebrated team in baseball, winning 26 World Series. The Red Sox? They were 0-for-84—and on several of those occasions, their World Series bubble had been burst by none other than the Yankees. The grandstands at every game were a combustible mix of Yankees smugness and Red Sox angst.

"We hear stories about somebody wearing a Red Sox hat in the bleachers at Yankee Stadium and just getting pelted with everything you can imagine," said Ed McGregor, a baseball editor for *ESPN The Magazine*. "There'll be cops just standing there. Somebody complains to them, and the cop says, 'What do you expect? You're stupid enough to wear a Red Sox hat in the bleachers at Yankee Stadium and you're going to get what you have coming.' It gets ugly. The Cubs-Cardinals series has a friendlier atmosphere. Part of that is the Midwestern ethic. I think the people are just kinder than on the East Coast."

Most years, Cubs-Cardinals games were little more than an excuse for fans of the respective teams to take a road trip. The two cities were only about five hours apart by car, connected by I-55 and a bunch of cornfields. "They like to drive down or even take the train," said Billy Williams, the Hall of Fame Cubs outfielder who participated in the rivalry for nearly two decades. "It gives a lot of people a chance to cheer for their team in the other city." And with few exceptions, those blocks of blue and blocks of red in the grandstands coexisted peacefully.

Peace, love, and understanding often prevailed on the field, too, even in the rivalry's most intense moments. For instance, on June 23, 1984—in a classic that became known as "The Sandberg Game"— the Cubs rallied from a 7-1 deficit to win 12-11 in 11 innings. Chicago second baseman Ryne Sandberg had the performance of a lifetime, going 5-for-6 with seven runs batted in, including game-tying homers in the ninth and 10th innings. How did the Cardinals retaliate for those crushing blows? Did they throw at Sandberg the next chance they got? Not unless bouquets counted. St. Louis manager Whitey Herzog gushed about the second baseman, calling him "probably the greatest player I've ever seen."

The teams kept playing and playing and playing. They played through the 1980s and the '90s and into the new century. Sometimes the Cubs won, sometimes the Cardinals won, and sometimes it rained. The names on the jerseys turned over again and again, but the theme remained essentially the same: Love thy neighbor. It would take something remarkable to end this march toward oblivion. It would take a series in which absolutely everything was on the line.

In 2003, that series arrived with brusque force. When St. Louis came to Wrigley Field for five games the first week of September, the fates of both teams hung in the balance. The Cardinals entered the series on a tear. They had won six of their past eight games and were in first place in the N.L. Central, a game ahead of Houston and two and a half ahead of fading Chicago. The Cubs had lost four of their past five games, and a poor showing in this series would effectively eliminate them from contention.

Forget those wimpy characters from *The Waltons*—the Cubs and the Cardinals now resembled the Hatfields and the McCoys. This series was bloody, bitter, and epic. It was all of those things, and more. Players were ejected. Knockdown pitches were thrown. Heated words were exchanged between the managers. The fans in blue hooted and hollered at the fans in red, and vice versa. There were extra-inning cliffhangers and dramatic comebacks.

It was among the most hard-fought and acrimonious series the two teams ever had played . . . against anyone. And when all was said and done, the Cubs had taken four of the five games and broken the spirit of St. Louis. The Cardinals never recovered from their swing through Chicago. They limped through the last month of the season and wound up third in the Central standings. The Cubs never were the same, either. They surged into the postseason by winning 15 of their final 22 games.

Eight months later, the effect of that series still resonated in Chicago's clubhouse. "It was the key for us going to the playoffs," Zambrano said as a smile spread across his boyish face. "Everybody was so excited to take four out of five. Then we just kept playing good baseball and going higher."

Now, though, the situation was reversed as the Cubs and the Cardinals prepared for their first series of 2004. This time, Chicago was in first place, a game ahead of Cincinnati and Houston and a game and a half up on Milwaukee. The Cardinals, meanwhile, were two and a half games behind and were struggling to find their footing. Their offense was as good as any in the National League, but they had been betrayed by their pitching.

Still, as St. Louis had learned the hard way against Chicago the previous September, everything could change here. This had the potential to be a pivotal juncture in the young season. Prior to the first of the four-game series on April 30, Cardinals slugger Albert Pujols told *MLB.com*, "They have a great team. Great bullpen and great pitching. Anytime you play with Houston or anybody in our division, it's always gonna be exciting. But it seems like every time we play the Cubs, it's even better. Everybody's ready to go."

The Cubs were ready to go, too. Their swagger was such that they even shrugged off a key detail: This series would take place in Busch Stadium, not Wrigley Field. Normally, that would have provided ample reason to worry; the Cubs were 20-47 at Busch Stadium over the past 10 years. But a lot had happened since the Cubs last had played there the previous August. For one, they had captured the N.L. Central title, and trampled over these Cardinals to do so. "Maybe Busch Stadium was tough," Zambrano said, "but now we have a great team. We are a competitive team, so I don't see the Busch Stadium stuff. They have a good team, but we can beat anybody."

Wood certainly pitched well enough to win the opener. He struck out 10 and allowed only five hits and three runs in eight innings. The Cubs also batted well enough to win, reeling off 10 hits. The most memorable hit, however, was the one that got away. Barrett seemingly put the Cubs ahead 4-0 in the fourth inning with a two-run homer down the left field line, but after a heated challenge by the Cardinals, the umpires ruled it foul.

Barrett wasn't quite sure what to make of all the hoopla accompanying this Cubs-Cardinals series. He was, well, overwhelmed by it. But like everything else, he figured it out quickly. "For me, it was awesome to be part of this whole rivalry and experience it for the first time," he recalled with his customary aw-shucks charm. "I had that home run called back, and it didn't really faze me because all that mattered was moving on." Indeed. The catcher finished the night with three hits, including two doubles.

So, if Wood pitched well enough to win and the Barrett-led offense hit well enough to win, how come the Cubs didn't win? Simple: The bullpen came about as close to throwing strikes as Bill Murray had before that home opener. On this occasion, however, no one was laughing. The bottom of the ninth inning began with the score tied 3-3 and Farnsworth on the mound in relief of Wood. Four pitches later, Pujols was on first base with a walk and Farnsworth was back on the bench. Now it was Kent Mercker's turn. After five pitches, Jim Edmonds was on base with a walk and Mercker, too, was back on the bench.

Chicago's hopes rested on the platinum arm of Hawkins. Surely he would be able to throw a strike, perhaps even several of them. Nope. Hawkins walked two batters on 13 total pitches, and when Pujols jogged across the plate for the winning run, Busch Stadium erupted. Said a stunned Baker afterward, "It was just a bad ending to a good game."

The following night was just plain bad—from a weather standpoint, anyway. A steady rain turned Busch Stadium into a wet and wild mosh pit, but Clement slogged through the conditions and slammed the Cardinals into submission. It was the fourth brilliant outing in a row for Clement, who lowered his earned run average to 1.95 by holding St. Louis to one run over eight innings. The man was in a groove. "I want to get more consistent every time I get out there," he said. "That's how you become a better pitcher. That's how you learn."

The bullpen, on the other hand, was not in a groove. Chicago headed into the bottom of the ninth inning with a 4-1 lead, but that offered little solace given the events of the previous night. The rain was coming down so hard that Sweaty Joe was dripping before he even stepped onto the mound. Minutes later, Baker and his fellow coaches also were dripping, even though the dugout was protected from the elements. Borowski got the save, but he gave up a run and put the tying runs on base before striking out Reggie Sanders to end the game. Baker, reeling again but this time victorious, shook his head and then clasped the hand of pitching coach Larry Rothschild.

After two straight stunners, what would the next night bring? Another stunner, of course. Zambrano shook off that poor start in Arizona and pitched perhaps the best game of his young career. In seven innings, he allowed no runs and three hits and struck out a personal-high 12 batters. However, St. Louis starter Matt Morris was even better, pitching nine shutout innings.

For the first time since June 1986, the Cubs and the Cardinals took a scoreless game into extra innings. St. Louis reliever Jason Isringhausen kept the score that way in the 10th inning; Farnsworth did not. Perhaps the problem was that the plan didn't call for Farnsworth to beat the Cardinals senseless. Instead, he had to pitch to them, which was when the trouble began. Farnsworth walked Tony Womack; he walked Pujols; and he walked Edmonds. The good news was that he didn't walk Scott Rolen. The bad news was that Rolen singled to finish off the Cubs.

Afterward, Farnsworth had nothing to say about his travails.

What could he say? What could anyone from the bullpen say? The numbers spoke for themselves. A relief corps that was supposed to be vastly improved had a 7.46 earned run average since April 10, and this latest meltdown had nullified Zambrano's banner night.

Zambrano, though, wasn't pointing the finger at the bullpen—that wasn't in his nature. He was a big and boisterous man who was so full of life that he'd talk to total strangers like they were his friends. A setback like this wasn't going to cut into his upbeat demeanor. "As a pitcher, you have to understand that you have 32 or 33 starts," he said in his thick Latin accent. "You have to agree with wins, losses, and no-decisions. Those are the three things that can happen to a pitcher. I always think that when I go out there, I want to give my team a chance to win the ballgame. I felt good after the game because I did my job. I felt bad because we lost the game, but like I say, you can only do what you can do."

Would a similar type of effort be enough for Maddux, the starting pitcher for the series finale on the afternoon of May 3? Or would the bullpen unravel yet again? Like Wood, Clement, and Zambrano before him, Maddux was in prime form, allowing only two runs in seven innings. And an offense that had scratched and clawed to score runs all series long came through, too, unloading for three home runs. The biggest one came from Lee in the top of the eighth inning. With the Cubs clinging to a 3-2 lead, he hit a two-run homer to open up the game. "It felt good to hit that home run," Lee said. "It's a big rivalry, St. Louis-Chicago. We needed to get out of there with a split rather than going 1-3 in that series, so that home run gave us a cushion."

As soon as Lee crossed the plate, the folks dressed in red began quietly filing out of the stadium. The ones in blue, however, didn't go anywhere; they weren't so sure the issue was settled. Sure enough, the bullpen's comedy of errors continued in the bottom of the inning, when Francis Beltran gave up a solo home run to Edmonds to narrow Chicago's lead to 5-3. No one breathed a sigh of relief—least of all Chicago's relief pitchers—until Sosa hit a two-run homer in the top of the ninth. Borowski followed by offering up a belated present to those Cubs fans who had trekked to St. Louis: a scoreless inning.

This latest round of the rivalry had ended in a draw. "We could have swept them or won three; they could have swept us or won three," Walker said. "It was all close. I think it ended the way it should have."

Cubs reliever Todd Wellemeyer was less charitable, saying, "We weren't satisfied with it. We could have easily won all four, and I think St. Louis knows that. They know we can beat them at any time."

Those sounded like fighting words.

DOOMSDAYS

NINE

When the Cubs left Chicago on April 25 following their sweep of the Mets, they were all smiles. When they returned on the evening of May 3, they were all scowls. They still were atop the N.L. Central standings, tied with Houston at 15-10, but something was amiss. The Cubs were in a tizzy.

Farnsworth was mad because he couldn't throw strikes. Borowski was mad because he thought the media and the fans wanted him bounced from the closer's job. Baker was mad because the media and the fans wouldn't cut Borowski any slack. And Hawkins was mad because everyone around him was so damn mad.

The bullpen was under siege. Trouble actually had started percolating way back in spring training, when it was noted that the velocity of Borowski's pitches was down about five miles per hour. Borowski said he was fine, but the radar gun said otherwise. Eyebrows were raised even farther when the regular season began and the first-pitch strikes that had been his saving grace in 2003 eluded him. Whenever Sweaty Joe took the mound, everyone around him sweated bullets.

Nevertheless, a soggy Baker was standing by his man. While the critics pointed to Borowski's 5.73 earned run average, the manager cited his six saves in as many attempts. Said Baker defiantly, "You get tired of hearing about what you're not doing. Joe is the same Joe. It's just that sometimes the media does change you. I've changed." Baker wasn't ready to pull a Lee Elia and launch into a profanity-laced ti-rade—but he no longer was smiling, that was for sure.

Adding to the foul mood at Wrigley Field, Arizona, which had out-scored the Cubs 23-4 in their series a week earlier, was coming call-ing for three more games. The Diamondbacks were National League bottom-feeders, but against Chicago, they had looked like the 1927 Yankees. "It's strange," Walker said. "If it's a bad team that's beating a good team, people will say, 'What's the deal?' But this is the big leagues. Everybody's got great players. Every day you go out there, you have a chance to get beat. Right now, the Diamondbacks just have our number."

The numbers the Diamondbacks hung on the Cubs in the series opener on May 4 were brutal. Darkness had fallen over Wrigley Field, and not just because it was the first night game of the season. Even though Arizona trotted out Steve Sparks, a knuckleball pitcher with a 4.56 earned run average, sparks did not fly off the bats of the Cubs. Over the pitcher's first seven innings, Chicago managed no runs and just three hits. Arizona, meanwhile, pounded Mitre and reliever Glen-don Rusch for six runs. There was a momentary glimmer of hope when Slammin' Sammy hit a three-run homer off Sparks in the eighth inning, but the black veil came back down in the form of a 6-3 loss.

Even though the lights were shining brightly over in the club-house, Chicago's players still were in the dark. When asked why the Diamondbacks were giving the Cubs such fits, Zambrano shook his head and said, "I don't know. I really don't know." Wellemeyer was asked the same question, and his response was equally illuminating. "I don't know," he said, staring blankly at his locker. "Whatever." And Lee's explanation for these bleak days? "I wish I knew. I'd be a rich guy if I knew the answer."

Following the next night's game, Wood didn't have any answers, either. It was a vintage outing for the right-hander: He pitched seven innings, limited the Diamondbacks to two runs and three hits . . . and lost, 2-0. For reasons known to no one, Wood was starting to resemble the hard-luck pitcher of 2003. He had a shimmering earned run average of 2.53, but it wasn't reflected in his 3-2 record. The right-hander offered the same old analysis of the same old story: "We gave up two, they gave up none."

That day, Alou joined the ranks of the mad, although it had nothing to do with the bullpen or Chicago's inability to beat Arizona. Assuming he was speaking off the record, Alou had told *ESPN.com* that he urinated on his hands to make them hard and prevent calluses from forming. *ESPN.com* let the story flow, and now everyone knew about the left fielder's pregame ritual. To his further chagrin, the revelation sparked a citywide debate over whether urinating on one's hands really did make them more resistant to calluses.

Both on and off the field, the Cubs were feeling pissy. The bullpen was running ragged, the offense was averaging just 2.1 runs per game since that sweep of the Mets, and the Cubs had fallen two games behind the Astros for first place in the Central. Desperate times called for desperate measures. The morning after Chicago's latest flop against Arizona, Baker canceled batting practice. "When you're not going good, you can overhit, overanalyze," the manager said. "Sometimes you have to go back to the way you were in high school, when you just put on the uniform and went and played. Take a little pressure off of them, let them get a little bit of rest today, put your uniform on and stretch and get loose, and go play."

The embattled Cubs used their morning respite to regroup. For Borowski, that meant focusing on what was most important: his family. He grabbed a helmet-full of baseballs and a bat and ambled onto the empty field with his four-year-old son, Blaze. "Right here, home plate," he said, handing the bat to Blaze. "Choke up."

Working from the stretch about 10 feet from home plate, Borowski threw the ball underhand. Blaze took a good hack at the pitch, but missed it. "Steeerike one," said Borowski, his face glistening in the sunlight.

He sent another soft toss toward the boy. "Steeerike two."

And another. "Steeerike three."

On the fourth pitch, however, little Blaze ripped a liner that nearly plunked his old man on the head. Some things just weren't changing.

Back in the clubhouse, Slammin' Sammy was trying to do his part to keep his team unified. One of the offerings from his boombox was the wedding-reception staple "Celebrate" by Kool and the Gang. It seemed to be having the desired effect, too. "The first thing you learn in baseball is that you don't let one day affect the next," Walker said while working on a crossword puzzle at his locker. "The second thing is, you don't get too high if you're doing well or too low if you're doing bad. We're all professionals in here. We go about our business every day like we're supposed to."

That was what Lee was trying to do, but it wasn't easy. Despite those clutch home runs against Cincinnati and St. Louis, his first season with the Cubs had been an uphill battle. The first baseman was big and strong, but so far, his numbers weren't: a .256 average, three homers, and 13 runs batted in. As Lee suited up for the series finale, he conceded, "I've probably been trying to do a little too much, with a new team and these great fans. This is a big game today. You don't want to get swept anywhere, but especially at home."

Those hometown fans were growing impatient, particularly when Clement's slider flattened out and the Cubs fell behind 3-1 after three innings. In the fourth inning, when the Cubs failed to score for the third straight time after putting men on base with no outs, boos began to ring out. Said Clement, "I just kept telling myself, 'Don't let this game get out of hand, don't let this game get out of hand. We're going to come back.'"

The Cubs did just that in the fifth inning. They scored five runs, and it was Lee who led the charge with a three-run homer. Lee finished the day with five runs batted in and a career-best five hits in as many at-bats. Following the 11-3 win, no one was happier for the beleaguered first baseman than Baker. "It's nice to see someone break out like that, especially him," he said. "He's worked so hard, and I know he's been a little frustrated."

Clement, meanwhile, raised his record to 5-1. It wasn't his smoothest outing of the season, but in some ways, it was his best. He proved conclusively that his heart was as strong as his arm. "It was a battle," Clement said. "Unlike the past couple of games I've pitched, where everything was working well, I had to find my stuff. This is a game I had to pitch pretty hard to get where I was at. It was a big win for us after losing the first two games."

Big wins rarely were delivered to Cubdom unconditionally. In one way or another, strings were attached. The day the Cubs beat Arizona, they learned they were losing Gonzalez. As usual, there was more to the matter than met the eye and some oddity was sprinkled in for dramatic effect. Gonzalez had been beaned on the wrist by a pitch from Mike Koplove in the second game of the Arizona series . . . or had he? Home-plate umpire Charlie Reliford didn't even award Gonzalez first base, thinking the ball had hit the shortstop's bat instead of his wrist. "You couldn't tell; the umpire couldn't tell," said a befuddled Baker. "Nobody could tell except Alex. Usually when you're hit like that, you show a lot more emotion."

Emotion wasn't part of the shortstop's game, even when he had an imprint of a baseball on his wrist. He once described himself as someone who didn't "try being too flashy," but this pushed his credo to ridiculous extremes. An X-ray machine ended up saying what Gonzalez apparently couldn't: He had a non-displaced fracture of the ulnar styroid bone. The injury would keep him on the disabled list for six to eight weeks.

Enter Ramon Martinez, the quintessential Dusty-type guy. Martinez had played for Baker on the Giants, and one of the manager's first orders of business in Chicago had been to recruit him. The 31-year-old Puerto Rican was a smart role-player who always had come through for Baker in a pinch. "Right now, our possibilities are right here with Ramon," Baker said. "Think where we'd be without

Ramon. I feel very fortunate that we have Ramon. Not a lot of teams have a Ramon. That's a pretty good backup."

If the arc of Gonzalez's rehabilitation followed those of the other wounded Cubs, good old Ramon wouldn't be a backup again for a long time. A lot of players were going on the DL, but no one was coming off it. Grudzielanek's return had been pushed back to late May, while Remlinger's now was scheduled for early June. And Prior's? The Cubs actually had formulated a concrete date—June 3—but they didn't want to commit to it, of course. The season had become a dizzying blur of infirmity, and it was all the Cubs could do to maintain their focus. Said Hendry, "It's just a matter of toughing it out and grinding it out for the next month, and hopefully, we'll still be in a good position where we can make a charge."

The Cubs were in dire need of a break, and not the kind that involved a bone. They received one on May 7, the day they began a three-game series against the Rockies at Wrigley Field. Shawn Estes would be Colorado's starting pitcher in the opener. The left-hander had been the one blemish on Chicago's pitching staff in 2003—going 8-11 with a 5.70 earned run average—but he was a welcome sight in something other than Cubs blue. It was an emotional homecoming for Estes, who was touched for nine runs in Chicago's 11-0 win. In fact, he was greeted so enthusiastically that no one seemed to notice that Zambrano pitched a two-hit, complete-game shutout.

The next afternoon, the Rockies placed another offering on the Wrigley Field altar: Jason Jennings, who had a 10.57 earned run average. Within the first three innings, Sosa and Alou hit solo homers onto Waveland Avenue and Walker launched one onto Sheffield to give Maddux a 3-1 lead. After that, however, the Cubs became the ones bearing gifts. Like they had done for the better part of the past two weeks, they gave away at-bat after at-bat by flailing away at pitchers' pitches.

By the bottom of the ninth inning, the Cubs were on the verge of losing 4-3. First, though, they had to provide a final example of their inability to manufacture runs. With one out and the tying run on third base, Walker and then Patterson whiffed to end the game. The nearly 40,000 fans in attendance didn't need to boo to express their displeasure; the hush that spread across the grandstands was deafening enough.

Earlier in the week, Baker had addressed the offense's shortcomings, saying, "Our team isn't such that we're going to get, like, five singles in a row. We don't have that kind of team. We depend on the long ball and walks and pitching and defense. That's the way it is. We only have a couple guys here with speed. What we have to emphasize is that when you get the bunt sign, you've got to get it down. When you have a runner on third with less than two outs, you've got to get him home. When you have a runner on second, you have to advance him." The players, it seemed, hadn't taken note of Baker's message.

Fortunately, another old friend from the Estes mold showed the Cubs the way in the rubber game on the afternoon of May 9. Jeff Fassero had pitched relief for the Cubs in 2001 and 2002, and not particularly well. His earned run average during his stay in Chicago was 4.57, but like Estes, he had one thing going for him: He was a left-hander. As a result, he always was able to find work. Now 41, Fassero was playing for the Rockies, his seventh major league team. Although he was gray and wrinkled from his Homeric odyssey through baseball, he looked pretty damn good to the Cubs.

However, they wouldn't have had the opportunity to reacquaint themselves with Fassero had it not been for the heroics of Ramirez in the bottom of the 10th inning. With two outs, no one on base, and Chicago trailing 4-3, Ramirez hit a Shawn Chacon offering onto Waveland Avenue to tie the score. But instead of embracing their new lease on life, the Cubs spent the next two innings flailing away. Luckily, Colorado was equally inept at the plate.

By the 13th inning, the Rockies had used up six pitchers and had no choice but to turn to Fassero. Old Faithful promptly did his thing, loading the bases before giving up a game-winning single to Patterson. The fans cheered, and the players hugged. Thanks to helping hands from Estes and Fassero, the Friendly Confines felt friendly again. The Cubs had won their first series in two weeks.

The Wrigley Field love-in was short-lived. For the next six games, the Cubs wouldn't be able to count on any acts of kindness from the opposing team. They were about to embark on a trip to the West Coast, which always had the potential to be harrowing.

In 2001, one of their swings through California all but ended any notions they might have had of October glory. When the Cubs arrived in San Diego on July 31, they actually were in first place, a comfortable four and a half games up on Houston. They split the first two games with the Padres, but fate still was smiling on the Cubbies in the series finale. Behind the nearly flawless pitching of starter Jason Bere, the Cubs took a 3-0 lead into the bottom of the eighth inning. But instead of sticking with the hot hand, manager Don Baylor inexplicably called for the ancient one, Fassero, who loaded the bases and then served up a game-winning grand slam to Ryan Klesko. Said Fassero, "You have all those things working in your favor, you make one bad pitch, and that's the ballgame."

And the season. The ghosts of failures past reappeared after that stunning defeat. Upon traveling up the coast to Los Angeles, the Cubs stumbled and bumbled to two losses in three games against the Dodgers. Before long, their lead in the N.L. Central had dried up, and they finished the season in third place.

This year, the West Coast terrain would be no less treacherous. The Dodgers and the Padres, in first and second place, respectively, in the N.L. West, were playing as well as any team in baseball. The journey began on May 11 in Los Angeles, where the Cubs threw everything they had at the Dodgers, namely Wood. From the get-go, however, something clearly seemed wrong with Chicago's ace. He looked uncomfortable on the mound and gave up two home runs in the second inning. When Glendon Rusch started the third inning instead of Wood, hearts began racing throughout Cubdom. Never mind that Chicago lost the game 7-3. What the hell had happened to Wood?

When he surfaced after the game, the dreaded p-word—precautionary—was bandied about. That same word had been used to describe Prior's injury in March, and then his Achilles tendon disappeared. Nevertheless, the Cubs had a story, and they were sticking to it. Wood's right triceps had tightened up, and, as the pitcher said, "It was something we didn't want to play with."

Tests the next day revealed no damage to Wood's triceps—in fact, the Cubs said he probably would be back within 10 days—but the team didn't play that night's game with any sense of optimism. Behind an offense that was as listless as ever, Chicago suffered a 4-0 loss. Wood had slipped into the abyss of injuries, and the Cubs now were three games behind first-place Houston. Had they arrived at doom's doorstep? It only seemed that way.

After Gonzelez's injury, Hendry had said something about the character of his club that was even more applicable now: "There's no sense in feeling sorry for yourself. [Injuries] are part of the business. Every team usually has some sort of traumatic injury over the course of 162 games. Last year, we got through them. I think everyone thought we were kind of done when Corey got hurt in the middle of July. This has been Dusty's forte. When things are going badly, he finds a way to reach down and find a positive."

Dusty was working overtime on the West Coast. In yet another test of the team's mettle, Walker had to be scratched from the last game of the series because of a sore right shoulder. Grudzielanek was out, Walker was out—and someone named Jose Macias now was up. At 5'8" and 190 pounds, Macias looked more like a redwood stump than a ballplayer. He barely had been used to this point, but Hendry had acquired him from the Expos in the off-season because he was another one of those guys who could come through when times were tough. Said Hendry of the seventh-year big-leaguer, "Jose isn't a household name, but he is a very, very good player." He sure looked that way against the Dodgers, going 3-for-5 as Chicago's offense roared back to life with 14 hits.

The depleted pitching staff also made a stand. No Prior? No Wood? No problem. The Cubs still had Zambrano, who was on the cusp of greatness. His performance—eight innings of two-hit ball—was the main reason for Chicago's 7-3 victory. Zambrano hadn't allowed an earned run in 24 innings, and his earned run average now was 1.82. "I feel great every time I go to the mound," Zambrano said. "When you have more experience in the big leagues, you know what to do in situations, and you know how to get out of situations. You make the adjustments. I always go out there and think I can keep going up at this level."

Onward to San Diego, where the Padres had a special surprise for the Cubs in the series opener on May 14 at newly built Petco Park. In celebration of the 20th anniversary of their National League championship, the Padres donned replicas of the uniforms they had worn when they broke the hearts of Chicago in the 1984 playoffs. The Cubs, however, had their own surprise for the suntanned masses at Petco Park. It also was throwback night for Maddux, who turned back the clock and pitched like he had in his prime. In eight innings, he allowed five hits and one run and, most tellingly, threw only 88 pitches. The 6-1 victory was the 292nd of Maddux's career, moving him ever closer to the coveted 300 mark.

Prior, meanwhile, filled out his day by picking up his bachelor's degree in business from the University of Southern California, which he had completed in the off-season. Since he had plenty of time on his hands, he addressed his fellow graduates while he was there. It was a definite step up from ringing the opening bell at the Chicago Board of Trade. Clad in a cap and gown, he said, "My message to you today is to trust your abilities. Be confident and positive. Let your abilities carry you to success, and take it one step at a time. It's what I tell myself every day. It's what gets me through the tough stretches."

Prior's pitching replacement was going through a tough stretch of his own. Mitre hadn't won a game since April 21 in Pittsburgh, and his earned run average of 5.01 was well above those of Chicago's other starters. As it turned out, all the young right-hander needed was some home cooking. Mitre had grown up blocks away from Petco Park, and with a healthy helping of friends and family in attendance for the next game of the series on May 15, he pitched six strong innings and got his second win of the season. "I took the same approach," Mitre said following the 7-5 victory. "The only thing different was pitching in my hometown." It also was a momentous evening for Sosa, who hit his 549th homer—a 434-foot shot that was the longest in Petco Park's 21-game history—to pass Mike Schmidt and move into ninth place on the all-time list. Sammy really was slammin' now. So far in May, he had five home runs and 13 runs batted in.

If there were any remaining questions about the heart of these Cubbies, they were answered in the team's 4-2 victory the following afternoon in the series finale. Rusch—who was subbing for Wood—gave up just one earned run in four and one-third innings. Martinez—who was subbing for Gonzalez—went 2-for-4 with a run batted in. Macias—who was subbing for Walker, who had been subbing for Grudzielanek—hit a home run in the fifth inning that put the Cubs in the lead for good. And Borowski—whom everyone wanted subbed out—got his 21st consecutive save, a new team record.

Somehow, some way, the Cubs were surviving, even thriving. Instead of going belly-up on the West Coast, they had become stronger. They were riding a four-game winning streak and were tied again with the Astros for first place in the N.L. Central.

"When you get a chance, you want to do good," said Macias, who had sparked the offense during Chicago's four-game run by going 11-for-20. "We need to win as many games as we can, and I have to do my job. I'm feeling very comfortable at home plate right now. It's something I can't even explain. I know my swing's there. We don't make excuses because of injuries or anything. Some people are out, and the people who are in try to do the job and make sure we continue to win. Give me a shot, and I'll be there and ready to go. Everybody's hot right now."

The black veil was lifting. Or was it? Sosa was scratched from the lineup just before that final game against San Diego. The reason? He threw out his back while sneezing.

HANGING ON FOR DEAR LIFE

TEN

The manager's office at Wrigley Field looked like a bunker. Separated from the clubhouse by a short flight of stairs, it was windowless and had cinderblock walls. Countless plans of attack had been formulated over the years in these colorless quarters, only to be blown to smithereens on the battlefield outside. It was easy to imagine Gene "Stick" Michael or Jim Essian, a tin pot on his head and a bayonet in his hands, cowering under the tiny desk and praying for mercy as another season was torched.

Baker had done his best to give the office a warm and homey feel, decorating it with pictures of family and friends and assorted knickknacks. But even with such adornments, it remained the bomb shelter it always had been. Next to Baker's desk, amid the collage of his otherwise blessed life, the Cubs' 2004 schedule was taped to the wall like some ill-begotten outline for world conquest. Directly above it was a cross.

Apparently, Baker needed a bigger cross. If Bartman's outstretched hands had been the first clue that forces well beyond the manager's control were at work—a curse, if you will—Sosa's sneeze was the second. On May 17, after the Cubs had returned to Chicago from San Diego, the slugger had an MRI. The procedure detected a sprained ligament in his lower back, which would sideline him for at least two to three weeks.

This latest blow would have been unimaginable anywhere but in

Cubdom. Sosa was a bigger-than-life character who had averaged 155 games played per season from 1997 through 2003. He had withstood beanballs and home-plate collisions and encounters with the ivy-covered brick wall in right field. Through thick and thin, the manager had known he could pencil Slammin' Sammy's name in the lineup. Now, though, Chicago's iron man had been felled by a sneeze. Said Baker, "I was always taught in church that the Lord won't put more on you than you can handle, but this is getting heavy."

On the night of May 18, as the Nubs staggered forward and began a three-game series against the Giants at Wrigley Field, Sosa received an epidural injection at Northwestern Memorial Hospital to relieve the swelling and pain in his back. The Cubs had undergone a radical transformation since Opening Day on April 5. Their batting order (excluding the pitcher) for that game against the Reds had been Grudzielanek, Patterson, Sosa, Alou, Ramirez, Lee, Gonzalez, and Barrett; in the series opener against the Giants, it was Walker, Martinez, Hollandsworth, Alou, Ramirez, Lee, Patterson, and Barrett.

Cubs Lite was no match for San Francisco starter Jason Schmidt, who yielded just one hit, a Texas Leaguer by Barrett, in his complete-game, 1-0 win. Chicago—specifically, Clement—really missed Sosa's bat in the middle of the lineup. With any kind of offensive support, the right-hander would have coasted to a victory. He allowed five hits and a run over eight innings, but his hard work went to waste. The night was a bummer all around. In addition to the Cubs losing while Sneezin' Sammy was prone at Northwestern Memorial Hospital, Houston beat the Marlins to regain sole possession of first place.

Baker, however, still was expecting the best, even though the worst was occurring at every turn. "Everybody who wants to play is now getting a chance to play," he said. "In spring training, I told them that there were going to be injuries, and if something happens, you don't feel sorry for yourselves. You just play, and you expect whoever is out there to do the job." Baker even was smiling again. No one was going to find *him* cowering under his desk in his bunker. "I don't have no emotional problems," he said. "Have you ever seen me down?"

Even when the chips were down again on the night of May 19, Baker wasn't. In fact, he was so confident in his ragged team that he all but dared the Wrigley Field ghosts to mess with him. With Chicago losing 3-2 to the Giants in the bottom of the seventh, he scanned his ever-thinning bench and fixed his eyes on Jason Dubois. It mattered little that the 25-year-old Dubois never had batted in a major league game. And it mattered less that, with one out and men on first and third, this was one of Chicago's few scoring opportunities of the game. Baker sent Dubois to the plate as a pinch hitter for Zambrano and expected the best. "He can hit," Baker said of his untested pinch hitter. "That man can hit." Dubois hit one just far enough, and the tying run scored on a sacrifice fly.

When the game went into extra innings, Baker was as upbeat as ever. It mattered little that the manager had used up the bulk of his bullpen—Farnsworth, Hawkins, and Borowski—and needed to end the game quickly. And it mattered less that the Cubs had scored just three runs the entire series. Baker expected the best. He got it, too, when Alou hit a walkoff homer in the bottom of the 10th. As if the game's outcome had been preordained, Baker said, "Moises hit it right on time."

Could anything stop these go-go Cubbies? They had done such a bang-up job of insulating themselves from reality that the next morning's pie-in-the-sky injury report almost seemed plausible. While his teammates were trickling into the clubhouse, Wood was out on the field testing his triceps. Afterward, Hendry gathered the media into the interview room and cheerfully announced, "Woody's session went extremely well. He feels about 95 percent." In Cubs-speak, that meant Wood was going on the disabled list . . . as a precautionary measure. The GM emphatically added that there was no need to worry. "This isn't something that's going to be a long-term thing. We can skip those questions. There's nothing else that you don't know. There's no different projection."

Wood then addressed the media in the interview room and seconded that motion. "I'm saying, why push it and miss two months?"

the right-hander reasoned. "I think we're doing the smart thing. Rather than go out there [on May 23] and hope, we're going to shoot for [May 28] and know."

This wasn't a setback, the flame-throwing Texan insisted. On the contrary, it was a breakthrough, a triumph of the human spirit. "Two years ago, I would have kept pitching," he said. "I think it's a smarter move than I would have made in the past." First Prior had received his business degree from USC, and now Wood had gotten in touch with his inner self. Chicago's ace pitchers were bettering themselves in every conceivable way . . . except on the mound.

Over in the clubhouse a few dark tunnels away, something else didn't seem quite right. The sound patterns were skewed. Since Slammin' Sammy wasn't around, his boombox, positioned at the entrance of the room like a welcome mat, wasn't cranking out its usual happy-go-lucky fare. In fact, it wasn't cranking out anything at all. Filling the void were the grittier riffs of ZZ Top, which emanated from the other end of the clubhouse. After batting practice, however, stereophonic order was restored. Sosa appeared for just long enough to cue up his beloved salsa on his boombox. Even after he walked ever so gingerly up the clubhouse stairs and left to continue his convalescence, the salsa played on.

On the field, the Cubs would have to continue to play on without Sosa . . . and Wood . . . and Prior . . . and Grudzielanek . . . and Remlinger . . . and Gonzalez. At least they could count on the services of Maddux, who was sharp again in the rubber game against the Giants that afternoon. And Alou, who hit a two-run homer in the bottom of the seventh inning to tie the score at 3-3. After Alou's home run, the noise level in the grandstands rose several decibels. The faithful smelled a win, especially after the previous night's dramatics. They, too, were expecting the best—but this time, it didn't happen. Borowski gave up a two-run homer to light-hitting second baseman Neifi Perez in the 10th inning, and Chicago lost 5-3.

The season wasn't even two months old, but Baker was weary. "When I signed up for this job, [the stress] comes with it," he said.

"Under the circumstances, you wind up sleeping better because you're tired like a dog after these games."

The faithful, or at least two of them, found a different way to cope with the stress of this latest setback. About a mile from the ballpark, at the intersection of Addison and Southport, a young couple continued to expect the best. Oblivious to the cars, pedestrians, and everything else, these twentysomethings were lying on the grassy parkway in a passionate embrace. They were, it appeared, on the verge of hitting a home run of their own, presumably a game-winner.

Love may have been in the air outside the ballpark, but within the white lines of the diamond, it was war. On the afternoon of May 21, the Cardinals arrived at Wrigley Field for three more games—and that touchy-feely stuff from years past seemed like a distant memory.

Walker was something of an authority on big-time rivalries, having played for Boston in 2003. He said his first taste of the Cubs-Cardinals rivalry had packed all the adrenal punch of his Yankees-Red Sox experience. "I thought it was very similar to the Yankees-Red Sox rivalry I was involved in last year. I don't know how much more intense you could get than the Cubs-Cardinals. It's as high as you could possibly be. As players, you have to put a lot more into it, more so than a usual game because everything is so focused on each pitch and each play and each inning. It's an incredible amount of energy that goes into those games."

By the end of this series, one team would be a lot more drained than the other. The logical candidate was Chicago, whose resources were depleted to begin with. In the opener, Mitre made his eighth start of the season in place of Prior; judging by how lost he looked, that seemed like about eight too many. When Baker directed him to the clubhouse after five innings, the Cubs were losing 7-3.

Had the go-go Cubs finally run out of gas? No, adversity was their fuel. Chicago had the Cardinals right where it wanted them. "Ultimately, you don't panic," Walker said. "That's the worst thing you can do. You just try to do what we know how to do, and it will work out." In short order, the complexion of the series changed. Chicago's relievers—Wellemeyer, Farnsworth, and Hawkins—stopped the Cardinals in their tracks, and Alou hit a three-run homer in the seventh inning. Although the Cardinals hung on and won 7-6, their momentum was all but lost. Said Alou, who had almost single-handedly kept the Cubs afloat since The Sneeze: "I know that without Sammy, I have a lot more responsibility."

The next afternoon, Rusch had the responsibility of standing in for Wood. The left-hander had played for the last-place Brewers in 2003 and had been so abysmal—1-12 with a 6.42 earned run average—that not even they wanted him for 2004. But as far as the Cubs were concerned, the 29-year-old Rusch met one key criterion: He was available. Desperate for left-handed bullpen depth because of the absence of Remlinger, they signed him on April 1. Now he had been unceremoniously elevated to the role of starter, and he was about to face a Cardinals lineup that featured some of the most prodigious sluggers in the league. This was the baseball equivalent of a Hail Mary pass.

Chicago, however, went right after St. Louis and scored four times in the bottom of the first inning. Then Rusch did the rest. On this day, anyway, the only way Rusch differed from Wood was that he threw the ball left-handed. He was ruthlessly efficient, striking out nine and giving up one run over seven and two-thirds innings. In all, the game lasted a mere two hours and 15 minutes. Not only did Rusch's Cubs win 7-1, but he also received a standing ovation when he exited the game. "That gives you the chills when fans get on their feet like that," Rusch said. "It's pretty neat."

The faithful cheered on another unlikely hero in the finale on the night of May 23: Borowski. Just as the Cubs had done the previous day, they knocked down St. Louis in the first inning by scoring four runs. This time, though, the Cardinals got up. They slugged away at Chicago's starter, Clement, who left the game after seven innings with a precarious 4-3 lead. Hawkins breezed through the eighth inning, but Borowski's job would be a lot tougher in the ninth. He had to take on the heart of St. Louis' order—Albert Pujols, Jim Edmonds, and Scott Rolen, who already had combined for 101 RBI in 2004—and the margin for error remained just one run. The odds weren't in favor of Borowski and his 6.35 earned run average, which meant, of course, that he had the Cardinals right where he wanted them. Pujols flied out to left; Edmonds struck out swinging; and Rolen flied out to center.

The Cardinals left Chicago with their tails between their legs, two and a half games behind the first-place Cubs and Reds. "It was big to win a series against these guys," said Clement, who got his team-best sixth victory. "I can't say enough about my team. They got me those runs early, and Hawkins and Borowski were super."

The laws of physics in Cubdom were unyieldingly strict: What went up had to come down. The spiral was barely detectable at first, starting a few hours before that final game against the Cardinals when Wood trotted onto the field to limber up his triceps. The right-hander's return was only five days away, and there was a lot of work to do. After just eight pitches, however, his trial run skidded to a halt. He abruptly left the field and disappeared into the trainer's room.

Hendry, the voice of reason, said there was no need to worry. "He's not in any severe pain." Wood would undergo a bone scan on May 24 . . . as a precautionary measure. "We're not expecting anything negative," the GM reassured. Sure enough, the bone scan didn't turn up any structural damage to Wood's arm. It was the usual stuff: Wood was OK—really, he was—but he wouldn't be seen on the mound anytime soon. The Cubs were shutting him down, and he would miss up to five more starts. Wood's triceps was going the way of Prior's Achilles tendon. Pretty soon, they'd have to send a search party out to find it.

When the Cubs arrived in Houston to begin a two-game series against the Astros on May 25, they had a problem. A team that was supposed to soar to the stars was coming apart, and many of the pieces—the ligaments, tendons, and bones—were hurtling back down to earth. "We still have a long way to go," Baker said, but the Cubs were going in the wrong direction.

This was one of those early-season series that had been circled on the calendar in thick red pen. The Astros, with a lethal blend of pitching and hitting, had been expected to be Chicago's main competition in the N.L. Central. "It's a big series," Macias said. "Houston's got a very good team. We need to put our mind on winning every game we can. They'll be there till the end."

But would the Cubs be there, too? If this short series did indeed provide a first glimpse of how the divisional race would unfold, Chicago was in worse shape than anyone had thought. Houston had its own issues entering the series—namely a five-game losing streak that had dropped the team behind the first-place Reds and second-place Cubs in the standings—but they were rectified in a hurry. Even Chicago's healthy pitchers looked sickly against the Astros. In his first 56.1 innings of the season, Zambrano had allowed two home runs; in five innings on the night of May 25, he gave up two more. The Astros, in contrast, were close to perfect, as starter Ray Oswalt and relievers Dan Miceli and Octavio Dotel combined to blank the Cubs 5-0.

Said Lee, who hadn't hit a home run since May 6: "It seems like we've been all or nothing. It seems like we've put up 10 [runs] or zero." The Cubs, in fact, had been more nothing than all. They had been shut out in six of their 44 games.

The next night, Maddux was the one who resembled roadkill. In addition to a liner that bounced off his shin and another that nearly decapitated him, he was drilled for three home runs. The Cubs didn't even score their first run of the series until the fourth inning, when Barrett tapped a roller up the middle that brought home Ramirez. By the end of the evening, the Astros had won 7-3 and had overtaken Chicago for second place in the N.L. Central.

The one sliver of light amid the gloom was the long-delayed appearance of Remlinger, who pitched a scoreless two-thirds of an inning in the opening game against the Astros. But his return was offset by more casualties. As soon as Remlinger came off the disabled list, Mercker went on it because of his chronically sore back. Then after the Houston series, the Cubs announced that outfielder Tom Goodwin (a strained groin) and Wellemeyer (a partial muscle tear in his right shoulder) were being placed on the DL, too. How was this possible? Had they hurt themselves while sitting on the bench? Wellemeyer had pitched only 13 innings and Goodwin had batted only 42 times in 2004, but not even they were immune to this injury curse.

The Cubs had ripped through so many contingency plans that it was becoming difficult to keep track of them. Was this Plan R, Plan Y, or Plan CC? Who knew? At any rate, the new one involved left-handed pitcher Jimmy Anderson and outfielder David Kelton, who were summoned from the Cubs' Triple-A minor-league team in Des Moines, Iowa. If the carnage continued at its current rate, the Double-A roster in Jackson, Tennessee, would be fair game by August.

The next cruel twist of fate involved the schedule. Because of that rainout against the Pirates in late April, the Cubs had to lead off their series in Pittsburgh with two games on May 28. A double-header? They barely had enough warm bodies to play a single-header. Eight players were out with injuries, including four pitchers. Baker said that in his 12 years as a manager, he had "never seen more injuries to the pitching staff," but his message to the players who still were standing remained the same: "You just have to deal with it."

The Cubs appeared to have the right man for the job—Clement—in game one. He had emerged as a leader in these trying times, rallying his teammates with gutty outing after gutty outing. "You win," he had said, "by going out and executing and getting everybody together and on the right track."

But in the bottom of the fifth inning, Clement's Abraham Lincoln goatee, which had held so stoically firm all season long, became a droopy mess again. He nailed the backstop with one pitch and hit Bobby Hill, Jason Kendall, and Craig Wilson with three others. And before the Cubs knew what had hit *them*, their 1-0 lead had turned to a 4-1 deficit. It was a new low in a season that quickly was being filled with them. Not since May 18, 1898, had a Cubs pitcher beaned three batters in the same inning.

The one player who didn't seem overwhelmed by the dark forces closing in was, ironically, Barrett. In the bottom of the seventh inning, with two outs and the bases loaded, he strode to the plate as a pinch hitter and came through with a grand slam that gave the Cubs a 5-4 lead. All that did, however, was set the stage for another spectacular failure. The Cubs lost 9-5 when Borowski gave up a game-winning grand slam to Rob Mackowiak with two outs in the bottom of the ninth inning.

In the second game, the Cubs took another lead into the bottom of the ninth inning—they were up 4-2, thanks to a third straight improbably strong outing by Rusch—but it was becoming increasingly difficult to expect the best. The question wasn't *if* the Cubs would lose—it was *how*. The answer came quickly. Hawkins gave up a two-run, game-tying homer to Mackowiak in the ninth, and Francis Beltran surrendered a game-winning homer to Wilson in the 10th. As Wilson rounded the bases, Baker was doubled over in the dugout. The manager later said he never had seen anything like this double-header, but it was important to note that the season was only 47 games old.

The next night's loss to Pittsburgh didn't come with any bells and whistles. Mitre got shelled early, and the final score was 10-7. It was strictly garden-variety fare, although that didn't make it any easier for Baker to stomach. "It doesn't matter how you lose," Baker said. "Nobody keeps track of tough losses or lopsided losses. A loss is a loss." All losses weren't, in fact, created equal. The Cubs reached a milestone with this one. Their losing streak now was at five games, the longest of the Baker era.

Late in the afternoon of May 30, the Cubs finally put themselves out of their misery. No, they didn't strap on cement boots and jump into the nearby Allegheny River. Instead, they won. They actually won. Zambrano flirted with disaster all day long, but he allowed only one run through six innings. Then the offense came to the rescue, scoring three runs in the seventh inning, one in the eighth, and seven in the ninth. There would be no last-inning implosions on this day; Chicago's 12-1 lead was bullpen-proof. After Borowski retired the Pirates in order in the ninth, a relieved Baker said, "I'm just glad we came out ahead."

On the final day of the month, Memorial Day, the Cubs were back in Wrigley Field for the first of a three-game series against the Astros. In some respects, it was a microcosm of the entire season. There was a glimmer of hope: Alou hit a two-run homer in the fifth inning to lift the Cubs to a 3-1 victory in a key matchup against a division rival. And at the same time, there was a nagging sense of impending doom: Maddux left the game in the seventh inning after tweaking a rib muscle, all the while insisting that he was perfectly fine.

Mostly, though, there was a glimmer of hope. Unlike so many other years, Memorial Day wasn't the right moment to eulogize the Cubs. "Things go in streaks," said Baker, Chicago's fearless field general. "You just have to ride it out." Despite their recent struggles, the Cubs remained in the thick of the N.L. Central race. At 27-23, they were tied for second place, a mere two and a half games behind the Reds. "You're going to lose games, you're going to win games," said Lee, whose bat finally was beginning to heat up. "At the end, you just want to be in the playoffs. So it doesn't matter how you get there, as long as you're where you want to be at the end."

The Cubs weren't dead yet. There was one other reason to still believe: Mighty Mark Prior's Achilles tendon had been found, and it was on its way home.

June

HE CAME TO CONQUER

ELEVEN

The future, always a mile or two beyond the horizon in Cubdom, finally appeared in June 2001. This wasn't the usual mirage, conjured by the baseball gods as a practical joke. It was flesh and bone. Standing a sturdy 6'5" and 220 pounds, it had a poker face festooned with dark sideburns, calf muscles the size of footballs, and a long right arm that seemed to impose its will effortlessly. The venerable publication *Baseball America* documented the sighting with a cover headline that read: MARK PRIOR MAY BE THE BEST COLLEGE PITCHER EVER.

As a junior at USC in 2001, Prior had led the Trojans to the College World Series and had collected more awards than anyone could count. He was a can't-miss major league prospect. Heading into that June's amateur draft, the 20-year-old Prior was coveted by every team except the one that mattered most: Minnesota, which had the first pick. The cash-strapped Twins couldn't afford the multimillion-dollar bonus required to sign the best college player ever, so they settled on catcher Joe Mauer. Although Mauer was an outstanding player in his own right and would be popular with the local fans because he was from the Twin Cities, he was no Mark Prior.

Something weird was about to happen to the Lovable Losers. Something was about to go right. The Cubs had the second pick, and not even they could screw it up. The 2001 draft wouldn't bring a Jeff Wehmeier, a Mike Harkey, or any other cadavers masquerading as bonus babies. All Chicago had to do was call Prior's name, then sit back and watch him shine.

When Prior officially became a member of the Cubs the first week of June, he was beside himself with excitement. "It's kind of mind-boggling that this is starting to become a little bit of a reality," he told *Cubs.com*. "Knowing that I get a chance to play in one of the most honored fields in America, Wrigley Field—I mean, who wouldn't want to pitch there and play for the Chicago Cubs?" Prior, a native of San Diego, obviously wasn't a student of Cubs history. He was bliss-fully unaware of what he had gotten himself into, which probably was for the better.

The faithful had their savior, but it would be a while before he came to the rescue. The Cubs weren't inclined to rush Prior along, especially since he had just completed a college season in which he had pitched 138.2 innings. "He can't come straight to the major leagues, or won't come straight to the major leagues," John Stockstill, the Cubs' scouting director, said to *Cubs.com*. "Every college pitcher needs to have a little bit of time to get ready." No one complained very loudly. After so many decades of suffering, what was another year?

Prior pitched his first professional game on April 7, 2002, and it was a beauty. Suiting up for the Cubs' Double-A affiliate in Jackson, Tennessee, he struck out the first six batters he faced en route to a victory over the club from Mobile, Alabama. There were five more overpowering starts for Jackson before Prior moved on to Triple-A Des Moines, where he cut a swath through the Iowa cornfields with a 1.65 earned run average and 24 strikeouts in three games. Like a conquering hero on a white steed who would liberate the masses from the curse's reign of terror, he was winding ever closer to the heart of Cubdom.

Prior crossed the Mississippi River and traversed the plains of Illi-nois, and on the evening of May 22, he rode up to the gates of Wrigley Field. A captive audience was waiting: 40,000 screaming fans and more than 150 curious members of the media. The Pirates were there, too, although they seemed less thrilled about it than everyone else. Prior's major league debut was everything the faithful had fantasized it would be. The Cubs won 7-4, and Prior allowed just four hits and two runs over six innings. What's more, he had 10 strikeouts, the most by a Chicago pitcher in his first big-league game since 1969.

For Prior, it was a typical outing; for Cubdom, it was something divine. The young pitcher found that out when he was mobbed by fans outside the ballpark after the game. "I got caught in a logjam on Halsted and Clark," he said. "I was driving, and they saw me in the car. I didn't sign [autographs] because I was in the middle of traffic. I didn't think it was the safe thing to do. I know my life's going to change. For me, I'm still just a simple guy, kind of low key. I'll just have to find some restaurants that aren't maybe so high-profile."

There was nowhere for Prior to hide. Although the remainder of 2002 meandered the way of most seasons—the Cubs finished 30 games out of first place—the future was in plain sight. In 116.2 innings that year, Prior struck out 147 batters and had a 3.32 earned run average. He was the perfect complement to Wood, who now was fully recovered from his career-threatening elbow injury in 1999. It would be only a matter of time before the future and the present intersected.

For once, the wait wasn't long. Prosperity came to Cubdom in a flash, in the form of the 2003 N.L. Central title. And that merely was the beginning of this new age; Prior, remember, was just 23 years old. After Chicago's loss to the Marlins in the National League Championship Series, Prior said, "I think we took a good step this year. Hopefully, we're in this position again next year."

Next year never came for Prior, of course. The present, the future, and everything in between vanished into thin air along with his Achilles tendon. It didn't make sense. When Wood blew out his elbow, few people were shocked. He had an erratic throwing motion that put his arm in peril. Prior, in contrast, was a finished product. His delivery was so smooth and mechanically sound that he was supposed to be immune to serious injuries. But in the grander scheme, technical issues didn't carry much weight. Like Wood before him, Prior ultimately succumbed to his destiny. Maybe this bold notion of a golden age of Cubs baseball, displayed so tantalizingly in front of the faithful, had been a mirage after all.

Prior's injury set the tone for the season. One by one, key players disappeared, leaving Baker to field a lineup that looked a whole lot more like the 1974 Cubs than the 2004 Cubs. Seemingly resigned to his fate, the manager said, "You just keep going forward. What happens if they're not back when you anticipate? Then you're disappointed. I don't like being disappointed."

Gradually, though, Baker and his players could allow themselves to hope for better days. Prior's Achilles tendon had been found, and it was on its way home. All the Cubs had to do was hold on until it got there. Once Prior returned, a new tone would be established and the rest of the missing pieces in this season of great expectations would begin to fall back into place.

"The team just has to take it slow, step by step," said Zambrano, who had been doing his fair share to compensate for the absence of Prior. "The losses are going to come, but if we can just maintain .500, that's good for us. Then when we have to put up a little bit more, we'll put up a little bit more."

Cubdom would have to be patient. Like Prior's first journey to the big leagues in 2002, this one featured several twists and turns. It began in earnest on May 1 at the Cubs' spring training site in Mesa, Arizona, where Prior pitched a simulated inning against minor-leaguers. Witnesses, presumably hidden behind cactuses with binoculars pressed against their eyes, claimed he looked great. Prior, however, was only moderately pleased, saying he was rusty. On May 5 in Mesa, he ratcheted up his workload to two simulated innings. This time, he said it was the best he had felt during his rehabilitation, and the good news was promptly relayed back to the anxious flock in Chicago.

Prior's comeback continued in this manner for the next couple of weeks. All the while, the *Chicago Tribune* charted his course with "The

Prior Watch." The pitcher was "turning the corner," he was "in the homestretch," he was "right on schedule," and he was "turning the corner" again. Mighty Mark Prior was galloping toward Chicago.

On May 20, the trail wound to a Cubs outpost in Lansing, Michigan, home of the Single-A Lugnuts. This was a pivotal juncture for Prior, who would be pitching in his first real game since that night Bartman bewitched the Cubs. The 10,000-seat stadium was jam-packed with people who had made the 200-mile pilgrimage from Chicago to Lansing, and the small-town press box was overtaken by the big-city media. Wearing the red-and-white colors of the Lugnuts, Prior didn't disappoint. After pitching three no-hit innings, he left the field to a standing ovation. "I wasn't holding anything back," he said. "I went out and pitched like it was a real game, like I was in Wrigley Field pitching to a big-league team."

Prior still had some miles to travel before he pitched to big-leaguers. Five days later, he suited up again for the Lugnuts, throwing four and two-thirds innings and giving up one run and two hits. It was another step in the right direction, although Prior wasn't satisfied. "I didn't feel like I had the life I usually do," he said. "As far as soreness and injuries, I felt fine. I just didn't feel like I had the adrenaline going as much as I usually do."

Prior then headed to Des Moines, the last leg of his trek. After he made his first start for Des Moines on May 30, in which he struck out 10 and allowed only one run and three hits in six and one-third innings, the Cubs' brass had seen enough. The date was set: On the afternoon of Friday, June 4, Prior would pitch at Wrigley Field against the Pirates, the very same team he slew when he first stormed the gates of the old ballpark two years earlier.

Considering the gauntlet Chicago had to run in June, his return couldn't come soon enough. The month would feature eight games against the Astros, three against the Pirates, seven against the Cardinals, three against the Anaheim Angels, three against the Oakland A's, and three against the Chicago White Sox. When June began, all of those teams except the Pirates were above .500, and the Angels and the White Sox were in first place in their respective divisions. It was the type of month that could make or break the Cubs, who were broken as it was.

"As a team right now, we're really struggling with a lot of injuries," said reliever Francis Beltran, a career minor-leaguer whose role in Chicago's bullpen was increasing steadily because of all those injuries. "Everybody knows that. We need to try to get healthy and keep doing better than what we've been doing. It'll be good when we start getting guys back because we really need them right now. But we're going to make it. We're going to be fine."

The Cubs sure didn't look fine in the second of their three-game series against Houston on June 1 at Wrigley Field, and their ineptitude had nothing to do with injuries. In fact, Rusch was perfectly capable in his fourth start as a fill-in, allowing three runs over five innings. The 38,000 people in attendance that night must have felt like they were living out some sickening version of the movie *Groundhog Day*. They had seen this same scene unfold over and over and over—not just this year, but every year. Anyone who had followed the team for any length of time knew this, and knew it well: The base paths were where Cubs players went to die.

And even though the wind was blowing out and a tomato can named Brandon Duckworth was pitching, they died all night against Houston. With the score tied 3-3 in the bottom of the fourth inning, the Cubs loaded the bases with no outs, but then Patterson struck out swinging and Martinez grounded meekly into a double play. Two innings later, with the score still 3-3, Chicago loaded the bases again with no outs. This time, Lee popped out to shallow right, Patterson struck out swinging, and Martinez struck out looking. As the final insult, the Astros provided a textbook example of how to hit in the clutch when pinch-hitter Mike Lamb produced a two-out, two-run double in the top of the eighth inning to give Houston a 5-3 victory.

If the Cubs had been unable to knock out Duckworth, they wouldn't stand a chance against future Hall-of-Famer Roger Clemens the next afternoon in the series finale. In his first season with the

Astros, the 41-year-old Clemens was rediscovering his youth. When the game started, he was 7-0 with a 2.38 earned run average; when it ended, he was 8-0 with a 2.27 earned run average. Over seven innings against Clemens, the Cubs scraped together just one run and five hits. Said Chicago's Clement, who was the loser in the 5-1 game: "We ran into a good pitcher who's 8-0. He threw the ball like he's been throwing it all year."

The Cubs had been playing miserably, losing seven of their past 10 games and falling to fifth place in the N.L. Central. But their fortunes were about to turn—Mighty Mark Prior had made it all the way home. Since there was no baseball on June 3, the Cubs had an opportunity to let the magnitude of the moment sink in. "It's going to be a tremendous boost," Baker said. "The fans will get into it. We've been waiting on Mark all year long."

A standing-room-only crowd filed into sun-splashed Wrigley Field on June 4 to see Cubdom's savior. This was no mirage. There he was, flesh and bone, warming up in the bullpen next to the left field foul line, his pitches popping as they hit the catcher's glove. The day of reckoning had arrived. It was exhilarating . . . and a little bit scary. What if—*what if*—the Cubs didn't win?

The way Prior looked after moving from the practice mound to the real mound, that didn't seem possible. His first pitch was a ground out to third base; his second was a ball; his third was a pop out to third base; his fourth was a ball; his fifth was a pop foul out of play; and his sixth was a ground out to third base. Three up, three down.

The Pirates didn't even hit the ball out of the infield until Craig Wilson flied out to center in the fifth inning. All told, Prior pitched six scoreless innings, allowing no walks and two hits while striking out eight. Much to the unbridled joy of everyone in attendance—and the relief of Prior himself—Chicago's conquering hero had returned with a vengeance. "I had some anxiety going into it," said Prior, who was taken out only because Baker didn't want to overextend him in his first game back. "I was probably a little nervous. You can't duplicate the intensity and adrenaline at this level, no matter how many rehab starts. But I felt like I made good pitches."

It would have been a fairy-tale ending to Prior's long and winding comeback, except the final words of the story had yet to be written. Pittsburgh starter Jason Fogg—he of the 6.90 earned run average—vexed the easily vexed Chicago hitters, and the score was 0-0 when Prior exited. With two outs in the bottom of the eighth inning, however, Hollandsworth singled in Alou to give the Cubs a 1-0 lead and put them in position to eke out the win and salvage their dignity.

The ninth inning began with Sweaty Joe on the mound. Leadoff hitter Jason Kendall hit a shot to left field, but Alou made a diving catch. One out. Jack Wilson then doubled, but Daryle Ward followed by hitting a pop fly to Ramirez. Two outs. In nervous anticipation of the final out, the faithful were on their feet, clapping and cheering with all the energy they could summon. Sweat was flying all over the ballpark. In a moment, so were baseballs. Craig Wilson singled in the tying run, and Borowski, visibly shaken, was whisked off the field. In came Remlinger, who promptly gave up a go-ahead single to Chris Stynes. The faithful slumped into their seats.

Chicago had three outs to turn a 2-1 deficit into a victory. Macias led off with a double and was advanced to third by Walker on a sacrifice bunt, but then Lee popped out to first base. As Patterson strode to the plate, the faithful were on their feet again, exhorting him to give this story a happy ending. Instead, he flied out to center field. Like so many Cubs players in so many games over so many years, Macias died a grisly death on third base, taking the final shred of hope down with him.

Now what? Mighty Mark Prior had come and he had conquered, just as everyone had imagined. Yet not even he had been able to save the Cubs from themselves.

AGONY . . .

TWELVE

It had been a long road for Borowski, too. In fact, Sweaty Joe may have traveled the hardest road of all. No one put him on the cover of a magazine and called him the best college pitcher ever, and no one followed his every move to the big leagues. He went it alone.

His existence barely even was acknowledged by the organization that first signed him, the White Sox, who took a flyer on him in the 32nd round of the 1989 draft and then let him founder in the Rookie League before giving him the boot in 1991. For the next nine years, Borowski slogged through an alphabet soup of minor-league burgs from St. Charles, Illinois, to Richmond, Virginia. In between, he pitched a handful of games for the Orioles, Braves, and Yankees, but he never was able to stick in the majors.

In 2000, Borowski slipped off the map altogether, landing in the netherworld of the Mexican League. "You look back, and that's pretty much the lowest point of your career right there," he said. "You're pretty much on the outs." At 29 and with his wife pregnant with their first child, Borowski briefly considered bagging the whole thing and becoming a fireman. But he was too thickheaded to give up. He kept riding broken-down buses through Mexico, still figuring they might lead him someplace good. "You don't want to hit rock-bottom in your career," Borowski said, "but sometimes it makes you a tougher person. I think that's what happened to me."

One day the bus took him to the town of Obregon, where he happened to come across Oneri Fleita, an old minor-league acquaintance who now was the Cubs' coordinator of Latin American operations. Fleita watched Borowski pitch, and he liked what he saw. It wasn't long before the Cubs signed the right-hander and assigned him to their Triple-A team in Iowa. "He exemplifies what the American Dream is about," Fleita said. "Most guys quit. People have no idea how hard it is to keep at it. Hats off to the guy."

By 2002, Borowski was entrenched as one of the Cubs' middle relievers. What he lacked in physical talent he made up for with guts and guile. "I don't have a 98-mile-per-hour fastball or anything like that," he said. "I'm not going to blow people away. I've got to be smart—get ahead of people and try to put them away as quick as possible." When Borowski was elevated to the role of closer in 2003, his kill-or-be-killed approach worked better than it ever had before. He laid out everything he had and became one of the most pleasant surprises in a season that was defined by them. "I'm going to go and ride this for as long as I can," he said. "My arm feels great."

In reality, Borowski's arm nearly was used up. All of those miles finally caught up with him in 2004. Sweaty Joe still had the will, but he no longer had the way. Even Baker, his staunchest supporter, acknowledged that in the wake of his collapse against the Pirates. That game had meant so much to the Cubs—the dreams of the season had been pinned to it—and Borowski had been unable to get the final out.

The next day, Borowski was given the boot from the closer's role and Hawkins was the primary man assigned to it. Then he was placed on the disabled list, even though the doctors weren't exactly sure what was wrong with him. A battery of tests didn't turn up anything. "I don't know how many more [tests] he can take," Baker said. "He's had every test known to man. Let's hope he's OK."

Borowski had personified the 2003 Cubs. Through blood, sweat, tears, and some more sweat, he had surpassed all expectations. Now he personified the 2004 Cubs, too. He was broken down, and no one could pinpoint the problem. Considering Borowski had been hurting all season long, as evidenced by his 8.02 earned run average, the timing for placing him on the disabled list was suspicious. Sweaty Joe, it seemed, had met the same fate as the Bartman ball: He had been offered up as a sacrifice to the baseball gods.

Fortunately, the Cubs didn't need Borowski, Hawkins, or anyone else from the bullpen to save the day in the second of the three-game series against the Pirates on the afternoon of June 5. For a change, the hitters provided a margin for error. Zambrano pitched nearly as well as Prior had the day before, going eight innings and allowing four hits and one run, and the offense exploded for three runs in the seventh and three more in the eighth to pave the way for the 6-1 victory.

The series finale the next afternoon brought another unexpected development. That rib muscle Maddux had tweaked six days earlier against the Astros? Well, it hadn't become fodder for the TV show *Unsolved Mysteries*. Maddux wasn't being read his last rites, nor was he in a body cast. He was perfectly fine . . . seriously. In holding the Pirates to just one run and four hits over seven innings, he looked as fit as ever. And Hawkins—making his first appearance in place of the fallen Borowski—slammed the door in the ninth inning to preserve the 4-1 win.

The following day Hawkins slammed the door on the media, as well. He had earned every penny of his big contract so far, compiling a 1.42 earned run average in 30 appearances. But being a middle reliever was a lot different than being a closer, and he seemed twitchy about moving under the red-hot lights. Maybe Hawkins was having flashbacks to his days in Minnesota. The Twins tried to make him a closer early in his career, but the experiment failed because he didn't throw strikes consistently. Or maybe he had taken note of what happened to Sweaty Joe. More likely, he just didn't like the media. Hawkins gathered the ink-stained wretches and laid down some ground rules:

"That's it, I'm not talking anymore. I've got nothing else to say to the media. That's why I did this. I'm completely done. Don't hover around my locker. I'm not going to be a guy to talk to every day like Joe. I'm not talking. I just want to do my job and go home.

"It doesn't matter what happens in the ninth, as long as you don't give up the lead," he continued. "I don't care who's sitting on the edge of their seat." Then Hawkins assumed the classic fallback position for an athlete under duress: "I'm not going to apologize for that, because I can do what you guys [the media] can do, [but] you guys can't do what I do."

Everyone was mad again. Hawkins was mad at the media. The fans were mad at Patterson. And Alou was mad at the fans. There was a whole lot of hatred going around, which could mean only one thing: The Cardinals were back in town.

Patterson had become Cubdom's scapegoat—the goat incarnate, even—for all that ailed the offense. The young center fielder had a bundle of talent, but he had regressed since his breakthrough season in 2003. It didn't matter where the pitcher threw the ball—in the dirt, over his head, a foot and a half outside the strike zone— Patterson would swing at it, and usually miss. The boos first rang out during that game against Houston on June 1 in which he struck out two times with the bases loaded, and they had grown louder since then. After several days, Alou had heard enough. The veteran had taken on a more vocal role in Sosa's absence, and he stood up and came to Patterson's defense, telling everyone to back off.

The fans, however, were in no mood to heed Alou's words. They were tired of waiting for these 2004 Cubs to click. They wanted results—and they wanted them now. Once again, they didn't get enough of them in the first of four games against St. Louis on the night of June 7. In losing 4-3, Chicago left three men in scoring position—including two by Patterson in the fourth inning—and blew other opportunities because of sloppy base-running. The score wouldn't even have been as close as it was if the pitcher, Rusch, hadn't hit a solo home run.

The electricity was being sapped from Wrigley Field, both literally and figuratively. The Cubs entered the next night's matchup against St. Louis four and a half games out of first place, then a power outage on the city's North Side wiped out the TV video feed from Wrigley Field. When the feed was restored in the third inning, however, the picture appeared slightly brighter. The Cubs strung together six hits in the bottom of that inning—only three fewer than their entire output the previous night—and scored four runs. That was good enough for Clement, who pitched eight innings and raised his record to 7-4.

Despite the 7-3 win, the picture over in the clubhouse remained one of edginess. As old and cozy as the rest of the ballpark, the clubhouse hadn't been designed to withstand a season like this one, a season of such great expectations. The main hub was the dressing area, which was about the size of four racquetball courts laid side by side and contained the lockers, some recliner chairs for chilling out, and a couple of tables where the team could play cards and read the newspapers. Under normal circumstances, it was a tight fit, but these days, the players were feeling particularly squeezed. The great expectations were embodied in an ever-expanding media contingent that trolled the dressing room for interviews before and after every game.

The morning after the victory over the Cardinals began in the usual manner. A glob of newspaper, Internet, TV, and radio reporters entered the clubhouse and sought out scraps of space to set up shop. Since the front of the room filled up quickly, several media members moved to the back, near the recliners. Unbeknownst to them, however, it had been decided that those recliners sat on sacred ground. Remlinger, who was nearby at his locker, peered at the recliners and said, "We try to keep this a players' area, unless you need to talk to us." Shortly thereafter, one of the team's public relations assistants came over and informed the lingering assemblage that there was a new rule: The recliner area was off-limits.

Now the media were mad, too. The recliner controversy was quite a load to bear in this heavy air. The media were led to the front of the clubhouse, where they huddled in a sweaty mass of discontent. Then they were led to the trench-like interview room for Baker's pregame press conference, where they again huddled in a sweaty mass of discontent. "There's a lot of herding going on these days," one reporter muttered while they waited for Baker. "There's a new rule," another said sarcastically. "All questions now must be asked in Greek." Not surprisingly, when Baker arrived—about 10 minutes late, to the further irritation of the media—the exchange focused on the negative.

REPORTER A: "Is it a difficult process talking about injuries every day?"

BAKER: "It's tough because I'm not a doctor, and I'm having to answer doctor questions. I'm not God, and I'm having to answer questions as to when people are going to come back. That's what's tough, when you don't have answers. And I hate to say, 'I don't know' or 'No comment.' That's as bad an answer as you can get. But we *don't know*. What else are we going to say? You can't make it up. Everybody's wondering. I mean, I'm wondering. But I try not to wonder to the point where it takes away what I've got to do today—because it goes on with or without me, them, or whoever it is. There are still going to be people out there wanting to see us play and win."

REPORTER B: "What are you being told about Wood?"

BAKER: "He's been to different doctors. They say that there's nothing structurally wrong with the ligament, elbow, or anything. He feels good until he gets to the point of extension. I don't know—there's something that spurs something. Sometimes you have to throw through it and find a lane for that thing."

REPORTER C: "Obviously, it's a fear to have him in any kind of discomfort when he's throwing."

BAKER: "Hey, man, you're always in some kind of discomfort. You just have less discomfort most days."

REPORTER D: "Could you bring him back then and have him throw through it?"

BAKER: "You gotta get into it before you go through it. I'm just saying maybe, man. I don't know."

REPORTER E: "There's no plan for a return at this particular point?"

BAKER: "Well, it's hard to plan when there's discomfort."

REPORTER F: "Are you, as a baseball manager, resigned that maybe you won't see Woody until the All-Star Break [in mid-July] or thereabouts?"

BAKER: "Man, I don't know. The All-Star Break? You know how long that seems like it's away?"

REPORTER F: "Well, let's do the math—"

BAKER: "You do the math. You've got more time to do the math than me. If I sat around and did the math, I could get really depressed. Understand what I'm saying?"

REPORTER G: "Dusty, how close is Wood?"

BAKER: "There you go. I just told you, man. Didn't I just tell you that? Honestly, didn't I just mention that I don't have the answers? I don't know."

To make a long story short, nobody had a clue—and it was pretty damn upsetting. But perhaps that afternoon's game would provide some clarity. Prior was pitching. Although his first start hadn't gone as planned, he remained the calm amid the storm. Clad in flip-flops, an untucked golf shirt, and cargo shorts when he got to the ballpark, he didn't seem to have a care in the world.

The second coming of Prior's second coming began with the requisite bluster, as Rex Grossman threw out the ceremonial first pitch. Grossman, a quarterback from the University of Florida, had been picked by the Chicago Bears in the first round of the 2003 draft, and much like Prior with the Cubs, he was being counted on to rescue the franchise. The strong-armed QB walked to the mound to a hardy round of applause, wound up . . . and bounced the ball into the dirt. A warning to Beardom: The curse was spreading.

First, though, it had to finish swallowing up Cubdom. Prior was uncharacteristically flustered against St. Louis, throwing 28 pitches in the opening inning and allowing a run. After that, he unraveled completely. The game turned on a fastball he threw in the third inning, which veered toward So Taguchi's head and sent the center fielder sprawling to the dirt. It looked uncannily like a brushback pitch, although Prior insisted that wasn't the case. "I think anyone who understands baseball would understand I wasn't trying to knock him down intentionally," Prior said. "I broke his bat his first at-bat [in the first inning]. He swung at an 0-1 pitch that was over his head. So I was trying to go back upstairs and got it in a little bit too much. There was no intent on my part."

The Cardinals begged to differ. They retaliated in the top of the fourth inning, knocking Prior out of the game by scoring four runs. Then in the bottom of the fifth, St. Louis starter Matt Morris threw two brushback pitches at Lee, the second of which nearly hit him in the head and caused both benches to clear. "I can understand trying to defend their team," Baker said. "The first pitch was close, and the second pitch was at his head. You don't throw at a guy's head like that. That's wrong." Added Prior: "I understand, obviously, that there are emotions in this rivalry. It's one thing to send a message. It's another thing to throw at a guy's head. I think we all understand there's a way to do things and a way not to do things."

The game really got out of hand three innings later, when the Cardinals scored six runs to extend their lead to 12-4 and drive most of the faithless to the exits. Said Prior, "I don't know that there are a whole lot of positives to take out of this game." The Cubs, a decidedly mercurial bunch, needed to find some in a hurry—before the season started getting out of hand, too.

WRIGLEY FIELD
HOME OF
CHICAGO CUBS

. . . AND ECSTASY

THIRTEEN

Leave it to Baker, whose hopeful smile had been tested all season long, to locate a positive. The very day Prior and company were annihilated by their archrivals, the manager issued a challenge to Cubdom, one that cut to the core of its belief system. For once, he implored, view that old, chipped-up glass as being half full and not half empty.

"We haven't had the team we thought we were going to break [spring training] with since Opening Day," he said. "Opening Day, we didn't have Prior. Then we didn't have this guy, we didn't have that guy. Let's get 'em back first, and I'll take my chances. No matter what, instead of thinking about what we haven't done, consider what we have done with what we've had to do it with. We could be three and a half [games] out [of first place] with everyone here, and we'd still be in pretty good shape with three and a half months to go [in the season]. How many teams in baseball would trade to be three and a half games back with everybody [healthy]?"

Maybe, just maybe, the portrait of these 2004 Cubbies wasn't so muddled after all. The key was to look at it from a different angle. For instance, erstwhile players had begun to reappear throughout the St. Louis series. Although they weren't ready to play yet, their presence among their teammates at Wrigley Field meant they were closing in on that end.

There was Grudzielanek, gimping through the heavy traffic in the clubhouse, his right calf wrapped protectively. "I'm very anxious to get back," the second baseman said after working out his Achilles tendon. "That's why I really have to control myself right now. I just have to make sure I'm right when I do come back. Everything else is fine. I mean, hitting and throwing and defense and all that kind of stuff is fine. It's when I start running—the explosion right out of the gate and then the top-end running is what really causes the pain. I'm going to have pain for a while. Right now, we're trying to control and moderate it to a point where it's very low and I can play with it on an everyday basis."

There was Slammin' Sammy, with salsa music blaring at his locker upon his return from a batting session in the cages under the outfield bleachers. "I just feel sore," he said. "I'll be OK in a couple or few days. The main thing is that I'm swinging OK. I was in the cage for a little bit, and I stopped. Yesterday I swung too much. In that situation, you're going to come back and your body is going to be sore. So we gotta slow down a little bit and give it a couple of days, and then come back again. If I don't feel ready, I'm not going to play. It's as simple as that."

There was Wood, too. He still was in no condition to unload a 98-mile-per-hour fastball, but he was there just the same, gripping a bat and chatting with his teammates by his locker before disappearing back into the trainer's room. And there was Gonzalez, his dark, Latin good looks on full display as he entered the stadium from the players' parking lot and strode down the concourse. Despite a cast on his right arm, he looked as chipper as could be, moving toward the clubhouse with an air of confidence and purpose.

No, the picture wasn't so muddled after all. "We've had some injuries and setbacks," said Wellemeyer, who was on the comeback trail himself. "As soon as we get those guys back, we're going to take off."

Why wait? In the final game of the series against the Cardinals on the afternoon of June 10, the Cubs didn't get mad—they got even. The bottom of the fourth inning proved to be their launching pad, as they scored 10 runs (their most in an inning since 2002) and had 11 total hits (tying a team record set in 1922) and nine consecutive hits (one shy of the major league record). "You had the feeling that eventually it had to happen," said Walker, who hit a home run in going 3-for-5 in the game. "We have a pretty good offense here, even without Sammy in the lineup." Chicago's offensive outburst gave its starting pitcher, Zambrano, a much-deserved breather, although he wasn't sure what to do with it. Said the right-hander following the 12-3 victory: "It's the first time I've spent a lot of time in the dugout."

As soon as the Cubs showered and dressed, they embarked on another dreaded trip to California. This one had a twist: In their inaugural interleague series of 2004, they would play the Angels for the first time ever. The Cubs had difficulty finding their way around Angel Stadium of Anaheim during the opening game on the night of June 11. Despite another solid start from Maddux, they managed just seven hits and lost 3-2. The next night, however, they seemed right at home, pounding Anaheim 10-5. Walker, Hollandsworth, and Ramirez all homered, while Patterson, who was starting to look less like a goat and more like the budding star he was supposed to be, was 2-for-4 with two runs batted in.

Was the glass half full or half empty? The series finale the following afternoon, a five-hour epic, didn't provide any definitive answers.

Half full: Clement was brilliant. In six innings, he allowed just one run.

Half empty: Chicago's offense was not brilliant. The score was 1-1 when Clement left the game.

Half full: The offense finally did something. A run in the seventh inning and two more in the eighth gave the Cubs a 4-1 lead.

Half empty: The bullpen tanked. The Angels tied the game in the bottom of the eighth by scoring three runs off Mercker and Farnsworth.

Half full: The offense did something again. Barrett's RBI single in the top of the 11th gave the team a 5-4 advantage.

Half empty: The bullpen tanked again. With two outs in the bottom of the 11th, Hawkins blew the save by allowing a game-tying single. Hell, anyone in the press box could have done that.

Half full: The Cubbies refused to go quietly into the California sunset. Walker's two-out single in the top of the 15th inning scored Patterson and put Chicago in yet another position to win.

Half empty: The Angels had last at-bats.

Half full: Somehow, some way, the Cubs prevailed. Jon Leicester, a no-name making just his second major league appearance, succeeded where Mercker, Farnsworth, and Hawkins had failed. He pitched three scoreless innings, the last of which sealed the deal.

To the pessimists, it was a seat-of-the-pants victory that said more about the Cubs' weaknesses than their strengths. To the optimists, it was a turning point. Was there any doubt about how Baker felt? "There were quite a few heroes today," he said.

The mystery was solved. Apparently, there had been more to Borowski's woes than a strained I-can't-get-anyone-out muscle. The belated diagnosis? He had a slightly torn right rotator cuff. His rehabilitation schedule remained sketchy, though. No one could say for sure when, or if, he'd be back.

Still, this was no time to mourn the passing of Sweaty Joe. Things were starting to look up. The day Chicago outlasted Anaheim in their marathon, Sosa was in uniform for the first time in a month, playing for the Double-A Diamond Jaxx in Jackson, Tennessee. The fact that he was there revealed as much about his attitude as his back. In 2003 he had declined a minor-league rehab assignment after recovering from his infected toenail, opting instead to work out the kinks in the spotlight of the majors. The consequences of that decision were dire. In his first two games back, against Houston, he went 0-for-11 with eight strikeouts. That, in turn, led to Corkgate.

But Sosa had learned from the past; he was indeed becoming Selfless Sammy. "[In 2003] he went to Houston without that rehab, and he wasn't ready," Baker said. "They were just blowing it right by him because he hadn't swung or nothing. We talked about that. He remembered that and didn't like the feeling. He didn't want to come in struggling."

Grudzielanek was in uniform, too, with the Cubs' Triple-A affiliate in Des Moines, Iowa. If all went well, both he and Sosa would be suiting up for the Cubs within a week. Slowly but surely, the pieces were falling back into place. "The character of this team is very strong and positive," said Walker, who didn't seem the least bit upset about the prospect of losing some playing time to Grudzielanek. "We all pull for each other, and all have the common goal to win our division and get to the World Series. We've kept our bench guys sharp. We've played well despite our injuries, so when we're at full strength, we're going to be a very tough team to beat."

Again, why wait? The future was now. When the Cubs arrived at Minute Maid Park on June 14 for a pivotal four-game series against the Astros, Prior was set to pitch the opener. However, Mighty Mark found himself in an odd position that evening: He wasn't the center of attention. That honor belonged to the game's other starter, Roger Clemens. With the best record (9-0) and earned run average (2.08) in the National League, the ageless right-hander was the talk of baseball. Prior? Well, he was feeling somewhat deflated. All he wanted to do was get his first win of the season and beautify his homely 4.66 earned run average. This would be an ideal chance for Prior and the Cubs to find out even more about the strength of their character.

Early on, Clemens versus Prior lived up to its billing. Clemens pitched a scoreless first; Prior pitched a scoreless first. Clemens pitched a scoreless second; Prior pitched a scoreless second. In the third inning, however, Chicago began to catch up with Clemens's fastballs, as Walker tripled with two outs and then scored on a single by Martinez. The Cubs then scored another run in the fourth inning, two in the fifth, and one more in the sixth. Houston, in contrast, couldn't catch up with anything Prior was throwing. When he left the game after five innings, he hadn't allowed a single run.

Not only did the Cubs become the first team of 2004 to beat Clemens, they beat him easily. The final score was 7-2. "Tonight was more personal," said Prior. "I wanted to make some improvements off my last outing. It was more of determination, kind of a personal battle with myself." After two false starts, Prior had draped the Cubs in glory. The team everyone had been waiting to see finally was here.

Buoyed by its win against Clemens, Chicago systematically dismantled the Astros:

- In game two, the Cubs scored three runs in the top of the ninth inning—highlighted by a two-run single by Martinez—to win 4-2.
- In game three, Maddux allowed just one run over six and one-third innings, and the Cubs triumphed 4-1.
- In game four, Chicago's supersub, Rusch, spearheaded a 5-4 victory by holding the Astros to two runs and four hits in eight innings.

Before the Astros even knew what had hit them, Chicago had swept them in a four-game series for the first time since 1967. These were heady days. The Cubs had won six straight on their road trip, knocked Houston into fifth place in the N.L. Central, and climbed into a second-place tie with Cincinnati. At 37-29—a season-best eight games over .500—Chicago now was only two games behind the Cardinals in the standings.

After the final out of the sweep against Houston was recorded, Lee pounded his glove emotionally. The first baseman, who had been waiting as anxiously as anyone for things to start going right, had every reason to be elated. He was the principal figure in Chicago's six-game run of good fortune, going 11-for-24 (.458) with six runs batted in. "We all know what's at stake, and we know that we're all going to have a part in the success of this team and how far we're going to go," said Lee, who had raised his batting average from .270

to .289 during the winning streak. "We just came off of a big road series in Anaheim and Houston. To win six out of seven games, including a sweep of the Astros, was a big lift to us. We're getting stronger as a club every day."

Of course they were. Chicago's heavy, Slammin' Sammy, had finished his minor-league rehab assignment and was back at Wrigley Field on the afternoon of June 18 when the team began its second round of interleague play, against Oakland. The sun was peeking through the clouds, and Sosa's biceps were bulging through the rolled-up sleeves of his uniform. It was a rapturous sight.

Sosa's first at-bat of the game was a swinging strikeout; his second was a fly out to right field; and his third was another swinging strikeout. But his fourth at-bat, in the bottom of the ninth inning, was the one that really mattered. With two outs, the bases empty, and the Cubs trailing 2-1, Slammin' dug into the batter's box as the crowd rose to its feet. One swing of the bat—one fly ball into the sea of hopeful fans out on Waveland Avenue—could tie the score. Instead, Sosa grounded softly to the shortstop, and Chicago's winning streak ended at six. As had been the case with Prior, Sosa's return didn't yield immediate results. Nevertheless, that glass remained half full. "I didn't get any hits," Sosa told the hot and sweaty mass of media, "but the most important thing is my back feels great."

The next afternoon, Grudzielanek also was in the lineup, but his understudy, Walker, stole his thunder. The Cubs were losing 3-2 in the bottom of the ninth inning when Walker came to the plate as a pinch hitter with one out and Hollandsworth on first base. Walker kept the rally alive by singling, then scored the winning run on a bang-bang play at the plate when Barrett doubled. "The chemistry on this team is great, and we all know what our roles are," Walker said. "Everybody in this clubhouse wants to win. That's the most important thing—to do your job, whatever Dusty may ask of you."

In the rubber game on the afternoon of June 20, Zambrano was the one who stepped to the forefront, although there wasn't anything unusual about that. In leading the Cubs past Oakland, 5-3, he lifted his record to a team-high 8-2 and dropped his earned run average to a team-low 2.25. Said Baker of his young star, "The guy doesn't give up many runs, and he knows how to pitch winning baseball."

Just like that, the Cubs were on another roll.

The Cardinals were on the move, too. They had won seven of their past 10 games and had been in first place since June 12. Chicago, however, was right on their tails, only two games behind them in the standings. So when the Cubs zipped into Busch Stadium on June 22 to play their nemesis three more times, a hell of a lot more than civic pride was on the line. The Cubs could be in first place by the end of this series . . . or they could be five games back. They seemed fixated on the former scenario, not the latter.

The Cubs were behind 4-3 after the first seven innings of the opener, but it didn't matter. Grudzielanek led off the eighth inning with a single and was advanced to second on a sacrifice bunt by Martinez. After Alou grounded out, Sosa kept the inning going by drawing a walk. Then Ramirez broke the game open, hitting a double into the right-center field gap to score Grudzielanek and Sosa. In the bottom of the ninth inning, with the Cubs still winning 5-4, nary a drop of sweat could be seen under the lights of Busch Stadium. Hawkins overpowered the Cardinals and recorded his ninth save of the season.

In the top of the sixth inning the next night, Chicago overcame a 5-3 deficit and took a 9-5 lead. A first-place tie with St. Louis was only three innings away. All was joyful, as evidenced by a chant that had reverberated through the enemy grandstands during the series: "Let's go, Cubbies." The Cubbies were going, all right. Unfortunately, they took a wrong turn in the bottom of the sixth inning. After a three-run rally by the Cardinals that made the score 9-8, Chicago's issues with anger management resurfaced. Mercker, unhappy with the ball-strike calls, yelled some choice words at home plate umpire Sam Holbrook at the end of the inning. Then Barrett entered the fray, and the two players were ejected. "I was trying to make a point to Sam," Barrett said, "and before I knew it we were both tossed out."

With Barrett out, Chicago's only other catcher, Paul Bako, had to go in. The best anyone could tell, Bako was on the team solely because Maddux liked him. Bako was batting .213, and he hadn't exactly stopped base runners in their tracks from his perch behind the plate. But he was Maddux's personal catcher, a role he originally assumed in Atlanta in 2000 and 2001, so he donned the tools of ignorance every fifth day. Of course, this wasn't the fifth day.

The Cardinals tied the score in the seventh inning and were threatening again in the eighth. With two outs and So Taguchi on third base, Farnsworth was called in from the bullpen. His first pitch, delivered high and tight at close to 100 miles per hour, bounced off Bako's glove and skipped to the backstop, and Taguchi scored what proved to be the winning run. Baker stated the painfully obvious after the game: "The ball just got away."

So, too, did the series. The next night, the Cubs played neither joyfully nor angrily. Instead, they looked comatose. Although Clement didn't pitch badly, he was done in by another Cubs player who had no business being there, shortstop Rey Ordonez. In the wake of Gonzalez's injury, Chicago had plucked the 33-year-old Ordonez out of forced retirement to fortify their bench. After Ordonez made an error in the fourth inning that led to three unearned runs, the faithful were wishing he still were fortifying a couch somewhere far, far away from St. Louis. Chicago's offense then reverted back to its *Groundhog Day* form, and the Cardinals won 4-0.

Was the glass half empty or half full? Half empty: The Flubs had squandered a golden opportunity. Instead of gaining ground on the Cardinals—and maybe even moving into sole possession of first place—they had dropped back by another game. Half full: It was only June, for crying out loud. And on balance, what a June it had been so far. Despite playing a schedule that was filled with topflight teams, the Cubs were 13-9.

Baker's view on the matter? His line of vision hadn't budged. "We're not even at the midpoint of the season," he said. "We'll just take it one game, one series at a time and keep our focus on winning. Whatever it takes to do that, we will do it."

It all starts idyllically enough, with the championship-starved faithful brimming with hope.

Manager Dusty Baker is determined to maintain his trademark smile, regardless of what horrors the season may bring.

After more than a decade in exile, Greg Maddux is back in the blue pinstripes, a sure sign that this year might be *the* year.

Jim Hendry, Chicago's ruffled general manager, spent the off-season feverishly dialing his cell phone. Now all he can do is stand back and watch what happens to the team he's assembled.

Anyone seen Mark Prior's Achilles tendon? The ill health of Chicago's prized pitcher is a mystery that fascinates the local media.

Anyone seen "Mighty" Mark Prior? Even when Prior returns to action in June, he isn't quite himself.

Outfielder Todd Hollandsworth scoffed at the curse when he signed with the Cubs in the off-season. Later, he injured himself fouling a ball off his leg and was out for the rest of the year.

Sammy Sosa keeps hopping with his usual theatrical vigor . . . until he is felled by a sneeze.

Kerry Wood argues balls and strikes during a game in April. Not long after that, the Cubs ace would succumb to the same injury fate as Prior.

First baseman Derrek Lee, one of the players who signed on for the 2004 title push, gets a taste of the vibrant Wrigley Field scene.

"Sweaty" Joe Borowski focuses his entire being on delivering a pitch. Now, if only he could get someone out . . .

Where, oh where, would the Cubs be without Aramis Ramirez, the most consistent hitter on a maddening offense?

Michael Barrett, one of the season's biggest surprises, does it all for the Cubs—on the basepaths, behind the plate, and in the batter's box.

"The Mad Venezuelan," Carlos Zambrano, doesn't need any divine intervention to get the job done—but just in case, the powerful right-hander looks skyward.

The cursed one: No matter how well he pitches, Matt Clement never seems to come away with a victory.

Maddux confers with his trusty sidekick, Paul Bako.

When he's not urinating on his hands, Moises Alou is driving in runs for the Cubbies—and lots of them.

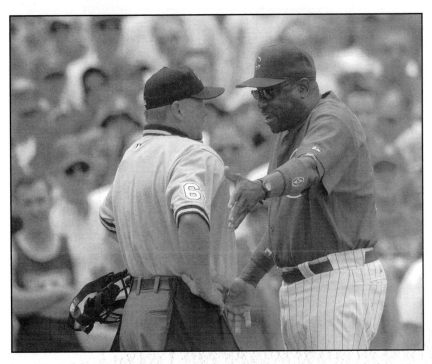

Even the ever-optimistic Baker is pushed to the brink in this season of great expectations. "It's been my toughest year," he says.

Todd Walker turned down more money from other teams because he wanted the once-in-a-lifetime chance to play for a World Series winner with the Cubs. Oops.

LaTroy Hawkins does what anyone in the press box can do: He blows a save.

Regardless of what life, or the Cubs, throws at player-turned-broad-caster Ron Santo, he somehow manages to keep coming back.

The Cubs are getting the better of St. Louis on this afternoon—but in the end, the Cardinals leave them in the dust.

Kyle Farnsworth unloads a fastball. Where it's headed, nobody knows.

Even after overcoming his triceps injury,
Wood remains star-crossed.

The faithful are sure the improbable arrival of Nomar Garciaparra will bust the curse.

Nomar is overjoyed to be donning a Cubs uniform for the first time—but instead of breaking the curse, the curse breaks him.

Unlike so many other players on the moody Cubs, second baseman Mark Grud-zielanek is both quiet and consistent.

From injuries to booing from the faithful to being dropped in the batting order, Slammin' Sammy's dream season turns into a nightmare.

As these Cubs are prone to do, Alou finds some time to bicker with an ump.

Wrigley Field may be crumbling, but it remains the shrine, the most beautiful stadium in sports.

Lee has played almost every inning of every game in this grueling season, so he richly deserves all the high fives his teammates give him.

Through thick and thin (mostly thin), the faithful always will love Prior and his fellow Cubs.

OF SOUTH SIDERS
AND SWOONS

FOURTEEN

It was late March, and everyone was trying to figure out what had become of Prior's Achilles tendon. Former big-league pitcher Jack McDowell had his own theory, one that bordered on the sinister. "You shouldn't have a problem like that that doesn't heal in a month," he told the *Chicago Sun-Times*. "That's what happens to guys who use steroids. I'm not saying I'm suspicious of Prior, but that's one of the telltale signs." McDowell's take on the situation might have been credible, except for one thing: Most of his career in the majors was spent with the White Sox.

In mid-April, after a Cubs-Pirates game at Wrigley Field, a taxi screeched up to a souvenir stand near the ballpark. One of the passengers stuck his head out the window and yelled to the vendor, "Hey, you got any shirts that say SOX SUCK?"

"No," the vendor replied, "but I wish I did."

The passenger ducked his head back inside the window, and the taxi sped away from the curb.

About a month after that, Wrigleyville was filled with partygoers following a game between the Cubs and the Giants. Two young men, one with a flask in his hand, were weaving aimlessly down Addison Street when they saw a codger wearing a White Sox cap. "White Sox suck," said the guy with the flask, slurring his esses.

"You suck," the codger in the black cap shot back.

The guy with the flask glared foggily at the codger in the black cap, then he and his compatriot staggered on.

From McDowell to the duo at the souvenir stand to the flask guy, it hardly seemed relevant that the Cubs and the White Sox hadn't played each other yet, and wouldn't until June 25. Anytime was the right time to talk some trash.

In Chicago, you either liked the Cubs or you liked the White Sox. If you claimed to be a fan of both teams, you were a liar, a sissy, or an outsider. It was a city divided. The White Sox played in a hardscrabble part of the South Side, 71 blocks away from Wrigley Field. U.S. Cellular Field, or The Cell, wasn't surrounded by a quaint little neighborhood like Wrigley Field was. Instead, the 14-year-old stadium butted up to the sooty Dan Ryan Expressway, giving the façade an industrial edge. Not surprisingly, many of the team's fans had blue-collar sensibilities.

"We have a terrific culture," said Scott Reifert, director of public relations for the White Sox. "I'm responsible for the market research we do of our fans. We use a firm outside of Chicago. The first time they came in, they said, 'Chicago is unlike any other place we've ever polled.' What they said was that Sox fans are blue-collar in their approach to life. They might be white-collar by the economic definition, but from a generational standpoint, they have roots they can trace to a great-grandfather who worked at the stockyards or somebody who was a South Sider. And they still have a South Side mentality, which is, You value hard work, and winning and losing matters."

That was precisely what drove White Sox fans nuts about their counterparts on the uppity North Side. Winning and losing didn't seem to matter nearly as much as having fun at the old ballpark. Really, everything about the Cubs drove the South Siders nuts. If you were to play a game of word association with White Sox fans regarding the differences between the two teams, the responses would be something like this:

Wrigley Field: A frat party. A boobs fest. Twenty-minute waits to get into the bathroom and urinate into a trough.

U.S. Cellular Field: Underrated. Modern amenities. Plentiful parking.

Typical Cubs fan: Drunk. Spends the entire game talking to friends on the upper-deck patio.

Typical White Sox fan: Watches the game. Knows something about baseball. Demands results.

Perfect day at Wrigley Field for a Cubs fan: Cubs win. Sammy hits a dinger. Plenty of beer vendors. Sun. An opposing outfielder to taunt from the bleachers. Not necessarily in that order.

Perfect day at U.S. Cellular Field for a White Sox fan: Sox win. A well-played game.

Brand of baseball, Cubs: Sorry. Lazy. Sammy homers; if not, pray for rain.

Brand of baseball, White Sox: The Go-Go Sox. Let's be aggressive, let's be smart.

Of course, Cubs fans would have their own views on these matters:

Wrigley Field: The shrine. The most beautiful park in sports.

U.S. Cellular Field: A faceless pile of concrete. Bring your rappelling equipment if you have tickets on the upper deck.

Typical Cubs fan: Loyal to the bitter end.

Typical White Sox fan: Toothless. Dresses in sweats.

Perfect day at Wrigley Field for a Cubs fan: Cubs win any way they can. Soak up some sun and a few beers along the way. A homer by Sammy can't hurt.

Perfect day at U.S. Cellular Field for a White Sox fan: Not getting carjacked after the game.

Brand of baseball, Cubs: Sometimes short on skill, but always long on heart.

Brand of baseball, White Sox: American League goonery.

This sibling rivalry transcended baseball. It was a clash of cultures, a battle for the hearts and minds of Chicago's populace. On that front, the Cubs were winning handily. From 1996 through 2003, the White Sox's highest attendance total in a season was 1,947,799 in 2000; the Cubs' *lowest* total during that same period was 2,190,308 in 1997.

But as Reifert was quick to point out, ticket-office supremacy could be fleeting. "You look at the history of Chicago, and just because the snapshot says [the Cubs outdraw the White Sox now], it does not mean in a decade it's going to be that way," he said. "It wasn't always that way in the past. Most Sox fans have been Sox fans forever, which means they remember a time when we were number one." Indeed, in the 1950s and '60s, the White Sox regularly outdrew the Cubs.

As for the quality of play on the diamond, the "You suck," "No, you suck" debate was pointless. Both teams pretty much sucked. Although the White Sox had fielded competitive teams more frequently than the Cubs had over the years, that was of little consolation. The Sox were in the throes of their own interminable championship drought. They hadn't won a World Series since 1917 and hadn't been to one since 1959.

Through thick and thin, the two feuding brothers always had each other to kick around. They began playing exhibitions in 1903, and sometimes these were the most anticipated games of the season. When interleague play was introduced in 1997 and the games counted, the rivalry became even more intense. This was particularly true for the White Sox, who viewed the two series the teams played each year as chances to shove the Cubs out of the spotlight they had been hogging. "This is a big stage for us," Reifert said. "This is a big opportunity for us to make some statements."

The White Sox made a habit of seizing the moment. Through 2003, their interleague record against the Cubs was 20-16. Those were 20 times when the Sox didn't have to feel like second-class citizens, 20 times when they—and not the Cubs—got the best tables at the restaurants around town. "I learned about [the rivalry] when I go into restaurants sometimes," Baker said. "They'll say, 'If you don't win the Sox games, you might have to wait for your table.'"

On June 25, 2004, the stakes—and the steaks—were bigger than ever. This was the first Cubs-White Sox series in which both teams were within five games of first place in their respective divisions. The Cubs were three games behind St. Louis; the Sox, featuring a lineup filled with sluggers, trailed the Twins by two games in the American League Central. The Cell, the site of the initial three-game grudge match of the year, seemed evenly split between people wearing CUBS SUCK and SOX SUCK T-shirts.

Played under a bright afternoon sky that created visibility issues for the players, the opening game was about as ugly as the language in the grandstands. In his second start ever at The Cell, Prior spotted the South Siders a 1-0 lead in the bottom of the fourth inning when he threw a wild pitch with a runner on third base. Not to be outdone, the Sox then spotted the North Siders four runs in the top of the fifth inning. Hollandsworth went from first base to third base on an errant pickoff attempt by Sox starter Jon Garland and scored on a ground out by Barrett. Later in the inning, Sox second baseman Juan Uribe dropped a pop fly, setting the stage for a three-run homer by Grudzielanek.

The White Sox couldn't overcome that mistake-filled fifth inning and wound up losing 7-4. For the Cubs, the game felt like a momentum-builder, particularly since they had just lost two of three games to the Cardinals. "Coming off a series like [the one in St. Louis], emotionally you can be a little down," said the hero of the day, Grudzielanek. "But when you come over here and see the fans, it definitely brings you right back up."

Game two the next afternoon looked like it would be a cinch for the Cubbies. The great Carlos Zambrano was going up against the not-even-good Felix Diaz, who had been called up from the White Sox's Triple-A affiliate in Charlotte the previous day as an emergency replacement for the ailing Scott Schoeneweis. It was such a mismatch that even the most boisterous members of the CUBS SUCK crowd were keeping a low profile.

They perked up in a hurry, though, when strange things started happening. The great Carlos Zambrano wasn't even good, and the not-even-good Felix Diaz was pretty great. Zambrano was on the ropes all day long against the vaunted White Sox offense, throwing 127 pitches and giving up five runs in six innings. Diaz, meanwhile, allowed only three runs over the same span, and the Sox won 6-3. "I tip my hat to [Diaz] for the way he pitched," White Sox manager Ozzie Guillen told the media after the game. "He threw outstanding."

In the finale the following afternoon, the Sox kept pounding the Cubs out of the spotlight. Maddux pitched his worst game since April (nine runs allowed in four innings), Chicago's offense failed to put Sox starter Esteban Loaiza away when he was in trouble in the early innings, its defense made three errors, and a photo of Bartman wearing a White Sox cap was flashed on the scoreboard. The SOX SUCK contingent was provided with only one reason to cheer: Slammin' Sammy hit a pair of homers, one of which traveled 454 feet. This, of course, initiated more mockery from the CUBS SUCK revelers.

Not only had the Cubs been thoroughly outplayed by the Sox, they had fallen five games behind the Cardinals in the standings. Furthermore, Remlinger had been put back on the disabled list because of shoulder soreness and Hollandsworth had been taken out of the series finale after fouling a ball off his knee. It had been a bad weekend for the North Siders, and it was about to get a little worse. As soon as Baker finished his postgame press conference in the interview room at The Cell, Reifert stepped in and announced that the White Sox had just acquired right-handed pitcher Freddy Garcia from the Seattle Mariners. Garcia was one of the better starters in the American League, someone who could push the White Sox over the top in the A.L. Central.

The Sox were the talk of Chicago. The two teams would begin their final series of the season in five days, but for the time being at least, the city belonged to the South Siders.

The Cubs might have lost their series against the White Sox, but they were holding their own in their bloody battle against destiny. They were on the verge of surviving June, the month the faithful feared most. It was called the June Swoon. Those Cubs teams that even made it past May often found themselves on life support as spring turned to summer.

Some snapshots of the Flubs in full swoon: a 4-21 record in 1954 . . . 10-20 in 1966 . . . 11-21 in 1975 . . . 10-17 in 1986 . . . 9-20 in 1995. The year most comparable to this one, however, was 1985. Like the 2004 Cubs, the 1985 edition was expected to be a World Series contender after winning the division title the previous year. Those '85 Cubs started the season well enough, going 12-6 in April and 15-11 in May. Entering June, they were just one game out of first place.

But as William Butler Yeats wrote in his poem "The Second Coming," the center could not hold. In other words, the Cubs were toast. Rick Sutcliffe, the Cy Young award-winner the year before, was hobbled by a bad hamstring; center fielder Bobby Dernier hurt his foot; and catcher Jody Davis was sidelined by a gastrointestinal infection. The Cubs lost 13 straight games that June and never recovered. Every pitcher in their starting rotation was felled by an injury in the ensuing months, and the team finished the season twenty-three and a half games out of first place.

No one would have been terribly surprised if history had repeated itself in 2004. Didn't history always repeat itself when it came to the Cubbies? Yet despite their ill health and that brutal schedule, they were 14-11 with two games remaining in the month. Regardless of what happened in those final games, against Houston at Wrigley Field, the Cubs would have a winning record in June.

The Astros had remade themselves since being swept by Chicago a couple of weeks earlier, trading closer Octavio Dotel to the A's and acquiring slugger Carlos Beltran from the Kansas City Royals in a three-team deal. The Cubs didn't know anything about this stranger from the American League, but they soon learned more than they wanted. In the first game of the series on the evening of June 29, he hit a solo home run off Francis Beltran in the top of the seventh inning to give the Astros a 5-4 lead. However, the Cubs bounced back with three runs in the bottom of the inning and won 7-5. The next afternoon, Houston's man of mystery struck again. With two outs in the top of the ninth inning and the score tied 2-2, he hit a solo home run off Hawkins, and this time Houston's lead held up.

Nevertheless, Chicago could take solace in the fact that the Pirates completed a three-game sweep of the Cardinals that same day. The Cubs, now three and a half games behind St. Louis, had slipped a grand total of one game in the standings in June. They still were well within striking distance of first place.

"Hopefully, the fans realize we have a good team and that we're just trying to be consistent," said Tom Goodwin, who recently had come off the disabled list and had resumed his role as one of Baker's most beloved bench players. "We'd hoped they wouldn't jump off the bandwagon in June, but I'm sure some years down the line the fans have done that when the team went into a tailspin that was too hard to come out of. Fortunately for us, we didn't do that."

The June Swoon had been averted. Another jinx down, a dozen or so more to go.

July

WRIGLEY FIELD
HOME OF
CHICAGO CUBS

NEVER GIVE UP THE FIGHT

FIFTEEN

If this season of great expectations panned out, it would be like Mardi Gras, Christmas, New Year's Eve, Chanukah, Thanksgiving, Cinco de Mayo, Valentine's Day, Fourth of July, Kwanza, and St. Patrick's Day rolled into one overwhelming package. The celebration would go on for weeks, perhaps even months.

Of all the revelers, none would be merrier than Ron Santo, the team's third-baseman-turned-radio-announcer. The heart of Cubdom beat inside his chest.

That heart actually stopped once, following surgery he had in November 2001. For a few moments, Santo was gone, but the doctors managed to bring him back from the beyond, back so he could watch some more Cubs baseball. Then there was the time his right leg was amputated. And the time his left leg was amputated. And the time his toupee caught fire when he moved too close to a portable heater that was hanging in the radio booth.

This was Cubdom: a man on peg legs with his hair ablaze, cheering on the Beloved with everything he had left to give.

Santo's life with the Cubs began when he was signed by them at age 18 in 1958. That same year, the promising third baseman was dealt what could have been a crushing blow: He was diagnosed with diabetes. But rather than succumb to the disease, he learned to keep it in check, eating candy bars or injecting himself with insulin whenever he felt his body waver. Santo became so adept at this routine that few people even were aware that he had diabetes. It was his secret, one he guarded closely because he was afraid the powers-that-be wouldn't let him keep playing ball if they found it out. Santo lasted 15 years in the major leagues, winning five Gold Glove awards, hitting 342 homers, and driving in 1,331 runs. When the nine-time All-Star retired following the 1974 season, his only regret—and it was a big one—was that he never was part of a Cubs championship.

Santo was afforded more shots at a World Series ring when WGN Radio hired him as the Cubs' color commentator in 1990. Santo didn't call a game as much as he *felt* it. The faithful forgave him for misidentifying the occasional player or for forgetting which team Chicago was playing. He was one of them.

Never was this more apparent than in "The Brant Brown Game" in 1998. It was late September, and the Cubs were clinging to a one-game lead in the race for a wild-card berth in the playoffs. In a critical matchup against the Brewers in Milwaukee, Chicago was ahead 7-5 with two outs and two men on base in the bottom of the ninth inning. A fly ball to Brown in left field seemed as though it would end the game, but he dropped it, enabling all three Brewers to circle the bases and costing the Cubs the victory. Santo's call of the play consisted of a primal scream that grew more anguished as each of those Brewers crossed home plate. The radio listeners didn't know what had happened, but they *knew*.

Although the Cubs still reached the playoffs, Brown's once-promising major league career was undone by that flubbed fly ball. Brown never again approached the numbers he posted that season—a .291 batting average and 14 homers—and by 2003, he was hacking away for the Single-A Flyers in Schaumburg, Illinois.

Santo suffered his own series of setbacks in the years following 1998. The first big one occurred in 2000, when he had a quadruple bypass. After that, he was beset by circulation problems in his legs from his diabetes. Santo underwent numerous surgeries, including the one when he flatlined, but his legs could not be saved; he lost his right leg in 2001 and his other the next year. Each time, though, he made it back to the radio booth. His never-ending pursuit of that Cubs championship, dangled before him like a carrot that moved a step backward every time he took a step forward with his prosthetic legs, kept him going.

That carrot seemed closer than ever in 2003, but when the Cubs captured the N.L. Central title, Santo was dealing with yet another setback. He had been diagnosed with bladder cancer, which meant, among other things, that he wouldn't be able to participate in the postseason from his seat in the radio booth. Instead, he would have to watch from his home in Arizona while he prepared for another round of surgery.

Santo, however, was not bitter. How could he have been? The Cubs retired his jersey number in a ceremony before the final game of the regular season, less than 24 hours after the division title had been clinched. With the team and the flock looking on, Santo stepped to the microphone at home plate and said: "First of all, I want to congratulate the divisional-champion Chicago Cubs, led by the best manager in baseball, Dusty Baker, and his wonderful coaches. I want to personally thank you guys because you have completed my life as far as I'm concerned. Thank you very much." He concluded his speech with words he had spoken so many times before: "We're going to go all the way. I know we are."

As usual, the Cubs didn't go all the way. But neither Game 6 against the Marlins nor the bladder cancer killed Santo. That spring, he was declared cancer-free and the Cubs were declared World Series favorites. Santo was back again, predicting with even more conviction than usual that this would be the year the Cubs went all the way. And despite the adversity the team went through during the first part of the season, he remained steadfast in that belief.

On the afternoon of July 1, Santo and the Cubs wanted a win in the worst way. It was the rubber game of their series against Houston, and a victory would enable them to keep pace with the first-place Cardinals and also knock the Astros further down in the standings. The Cubs had the right man for the job in Prior, who was nearly flawless in his first seven innings as his team jumped out to a 4-1 lead. Prior ran into trouble in the eighth inning, however, when the Astros put two men on base with only one out. Since Houston's newest slugger, the switch-hitting Carlos Beltran, was next up, Baker decided to bring in the left-handed Mercker from the bullpen so that Beltran would have to hit from the right side. Said Baker, "We were told by everyone in the American League we talked to, 'Don't let him hurt you left-handed.'"

So Beltran hurt them right-handed. Mercker's first pitch traveled from Beltran's bat to Waveland Avenue in about two seconds, and the score now was 4-4. "I made a terrible pitch," Mercker said. "Mark pitched his butt off today, and I ruined it for him."

Mercker ruined Santo's day, as well. Between innings, Santo made his way from the radio booth to the bathroom in the media center, located in the upper deck behind home plate. "Fuck, fuck, fuck," he muttered to himself as he waited in line with several reporters. Wasn't Santo supposed to be back on the radio soon? Who knew? He didn't seem to be in a hurry to return to the booth, giving one and all permission to cut in front of him in line. "Fuck, fuck, fuck," he continued.

Finally, Santo sidled up to a urinal, next to a local reporter who happened to be blind. The two men tried to piece together what had just transpired on the field below. After engaging in as analytical a discussion as was possible while conducting their business at the urinals, they concluded that Baker had done the right thing by bringing in Mercker to face Beltran. "You want to turn Beltran around, that's for sure," Santo said. He paused to think about that home run landing on Waveland Avenue. "But why does it happen?"

Why does it happen? Santo undoubtedly had been asking himself that question for the better part of his life, and he still didn't have any answers. But perhaps this year—2004—really was *the* year. With the score still 4-4 as the bottom of the 10th inning began, Santo was back in the radio booth, Slammin' Sammy was in the batter's box, and Brad Lidge was on the mound. Lidge delivered his first pitch,

Slammin' Sammy connected with the ball and then hopped, and Santo made the call:

"Oh, yeah!"

"Oh, yeah!"

"Yes!"

The radio listeners didn't know what Sosa had just done, but they *knew*.

Take that, South Siders. Slammin' Sammy had hit a home run that mattered—one that had beaten the division-rival Astros in an extra-innings cliffhanger—and the White Sox were up next on the schedule. At Wrigley Field, no less.

First, though, there was a victory to savor. Following his dramatic homer against Houston, Sosa didn't follow normal procedure and go to the interview room to dissect his deed. Slammin' Sammy didn't do the interview room. Instead, the media came to him. While Sosa showered, they waited by his locker. And waited. And waited. At last, Slammin' emerged triumphant from the showers, with a towel wrapped around his waist and an "are you waiting for little old me?" expression on his face.

After cutting through the jumble of cameras, microphones, and notebooks, he kindly turned down his boombox. The hero of the day then grabbed a can of deodorant from his locker and sprayed his armpits, as well as everyone standing closest to him, including a young and perky female reporter. "Sorry," he said sheepishly to the damsel in distress.

Slammin' was ready to address his adoring audience: "My timing is starting to come back. I never doubted I was going to come back and help the team the way they want me to help. It's going to take probably a couple more games. Be patient, because I'm not going to do it every day."

Baker simply was grateful Sosa had done it on this day, particularly with the series against the White Sox looming. "This means a lot," Baker said. "If you lose this game, it's a downer going into the next series. It was a great emotional lift."

The White Sox were on an emotional high, too, having won five straight games to open a two-game lead on the Twins for first place in the A.L. Central. But with one swing of the bat in the series opener at Wrigley on the afternoon of July 2, joy turned to sorrow for the White Sox. Zambrano loaded the bases in the top of the first inning, then gave up a shot down the right field line to Ross Gload that initially was called a home run. After conferring, however, the umps ruled that the ball was foul. Although the White Sox did score two runs in the inning, their momentum was reversed by the grand slam that wasn't. "That was a huge play," Baker said of the foul call. "We were lucky to get out of there with two runs."

With his new lease on life, Zambrano allowed just one hit over the next five and one-third innings before exiting the game with a cramp in his right forearm. By that time, the Cubs were winning 5-2, a lead they ultimately extended to 6-2. "We did a lot of little things right," Baker said, "and if you're going to beat a team like the White Sox, you're going to have to do those little things right."

The spirits, as well as the bodies, of the CUBS SUCK fans peppering the stands at Wrigley Field were further dampened the following afternoon. In between four rain delays totaling three hours, the Cubs and the White Sox squeezed in five and a half innings of baseball, enough to make the game official. The final burst of rain came not a moment too soon for the Cubs, whose 4-0 lead was cut to 4-2 in the top of the sixth. For those CUBS SUCK fans, the most painful image from the abbreviated game was this: Slammin' Sammy heroically rounding the bases after muscling a home run through the driving rain in the fifth inning. The *Chicago Tribune*—which (ahem) coincidentally was owned by the same company that owned the Cubs—captured the moment for posterity by making it the lead picture on the front of its sports section. The headline was every bit as precious: WHEN IT RAINS, CUBS ROAR.

The rain stopped that night, and some time the next morning—after the Fourth of July had dawned—the preparations began for the series finale. Since ESPN had opted to televise the game, the start time was shifted to 7:05 p.m. The Cubs versus the White Sox . . . on a holiday . . . at night. Who came up with this idea? The same whiz who decided to pay Hell's Angels in beer to keep the peace at the Rolling Stones' 1969 Altamont concert? "People can get started drinking, like, extremely early, right?" Baker said with a chuckle. "Sunday night, July the Fourth. It's a night game now, so they can start [drinking] earlier than before. Oh yeah, there's going to be plenty of excitement out there."

There was indeed plenty of excitement, although not because of more drunken brawls than usual in the stands. The battle of wills was, for the most part, limited to the field of play. In his best game yet as a member of the Cubs, Rusch pitched eight scoreless innings. The offense, however, was able to scratch across only one run—on a homer by Lee in the second inning—so Hawkins had to be in prime-time form when he was summoned to close the game in the top of the ninth. Instead, he did what anyone in the press box could have done, blowing the save by allowing a solo home run to Carlos Lee.

The Cubs had come too far to give up, though. In the bottom of the ninth, with the bases loaded and two outs, Walker stepped up to face Damaso Marte as a pinch hitter. Walker quickly dug himself into an 0-2 hole, but Marte could not bury him. The third pitch of the at-bat was a ball, the fourth and fifth were fouls, the sixth was a ball, the seventh was a foul, and the eighth and ninth were balls. The grittiest at-bat of the Cubs' season had produced their first sweep of the White Sox since 1998. "It's not the way you draw it up," Walker said. "Those are the kind of at-bats that give people heart attacks." Only if you were a South Sider. The North Siders were swinging from the rafters.

But this being Cubdom, an undercurrent of negativity ran through the series. Ramirez strained his left groin while sliding into third base during the opener and was forced to sit out the final two games.

Although the injury wasn't serious—he wasn't expected to miss more than another week or so—any time without Ramirez was too much time. He had been the one sure thing on Chicago's wildly inconsistent offense, leading the team in batting average (.326), hits (100), and runs batted in (56).

The outlook was much bleaker for Hollandsworth, whose .318 batting average and nine pinch hits had transformed him into the team's most revered bench player. Hollandsworth hadn't played since fouling that ball off his leg in the final game of the first series against the White Sox, and he was beginning to have flashbacks to his 2001 season with the Rockies. He suffered the same type of injury early that season—nerve damage in his leg—and never returned. "You guys don't know what I dealt with in 2001," he said. "Basically, in my mind, [missing] anything less than two months [in 2004] is a glorious celebration." The countdown began the day of the rain-shortened victory over the Sox, when he became the 15th Cubs player of the season to be placed on the disabled list.

Finally, there was that little matter of the N.L. Central standings. The Cubs had been fighting like hell. They had just swept the White Sox and had pushed their record to a season-high 11 games over .500 (46-35), yet they hadn't gained any ground on St. Louis. Zero. Zilch. *Nada.* St. Louis had matched the Cubs sweep for sweep over the Fourth of July weekend, lighting up Seattle to maintain a three-game lead in the Central. Those hated Cardinals were on a tear, with 14 victories in their past 19 games. "Sweeping the Sox was nice," Baker said, "but more important is, we're trying to win this division." It was a challenge that was becoming more daunting each day.

THE CURSE STRIKES BACK

SIXTEEN

There were six games remaining before the All-Star Break, the ceremonial midway point of the season. Baker viewed this as one of the most crucial stretches on the schedule, and he told his players the worst thing they could do was let up as their three-day reprieve neared. More than ever, Baker was expecting the best.

"I want my team to win all of [these games]," the manager said. "I'm serious about that. My goal is to think like a basketball coach. The last two minutes of the second quarter, right before halftime, you can reel off a couple three-pointers and cut that deficit real quick. And everybody else is thinking about going on vacation. It's tough on any job not to think about vacation. And it's tough on any job to come back from vacation and not still be in vacation mode. In our case, we're looking forward to coming back."

But whether the Cubs wanted to admit it or not, they were tired. In addition to dealing with the never-ending onslaught of injuries, they had been embroiled in emotional series after emotional series. Since the first week of June, Chicago had played nine games against Houston and seven against St. Louis, its staunchest division rivals. And, of course, there had been those six games against the White Sox, which always were spectacles unto themselves. "I can see how [the series against the White Sox] could be a distraction," said Goodwin, who got his first taste of the rivalry when he joined the Cubs in 2003. "For those six games, it's like end-of-the-world stuff. Then we've got to go back to playing our regular schedule, and it's kind of ho-hum. But as long as we don't take the other teams as ho-hum, I don't see it as being a big distraction."

On the surface, Chicago's next series, three games in Milwaukee beginning the afternoon of July 5, was a real ho-hummer. The Brewers had been the doormats of baseball for years; they hadn't finished with a .500 record since 1992. Furthermore, Chicago had their number at Miller Park, going 7-0 there in 2003. But these weren't the Brewers of seasons past. They had been revitalized by an off-season deal in which they sent All-Star Richie Sexson to the Diamondbacks for a slew of productive starters, including Lyle Overbay and Craig Counsell. Heading into their opener against the Cubs, the Brewers were holding their own in the N.L. Central with a 41-38 record.

From the get-go, it was obvious the Cubs were in grave danger. Brewers starter Ben Sheets struck out Walker and Lee in the first inning, then he fanned Patterson, Barrett, and Clement in the second inning. By the end of the game, the Cubs had K'd a season-high 17 times. Even worse, they had been shut out, 1-0. The loss was another bitter pill to swallow for Clement, who allowed only one run and three hits over seven innings. Clement, now 7-7, hadn't won a game since June 8 despite posting a 1.73 earned run average during that period.

However, with Prior pitching the next night, the defeat in the opener would be remembered as just a slight stumble in the sprint to the season's halfway point. Right? It looked good on paper, but once the game started, Prior couldn't locate the plate with either his curveballs or fastballs. In only four innings, he threw 92 pitches and gave up four runs and three walks. Chicago's hitters, meanwhile, couldn't locate the baseball, eking out six hits. The Cubs lost again, 4-2, and Prior didn't know how to deal with this latest snag in the fairy tale that was supposed to be his baseball career. His statistics since galloping back to Cubdom in no way resembled those of a conquering hero: a 2-2 record and a 4.00 earned run average. "We lost," he said with a snarl. "Bottom line." And that was that.

The Cubs had stumbled with Clement and had fallen with Prior, but there was no possible way they were going to get swept in a three-game series for the first time since September 26, 2002. Not against the Brewers. And not with "The Mad Venezuelan," Zambrano, pitching. Under the Miller Park big top on July 7, Zambrano played with all the gusto the faithful had come to expect. He pointed toward the heavens after retiring the side, he kicked the dirt and flapped his long arms all over the place, and he even broke a bat over his knee. But here was something the faithful *didn't* expect: Zambrano got shelled, allowing four runs in five and two-thirds innings. The faithful didn't expect this, either: The Cubs were swept in a three-game series for the first time since September 26, 2002. "Just three bad days," Baker said following the 4-0 loss. "There's not much to say."

Actually, there was. By being shut out twice, the Cubs raised their season total to nine, ever closer to the ignominious team record of 22 that was set in 1915. Their batting average for the series was .167, and the big boppers—Sosa, Alou, and Lee—were a combined 2-for-28. There was no need for Baker to say much. The sad-sack numbers spoke for him.

The curse was a tricky little devil. The faithful had breathed a sigh of relief when June came and went without the Cubs suffering any significant damage. But the intent now seemed clear. The curse had employed the element of surprise. It had spared the Cubs in June because it had something even more diabolical in store: a July Swoon.

The sweep at the hands of the Brewers revealed only part of what was happening. While the Cubs were getting their brains beaten in by Milwaukee, the Cardinals were continuing to win. By sweeping the Reds, they opened a six-game lead on Chicago. The Cardinals were surging and the Cubs were slumping, and those two disparate worlds, one made of steel and the other consisting of a half-full/half-empty glass, were about to collide. It was only July, but Chicago's season hinged on this three-game series at Busch Stadium. If the Cubs were to be swept, they would be nine games behind St. Louis and the division race would be all but over.

The faithful were not optimistic. In fact, they were in a full-blown panic, as reflected by the chatter on the airwaves of WSCR, a sports-talk radio station in Chicago:

- David in Bloomington was ready to make some major changes. "I was wondering what you guys would think of a trade involving Matt Clement for Randy Johnson—working that out somehow. Think about for the rest of the year. How big of a push would he give the Cubs right now? Over his whole career, minus the Expos, he's been an incredible pitcher."

- John, a Cubs fan up in Milwaukee, was ready to throw in the towel. "You know what? We're not in contention. That lineup we have, the position players we have, with the exception of maybe two or three players—heartless. Heartless wonders. They have no chance. None. They'll get swept. They'll be nine out on Monday morning when we wake up. I loved Sosa back when he was in his prime, but I think he's done."

- John B. in his car was ready to drive off the road. "Everybody had better quit looking back at last year. I was watching Milwaukee. They've got what the Cubs had last year—that look in their eyes. The Cubs do look heartless. I don't like what Dusty Baker is doing to this lineup on a daily basis, moving guys around. This team's in trouble. Everybody else has played the same amount of games. I don't want to hear that they're tired. This isn't last year. Everybody keeps saying, 'Don't worry, don't worry.' They're gonna be nine games behind."

First they had to fall seven games behind, which happened in short order. In the opener on the night of July 9, Maddux gave up his 18th, 19th, and 20th home runs of the season. With a 4.51 earned run average, he was looking more like the franchise's latest symbol of futility than the final ingredient for the World Series brew. He wasn't much of a quote, either. Of those despised Cardinals, he said, "Tip your hat and move on." If only it could have been that simple. Chicago's offense still couldn't go anywhere, mustering just one run to St. Louis's six.

Never underestimate the intelligence of people who call sports-radio talk shows. John in Milwaukee and John B. in a ditch had offered sage analysis. However, with Clement scheduled to pitch the second game of the series the following afternoon, just about any of the faithful could have predicted the outcome: (1) The offense would sputter and (2) he would lose. And like clockwork, the offense sputtered and he lost. "We picked a bad time to do it," Baker said of his team's five-game skid. "We all kind of went cold at the same time." Well, not *everyone*. Slammin' Sammy homered in the 5-2 defeat.

The Cubs now were eight paces behind St. Louis. They hadn't so much as led in a game since Walker drew the walk that beat the White Sox. That constituted 45 innings of baseball, 45 innings of unspeakable horror. The Cubs were down to their final bullet, but at least it was a good one: Kerry Wood.

BRING THE WOOD

SEVENTEEN

It was a blessing and, of course, a curse. Kid Wood reached the mountaintop that day in 1998 when he hung a major league, record-tying 20 strikeouts on the Astros. Two years removed from his high school prom, he was at the top of his game. At the top of *the* game. There was nowhere to go except down.

During the flickering period when he was positioned high above Cubdom, he seemed only vaguely aware of his exalted status. At the media social before the team convention in January 1999, he was surprised when he was besieged by reporters as he entered the downtown Chicago Hilton's Boulevard Room. "I got farther than ten feet in the door last year," he said, "so it's a little different." Wood was even more surprised when a reporter asked him if he felt like one of the leaders of the team. After thinking briefly about the question, he rubbed the peach fuzz on his chin and answered, "I'm just another player on the team. I'm just another part of the puzzle. There are guys on this team who are big parts of it, and I just try to fit in the puzzle. I got the first year out of the way, had some luck. It was a good year, and I had fun."

His nonchalance, as genuine and true as the 99-mile-per-hour fastballs he unleashed, lent even more vibrancy to the Kid Wood mystique. "He doesn't get impressed by a lot of things," said Marty DeMerritt, who had just taken over as Chicago's pitching coach. "If you gave him two things he would like to do in his life, it would be toeing the [pitching] slab and going fishing. He's a simple kid."

But Wood's simple life became hopelessly tangled after he blew out his elbow during spring training that year. Everything that had come to him so naturally suddenly was in doubt. When—*if*—he returned to the big leagues, would he still be Kid Wood? For the next year, he went underground and applied himself like he never had before. The faithful, meanwhile, settled back into their old routine, finding joy in the ivy, the beer, and the majestic home runs hit by Slammin' Sammy.

Then, like lightning flashing in the night sky, Kid Wood reappeared. The date was May 2, 2000, and the faithful were at Wrigley Field en masse that evening, waving signs that read BRING THE WOOD. Since Chicago was 10-17—well on its way to another losing season—this was the faithful's World Series. It was Game 7. And the kid did indeed bring the wood. On the very first pitch he saw from Houston starter Jose Lima, he hit a two-run homer. Wood's work on the mound was equally impressive. He allowed just one run and three hits in six innings as the amped-up Cubs scorched the Astros 11-1.

But again, there was nowhere to go except down. Struggling to get a feel for his reconstructed elbow, Wood was uncharacteristically tentative the rest of the season and finished with an 8-7 record and a 4.80 earned run average. This trip back to the mountaintop was going to be a long one, and somewhere along the way, Kid Wood would become a man.

In the summer of that 2000 season, Wood and one of his best buddies, Cubs first baseman Mark Grace, were making the rounds on Rush Street. They stopped at Cactus Bar & Grill, where an attractive brunette waitress named Sarah Pates caught Wood's eye. He was smitten, but Pates didn't know this Kerry Wood from Woody Guthrie. "I'm from Chicago, but I didn't really know too much about the Cubs," she recalled. "I really didn't follow them too much. A lot of families had traditions of bringing their kids to the Cubs games, but we never did that." Nevertheless, they hit it off. "He came in the next couple nights," she said, "and we got to know each other a little more. We've been best friends ever since."

They were married in November 2002, by which time Wood had a better understanding of his place in both the baseball universe and the universe at large. "[Marriage] makes you realize that no matter how bad you're doing, you come home and you have the same person who supports you," he said. "No matter how bad it gets, you come home to someone who's your best friend. That's what it's like."

Wood seemed even more driven to make something of himself, in no small part because of Sarah's influence. Like any good wife, she kept him on the straight and narrow. "He always says that I get him off the couch," Sarah said. "That's probably my biggest achievement." Wood was leaner than ever, his baby fat having melted away. He was meaner than ever, too. The shoulder-shrugging rookie of 1998 had become a fiery competitor who was calling out his teammates if he sensed they weren't giving their best.

Chip Caray, the Cubs' play-by-play announcer for WGN-TV, had seen all the ups and downs of Wood's big-league career. Following the 2002 season, Caray said, "In the midst of a 95-loss season, Kerry Wood pitched 200 innings, stayed healthy, made all of his starts, and wound up with around 200 strikeouts. What I told him after the last plane ride home [of the season] was, 'All of those things are great, but you stepped up as a leader.' When you see a player not only accept that mantle, but do it in a way that opens everybody's eyes, that's really great. He has grown up. He's a guy who cares passionately about his craft. He's overcome an incredibly devastating injury."

Still, Wood remained star-crossed. It seemed as if every time he left a game with the lead, the bullpen blew it for him. And if he wasn't leading, the score was something ridiculous like 2-1. Wood was pitching better than he ever had, but his statistics didn't bear that out. Through 2003, he still hadn't won more than 14 games in a season. But Wood didn't sweat the numbers. After everything he had been through, his aspirations had been scaled down. "I set a goal for myself in spring training every year," he said. "It's always the same: stay healthy and make all my starts. That's all I ask of myself. I don't go any further than that."

Even from that relatively humble vantage point—nearly a mountain lower than the mountaintop—there was nowhere to go except down. As in shut down. After hurting his triceps in May, Wood had to revise his goals again. "I obviously would like to get back in before the All-Star Break, but we'll have to wait and see," he said. "That's kind of why we took our time doing this and didn't rush back so soon and have something I had to deal with the rest of my career or even the rest of the season. This is something I wanted to get through so I could pitch the second half of the season and not have to worry about it."

There was no "Wood Watch" charting his progress. What was newsworthy anymore about Wood trying to work his way back from something calamitous? It was garden-variety fare. Nevertheless, at least one person was watching Wood with a keen eye. "Obviously, he's a big part of this," said the other half of Chicago's one-two pitching punch, Prior. "Where we want to go, we need him. He's going through the same thing I went through. I want to get him back as much as anybody. It'd just be nice to get him back in the rotation."

By early July, Wood was approaching the base of the mountain; his arm was feeling strong again. One morning at Wrigley Field, it was put to the test in a four-inning simulated game. The stands were empty and a ragtag assemblage of fielders stood behind him— Maddux at third base, Hawkins at shortstop, and seven-year-old Chase Maddux at second base—but at least live bullets were flying.

However, even in a controlled environment, there were no assurances that those bullets would fly in the right direction. Not where Kerry Wood was concerned. The batting order consisted of Bako, Macias, and Goodwin, and in the early going, Wood overpowered those sacrificial lambs. Then, for seemingly the first time all season, Bako hit a ball hard. Not only did he hit it hard, he hit it right at

Wood. Right at Wood's face. Destiny was traveling toward him at light speed, but the ball ricocheted off his outstretched mitt and only grazed his body. This time, anyway, disaster had been narrowly averted.

As Wood walked to the bench between "innings," he passed Mercker on the dugout stairs. "Fucking Bako," Wood said to his fellow pitcher.

"He hit you?" Mercker asked.

"In the fucking throat."

"Guys aren't supposed to hit your shit," said Mercker.

"I was behind in the count."

Bako was not released by the Cubs, but something good still came out of the simulated game: Wood was ready for a real start. On July 6, he slipped into an Iowa Cubs jersey and fine-tuned his arm against Triple-A competition. Those minor-leaguers were no match for Wood, who pitched four innings and allowed no runs. More important, he felt nothing beyond the normal aches and pains. After taking inventory of his body parts, he said, "Everything feels good."

The Cubs wasted no time sending him to St. Louis, where he would start the series finale on the afternoon of July 11. Prior's comeback had produced only mixed results so far; now it was up to Wood to save the season. After two straight losses to the Cardinals—after sliding an incomprehensible eight games out of first place—Chicago absolutely had to win.

Even though it was daytime, the flash of lightning was unmistakable. Behind Wood, the Cubs played with a spark for the first time in a week. They scored four runs in the top of the fourth inning, giving Wood something he wasn't accustomed to: breathing room. Not that he needed much. In five innings, he held the hard-hitting Cardinals to one run and struck out five. Although St. Louis rallied after Wood left the game, the Cubs hung on for an 8-4 victory. "When you start the year, you have everything on paper and everybody is talking about the starting pitching," Baker said. "Here it is, July 11, and it's the first time we've had [both Wood and Prior]. It's a tremendous boost for us."

While Sosa, Zambrano, Alou, and Ramirez headed to Houston to participate in the All-Star Game, the rest of the team started contemplating the task at hand. "I think we've got a great team, and we still haven't gone on a run where we've won seven of eight or 15 of 17, something like that," Wood said. "I think we're capable of doing that. We had a rough ending to the first half, and I think we can make up those games after the break."

If only for a moment, hope was restored.

WRIGLEY FIELD
HOME OF
CHICAGO CUBS

THE CIRCLE OF STRIFE

EIGHTEEN

The second half of the season began the same way the first half did: with Cubdom fixated on the health of Mighty Mark Prior. Thirty-six pitches into the era of restored hope, during the second inning against the Brewers at Wrigley Field on the night of July 15, Prior grimaced as he ran to cover first base on a ground ball to Lee. Minutes later, he disappeared inside the clubhouse. No one was sure what had happened, but it didn't look good. So ended the run of good health for Chicago's vaunted starting rotation. It had lasted four days, three of which had spanned the All-Star Break.

The remaining players, possibly in shock, seemed unaware that the era of restored hope had just concluded. As Rusch warmed up, the infielders huddled together and chatted casually, even cracking occasional smiles. And when the game resumed, Rusch promptly retired the side and then Lee led off the bottom of the inning with a home run that tied the score 1-1. Thanks to five more shutout innings from Rusch and a three-run outburst from the offense in the sixth inning, the Cubs left the field as 4-1 victors.

Then reality set in. "You can't get any more worried than being sick to your stomach," Baker said. He was referring to Prior's prognosis, which fell soundly into the "certain doom" category. Prior hadn't tweaked his Achilles tendon again, as some onlookers had suspected. This was something worse, much worse. His right elbow was ailing— and, apparently, it had been all along. If tests the following day showed that he had torn his ulnar collateral ligament—the same injury Wood had suffered in 1999—Prior would have to undergo reconstructive surgery and would be out for at least a year.

"It's something I've been dealing with on and off since spring training," Prior said in a press conference after the game. "It has been kind of a mental battle, going in every game and battling to make sure I'm all right, make sure I'm healthy. Hopefully, we can get some answers this time on what it really is. I can't tell you where I'm at or where I'm going to be."

While Prior was being poked and prodded the next day at Northwestern Memorial Hospital, Clement was being poked and prodded at Wrigley Field. The Cubs scored just two runs, one of which he had to drive in himself, and he lost. Still, Clement wouldn't allow his Abraham Lincoln goatee to droop. Someday he'd win again. "I'm just trying to win and keep my team in the game," he said following the 3-2 defeat. "I feel like I've done a decent job of that."

The outcome at Northwestern Memorial Hospital seemed infinitely more promising. Prior's elbow ligament wasn't torn after all. It wasn't nicked or even scratched. According to the team of medical technicians working tirelessly on the case, his elbow had "shin splints." In other words, it was sore. The doctors said he wouldn't cause any structural damage to the elbow by continuing to pitch and that he could take the ball for his next start on July 20 if he felt up to it.

Hope was restored again . . . until Prior said he might not feel up to it. That was when the whispering began among the faithful. Dare it be asked? Was Prior—Cubdom's conquering hero, the baddest ass in the big leagues—*soft?* There wasn't a major league pitcher who didn't have arm soreness from time to time. Why, with Chicago's season on the line, couldn't he suck it up and take the damn ball? Prior's response to the criticism: "Everybody has their own opinion, and I respect that. Deep down, I know what I'm doing. I know what's really going on. Respect my opinion and don't think I'm copping out."

Both the present and the future were once again in doubt, but on the afternoon of July 17, the Cubs got a blast of the past. Maddux took the ball for the 594th time in his major league career—enough mileage to produce major arm soreness, maybe even some arthritis—then the old-timer put on a clinic for the youngsters on Chicago's pitching staff. He baffled the Brewers with his pinpoint control, throwing his first complete game in a year and his first shutout since 2001. It also was a milestone day for the offense, which scored five runs in a game for only the third time in July.

In the series finale the following afternoon, however, there was nowhere to go except down. Wood pitched with the same intensity he did in his start after coming off the disabled list—six innings, one run, eight strikeouts—but this time, his teammates didn't follow his lead. There were gaffes on the basepaths and in the field, as well as the usual lack of clutch hitting. The Cubs should have won 5-1 or 6-2, but instead they lost 4-2. Said Wood after the game, "I think we're in a little bit of a funk."

This wasn't the second-half run Wood had envisioned. The Cubs were running, but they resembled a dog chasing its own tail.

So far, the Cubs had been stripped of their offense and their conquering hero. This July Swoon was nasty. And for good measure, the curse had thrown something else into the mix: a scheduling quirk. The Cubs had only two more cracks at the Cardinals, on July 19 and 20 at Wrigley Field. It was an absurdly early ending to the season series between the two teams, the earliest ending since World War I. If ever there were a year when the Cubs needed a slew of late-season games against the Cardinals, this was it. Now Chicago would have to rely on other teams to do its bidding and cut down St. Louis.

Still, Baker's glass was half full, maybe even two-thirds full. He saw this as a perfect chance for his go-go Cubbies to make a statement. "We're close," he said. "We're real close. And we're getting better and closer the longer I have my lineup." Even though Prior was temporarily out of commission, Ramirez had returned for the final game against Milwaukee and Gonzalez would be back for the opener against St. Louis. The Cardinals' eight-game lead wasn't nearly as formidable as it appeared. "At this particular point, [the Cardinals] are playing on all cylinders," Baker said. "I'd love to get to that point. We will get to that point. We haven't been there yet; we haven't had our guys play together. The more our guys play together, the more they'll act like a unit. The Cardinals haven't had any injuries, other than [Albert] Pujols out for a couple days and [Jim] Edmonds out for a couple days. They've had their total unit. As long as we stay together, things are going to be fine."

The Mad Venezuelan must have missed the meeting in which Baker had preached togetherness, because he began to fall apart in the fourth inning of the opener. After Edmonds hit a two-run homer to give the Cardinals a 2-0 lead, Zambrano took exception to the outfielder's casual gait around the bases. "Run the bases," Zambrano shouted to Edmonds. "Don't try to be cocky." The Mad Venezuelan exacted his revenge in the eighth inning, when he tagged Edmonds on the butt with a fastball. Zambrano was immediately ejected, but by then, both he and his teammates already had passed the point of no return. Not only had they lost their composure, but they also were on the verge of losing the game, 5-4.

The 40,000 people in attendance that evening probably would have felt better if Zambrano had taken out his frustrations on Cubs third base coach Wendell Kim rather than Edmonds. "Wavin'" Wendell had been giving the faithful fits ever since Baker hired him in 2003. Whenever Wendell waved a runner home, the faithful ducked and covered. Wendell waved and he waved and he waved, sending base runner after base runner after base runner to a fiery death.

He was at it again in the sixth inning against the Cardinals. With no outs, the score tied 3-3, and Ramirez on second base, Barrett hit a single. Even though Ramirez still was bothered by his strained groin and was scraping along like a car with three tires, Wendell waved. Ramirez was blown to smithereens about 20 feet shy of home plate, and Chicago came away with no runs in what could have been a game-turning rally.

To wave or not to wave? That was the question, and even Wendell knew the answer. After the loss, he stood in the clubhouse and said he had disgraced the team, the front office, and the fans. Cubdom had hoped for a different type of statement regarding this first of two statement games, but Baker was undaunted. Loyal to the bitter end, he said this of the apology issued by his embattled third base coach: "Wendell felt terrible. That's Wendell. He doesn't shun responsibility. That doesn't surprise me."

By 11 o'clock the next morning, the heat and humidity already were oppressive. It was the type of summer day when fire hydrants were opened to cool down the city. At Wrigley Field, where the infield was hot to the touch, Wavin' Wendell was throwing batting practice. The young and robust hitters were shaded from the sun by the batting cage, but 54-year-old Wendell, all 5′6″ of him, was fully exposed on the pitcher's mound. As if this were penance for his transgression the night before, Wendell focused his entire being on firing fastballs in rapid succession. After a while, though, his body began to buckle in the unforgiving heat. His warm-ups soaked with sweat and his chest heaving, he took progressively longer pauses between pitches. But there was a job to do, and Wendell somehow managed to finish it without keeling over.

The heat was just as stifling in the visitors clubhouse, which was about half the size of the home clubhouse and had all the frills of a homeless shelter. If the Tribune Company had wanted to spend its dollars wisely, it would have decked the place out with a putting green, hot tubs, and scantily clothed women serving ice-cold drinks. Maybe that would have softened up the opposition. But as it was, there wasn't even enough space for the players, so the amenities consisted of a small TV that was lodged in a spot where no one could see it. With nothing to occupy them, the Cardinals sat silently in the metal folding chairs by their lockers—staring at the grungy carpet, sweating, festering, growing angrier by the second.

This group looked single-minded and mean. It looked hellbent on winning the N.L. Central title, and kicking some Cubs butt along the way. "It's a very fragile thing to play at this high level," said the manager, Tony LaRussa. "One of the realities is there's no way you're allowed to celebrate this thing during the season. If you start celebrating too soon, you lose the edge. So you never really enjoy it. You feel good about it, but you don't enjoy it because you still have so much to do. We're going to keep pushing."

And the Cubs? They were falling back into the wishy-washy role they had played to perfection over the decades. Their manager was waiting for the sea to magically part and reveal a path to the Promised Land. "It's going to turn," Baker said of his team's sinking fortunes. "I know it's going to turn."

On this day—on this last-ditch attempt to make a statement and maintain at least the illusion of hope in the division race—the parting sea revealed Rusch. It was supposed to have revealed Prior, but he still wasn't feeling well enough to take the ball. Prior had, however, pitched a simulated game early that morning, looking particularly grizzled and fearsome with his face unshaven. Simulated games were becoming a rite of summer at Wrigley Field, and of this one, Prior said, "I was able to figure some things out mechanically that I think are going to help."

While Prior pondered, Rusch pitched. And the Cubs hit—boy, did they hit. In the second inning, they turned a 1-0 deficit into a 7-1 advantage behind six hits, including homers by Lee and Barrett. After St. Louis answered with a run, Ramirez hit a solo homer in the bottom of the third inning that extended Chicago's lead to 8-2. The Cubbies were well on their way to making a statement—and the good kind at that. Lo and behold, the season was turning.

But these were the Cardinals. They were 25 angry men, of whom LaRussa had said earlier that day, "They enjoy competing. That's why they put on a uniform. It's not to generate some stats and collect a check—it's to go compete against the other team." They scored four runs in the sixth inning, one in the seventh, and one in the eighth. The score was 8-8, and Hawkins was called upon in the top of the ninth inning to stave off doom. Instead, he did what anyone in the press box or the wheelchair-accessible section could have done, giving up home runs to Pujols and Reggie Sanders to make the score 11-8.

As Hawkins was leaving the mound after the inning, he asked home-plate umpire Tim Tschida about the ball-strike calls. Then perhaps the heat finally got to the middle reliever-turned-closer. Very simply, he went mad. With fire in his eyes, Hawkins rushed toward Tschida. Five Cubs coaches tried to restrain him, but he was a load to handle, hollering at Tschida and continuing to surge forward. The scene, by far the strangest of this quintessentially strange day, raged on until the coaches were able to wrestle Hawkins down into the dugout and then into the clubhouse.

Once again, the Cubs had lost their composure. And once again, they were about to lose a must-win game—although not without a final flicker of false hope. What would a year in the life of the Cubs be without some flickers of false hope? The team loaded the bases with two outs, then Ramirez stepped to the plate. With one swing of his bat, he could win this game. Ramirez swung his bat . . . and flied out.

In the clubhouse, amid the burned-out ruins of this season of great expectations, not a sound could be heard. Except for Hawkins. He had broken his code of silence and was talking to the media. "Do I regret it? No," said Hawkins, his eyes bloodshot. "I talked to [Tschida] like a man at first, and it didn't work. Do you think I was going to hit him? I wasn't going to hit him. I was mad. I talked to him like a man, and he threw me out of the game. I didn't curse at him, I didn't yell at him. I just asked him a question."

Throughout that ninth inning, Barrett had sensed a weird vibe between Hawkins and Tschida. "I felt like there might have been something there," the catcher said. "There's obviously something there between him and the umpire." In fact, there was. It was a chair that had come between Hawkins and Tschida and ultimately created this unsavory spectacle, this exclamation point at the end of the sentence that was the N.L. Central race. In 2002, when Hawkins was playing for the Twins, he was sitting in a chair in the bullpen that Tschida said was in the field of play. Hawkins refused to move it, claiming he had been sitting in that exact same spot all season long. The stalemate continued for a bit, then Tschida ejected Hawkins from the game.

The curse, a master of disguise, had appeared in many different forms over the years. As a goat. A black cat. The pickled brain of a general manager who decided to trade Lou Brock to the Cardinals or allowed Greg Maddux to sign with the Braves. A hole between Leon Durham's legs. A faulty ligament in Kid Wood's elbow. Bartman. And now—the devil be thy name—a chair.

THE CUBS STRIKE BACK

NINETEEN

Back in 1994, Major League Baseball created a device that manufactured hope for teams that wouldn't otherwise have any. Teams like the Cubs. It was called the wild card, and since the curse hadn't yet figured out how to do away with this nifty apparatus, Chicago's 2004 season was, believe it or not, still alive. The Cubs were right in the thick of the wild-card race, along with several other teams.

The wild card had worked for Chicago once before, in 1998. Although the Cubs finished 12 and a half games behind first-place Houston in the Central, they had a good enough record to be the National League's wild-card representative in the playoffs, where they were swept by the Braves in the opening series. It had worked even better for the 1997 and 2003 Marlins and the 2002 Angels, who won the World Series.

Baker didn't care how the hell Chicago got to the playoffs. It was all the same to him. "I think [about the wild card] all the time," said the manager, whose Giants reached the World Series as a wild card in 2002. "I think division and/or wild card. Just as long as you get to the dance."

To reach that dance, the Cubbies first would have to fuel up the old World Series Express. It was running on empty. Following the loss to the Cardinals, Barrett seemed as spent as the rest of Chicago's players, maybe more so since he had been wearing catcher's gear in the searing heat. He limped from the trainer's room to his locker, where he was asked by the media if he would be willing to answer a few questions. Ever the gentleman—even in the face of this crippling defeat—he complied. The catcher did, however, have one request: He politely asked if he could sit down. After sinking into the chair by his locker, he began the arduous process of thinking about the remainder of the season.

"We have a lot of good things going for us," Barrett said. "We haven't lost confidence. We haven't lost faith that we can win this thing still. We still have a lot of games left. We obviously passed up an opportunity to win two games and move closer, but now we have to go forward. I would have wanted to win that game today more than anybody, but it didn't work out.

"I'm a firm believer that anger is a gift," he continued. "It depends on how you approach it and how you control it. I think we're all in the same boat here; I think we all feel the same way. I think we're all a little frustrated, but at the same time, we all know we have a job to do, and that's to win as many ballgames as we can. Tomorrow we start over. It's a new day tomorrow."

It didn't start that way. In the early going of the first of two games against the Reds at Wrigley Field, everything appeared pretty much the same. Clement was pitching, and the Cubs weren't winning. Then in the top of the seventh inning, with the score tied 4-4 and Clement out of the game, the skies opened like some heavenly fire hydrant and finally cooled down smoldering Wrigley Field. It was as if a new day really had dawned. Sosa hit a home run in the rain, and the Cubs won 5-4.

Afterward, however, Slammin' Sammy wasn't elated. On the contrary, his feelings were hurt. Before hitting his home run, he had been booed by the disenchanted flock. Never mind that he had gone 4-for-26 since the All-Star Break and the team—*his* team—was in the toilet. Slammin' needed some love. "We're just human beings," he told the media messengers. "Sometimes when they want us to come through, it's not going to happen. They have to understand we need some support."

The Cubbies still were bruised and smarting, but they took another small step on their road to recovery the following day. Behind four home runs, as well as a second straight complete game from a resurgent Maddux, they smoked Cincinnati 13-2. Where, though, was the love? "You don't want any sympathy," Baker said, "but at least give us some understanding about what's happening and where we are." The second-year manager had a message for the sons and daughters of the fathers and mothers who had lived and died without ever seeing the Cubs win a championship: "You're either with us or against us."

Perhaps the Cubs would find what they were looking for in the City of Brotherly Love, where they began a three-game series against the Phillies on the evening of July 23 at brand-new Citizens Bank Park. To ensure that they did, they brought the wood, as in Kerry and their bats. Sosa, Alou, and Lee all homered in that opening game, and Wood allowed one run in six innings and was the pitcher of record in the 5-1 victory.

Chicago had bounced back with three straight wins since doomsday against the Cardinals. Things were starting to go right, which meant, quite obviously, that they were about to go wrong. The next afternoon, the Cubs entered the top of the ninth inning trailing 4-3, having squandered several scoring opportunities. Goodwin led off with a pinch-hit double, but he died out there on second base after Grudzielanek flied out to right field, Patterson struck out, and Sosa struck out.

In the rubber game the next afternoon, not even Prior—yes, he finally was ready to take the ball—could make things right again. Prior pitched like the conquering hero Cubdom had come to know and love seemingly a lifetime ago, but he didn't measure up to Philadelphia starter Eric Milton. Going into the top of the ninth inning, the Phillies were winning 2-0 and Milton was three outs away from becoming the first pitcher to throw a no-hitter against Chicago since 1965.

Then in a stunning turn of events, Barrett broke up the no-hitter with a bloop double to center field, Grudzielanek singled, and Patterson drove them in with a double off the center field wall. Now it was up to Hawkins to hold Philadelphia in the bottom of the ninth and send the game into extra innings. Suffice it to say that Pat Burrell singled home Jim Thome, and the Cubs lost another heartbreaker. Where, oh where, was the love?

It seemed another sacrifice was in order. This latest experiment at closer wasn't working, and the faithful were ready to blow it up—blow it up like the Bartman ball. Since taking over for Borowski, Hawkins had posted an earned run average of 5.14 and had allowed five home runs. The faithful were buzzing like a swarm of hornets, but Baker stood his ground. "You have to stick with somebody for a while," he said. "When Joe was here, they were hollering for LaTroy. Now they're hollering for someone else."

As if to prove his point, Baker went back to Hawkins the first chance he had. A little more than 24 hours after the stinging loss to Philadelphia, the Cubs were in Milwaukee playing the first of four games against the Brewers. When Chicago entered the bottom of the ninth inning with a 3-1 lead, Baker didn't call for Farnsworth, Wellemeyer, or one of the bratwurst vendors working the grandstands at Miller Park. He called for Hawkins, and the beleaguered closer did what none of the pantywaists in the press box could have done, retiring the Brewers in order.

Redemption was the theme of the evening. Clement was the winner, and he didn't even have to throw a shutout to accomplish that elusive feat. Although the first six innings followed the same sad script—Clement was losing 1-0—Lee led off the seventh with a homer and then Grudzielanek had a two-out, two-run single. After Grudzielanek rolled that clutch hit up the middle, Baker gave Clement a hug in the dugout. "It was nice," Clement said of the win, not the hug from Baker. "It's been a strange month or two where things just haven't worked out."

The Cubs made a little more history the next night, as Maddux closed to within one victory of 300. Chicago coasted to a 7-1 win behind its 38-year-old starter, who limited the Brewers to one run and four hits in six innings. In his last three games, Maddux had transformed himself from a symbol of futility into a pillar of hope. He had shaved more than half a point off his earned run average since that rocky start against the Cardinals on July 9 and now had a team-leading 10 victories. "He has a lot of miles left, a lot of victories left in him," Baker said. "As an older player, it usually takes a little longer to get your stuff together, but when you get it, you usually keep it longer."

For everyone else, that winning vibe was more transient. Wood felt sensational in the third game of the series on the evening of July 28—"I thought I threw the ball pretty well," he said—but was roughed up for five runs in six innings. The offense came out swinging—Barrett hit a long home run in the second inning—but then faded away. And the Cubs—who had arrived in Milwaukee looking for a sweep—were 6-3 losers.

Zambrano hadn't had that winning feeling since the All-Star Break. The Mad Venezuelan had been working like the dickens—yelling at batters, throwing at them, bouncing around the field like he was on a Pogo Stick—but his victory total had remained stuck at nine. In the series finale against Milwaukee, however, he finally channeled his boundless energy in the right direction. The 6'5", 255-pound right-hander slammed the Brewers until they were punch-drunk, throwing eight shutout innings to lead Chicago to a 4-0 win.

The Cubbies hadn't gotten their sweep, but they had taken three of four games. It was something to build on. "Whatever it takes for us to win the N.L. Central, to win the wild card—whatever it takes, we just want to go to the playoffs," Zambrano said. "And the sooner we're there, the better. The Cardinals, we don't have to worry about them. We have to worry about being in the playoffs."

St. Louis was long gone, now 10 and a half games ahead. The Cubs were well into Plan B, and Plan C didn't exist. It was wild card or bust. "We're the Cubs," said Prior. "We don't do anything as easily as we should."

Securing a wild-card berth certainly wouldn't be easy. The Cubs trailed front-running San Diego by two games and were tied with San Francisco in the hunt for a blue October, and neither of those teams was showing signs of letting up. Worse yet, Philadelphia, Florida, and Houston were positioned close behind Chicago. If an August Swoon were to follow this July Swoon, the Cubs would become lost in the wild-card shuffle.

Understandably, the faithful were on edge when Chicago began a three-game series against Philadelphia at Wrigley Field on the afternoon of July 30. The mood became even more tense when Philly deposited Cubdom's conquering hero into the proverbial recycling bin like yesterday's newspaper. Prior was hauled out to the curb after only four and one-third innings, having put his team into a 6-3 hole by allowing a career-high four homers.

Thanks to four home runs of their own—including three solo shots by Ramirez—the Cubs won 10-7, but the stirring comeback was more of an exercise in false hope than the genuine article. Ramirez himself admitted as much after the game. Although he had become only the 24th Cubs player ever to hit three home runs in a game, he didn't feel like patting himself on the back. "Everybody's right about the home runs," the third baseman said. "We lead the league in solo home runs, and that's not a good sign. We have to start playing small ball." The problem was, the Cubs lacked the means to do that. They had plenty of thumpers, but not enough of the types of players who could generate a small-ball spark on those days when the home runs dried up. The hour was growing late—only 59 games remained in the season—and a vital ingredient still was missing from the World Series brew.

July 31 was among the busiest days on the Major League Baseball calendar. It was the trade deadline, the last real chance contending teams had to acquire vital ingredients for their World Series brews. Jim Hendry lived for days like this one. His cell phone unsheathed, the GM was working frantically to make Cubdom's dreams come true. "When I got out of the car this morning at about seven," he said, "I was prepared for it to be a real big day for the Cubs."

By late afternoon, Hendry's work was done. The transaction was extremely complicated, involving the Twins, Expos, and Red Sox. In a nutshell, the Cubs said goodbye to Gonzalez, Francis Beltran, and minor-leaguers Justin Jones and Brendan Harris—then said hello to Boston shortstop Nomar Garciaparra. This wasn't *a* deal. It was *the* deal. It went way beyond being an upgrade on Gonzalez, who was hitting .217.

Garciaparra was one of the best all-around players in baseball, a slick fielder and a two-time batting champion who had a career average of .323. He had power, but more important, he was capable of playing small ball. Not only would Garciaparra be a contact hitter in a lineup dotted with players who struck out too often, but he also would do those little jobs the Cubs had butchered regularly, such as moving a runner from second to third base with a ground ball to the right side. The deal had the requisite element of impending doom— Garciaparra missed most of the first half of the season with a strained Achilles tendon, an injury that was hauntingly familiar to Cubdom— but he was batting .321 since returning.

No one really cared that Chicago dropped a 4-3 decision to the Phillies that day. Out of nowhere, hope had been restored—and with a vengeance. "His accomplishments and his abilities speak for themselves," Hendry said of his new acquisition. "Obviously, he's a tremendous player, and I think he's capable of giving us a huge shot in the arm down the stretch."

Garciaparra, who had spent his entire nine-year big-league career with the Red Sox, was warming up for his team's game at Minnesota when he heard the news. Initially, he was dazed and confused, but the 31-year-old shortstop quickly resigned himself to his fate, whatever that fate might be. Surrounded by a cluster of reporters, he said, "If it was in my control, I would still be wearing a Red Sox uniform, because it's the place I know, I love. All of those fans, I'll always remember. But I'm also going to another great place. I'm going to a phenomenal city with great tradition as well—phenomenal fans, great organization. I'm also excited about that." His parting words spoken, Garciaparra headed for time-worn Wrigley Field, where he would play the following afternoon.

Just 11 days earlier, the Cubs had been down for the count. Now, though, they had reinvented themselves, come back stronger than ever with an offense that suddenly rivaled any in the National League. Maybe that would be enough to push them past San Francisco and San Diego and into the playoffs. Maybe, just maybe, it would be enough to bust the curse and end this mortal struggle once and for all.

August

WRIGLEY FIELD
HOME OF
CHICAGO CUBS

A NEW LOOK FOR THE OLD SHRINE

TWENTY

The faithful knew how it felt when the sky was falling. That happened all the time. But this, *this* was something distinctly different. It seemed more like concrete than atmospheric matter. In June, a piece of the stuff landed near the foot of an elderly woman who was attending a game against the Cardinals. And the following month, another chunk came hurtling down to Earth after a game against the Brewers, narrowly missing a five-year-old boy. The sky wasn't falling . . . well, not exactly. Wrigley Field was.

Perhaps it was a stern warning from the curse in this season of great expectations. Or maybe the place was just plain old. Only Boston's Fenway Park had been around longer. In the beginning, circa 1914, Wrigley Field wasn't a shrine, a spiritualistic vessel. It was just another turn-of-the-century ballpark, made of steel, brick, mortar and, of course, concrete, at a cost of about $250,000. It wasn't even Wrigley Field back then. When the Cubs moved into the venue in 1916, it was called Weeghman Park. Not until 1926 was it christened with its current name, in honor of the team's owner, chewing-gum magnate William Wrigley Jr.

The Cubs had played about 7,000 games at 1060 West Addison Street. That was a lot of wear and tear, and as with the team that occupied Wrigley Field, nothing seemed to work quite right. The drains in the dugouts backed up when it rained too hard. There weren't enough bathrooms, and the concourses were too narrow to comfortably accommodate sellout crowds. Visiting teams complained for years about the lack of hot water in the showers. Inside the home clubhouse, a piece of paper haphazardly taped to the latch-impaired door leading to the concourse instructed, IF YOU ARE THE LAST ONE TO LEAVE, PUSH THIS DOOR CLOSED AND LOCK. The list of defects was endless.

There was some fourth-hand account—it was a Wrigley Field ghost story—of a time the night watchman was making his normal rounds and heard the bullpen phone in the Cubs' dugout ringing. This was mighty creepy, considering its line ran only to the corresponding phone in the team's bullpen, which was as deserted as the rest of the ballpark. Was the curse calling? More likely, the wiring was faulty.

Wrigley Field was a wreck, but it was redeemed by the intimacy and sheer beauty of its playing field. This was the one aspect of Cubdom that had stood the test of time. Wrigley Field became *Wrigley Field* in 1937, when the outfield bleachers and the center field scoreboard were constructed and ivy was planted on the outfield walls. The soothing, bucolic shade of green throughout the park, combined with seating areas that rested so close to the field they seemed to be part of it, created something that felt a little like paradise.

It cast a spell on one and all, particularly the home team. Players through the years would don that Cubs uniform for the first time and marvel at their surroundings. Then they would stink up the pristine field, seemingly anaesthetized by its bewitching powers, until they were dispatched elsewhere. Brant Brown, he of the infamous Brant Brown Game, spoke about Wrigley Field in 2000: "I've always felt really comfortable here at Wrigley Field. Maybe it's the day games. Maybe it's the sunshine or the atmosphere. I don't know what it is. It's like you never really want to leave this place." Brown left it for good after batting .157 in that 2000 season.

In recent years, architects who were designing other stadiums attempted to replicate Wrigley Field's nostalgic feel. Brand-new Petco Park in San Diego even featured a rooftop reminiscent of the ones overlooking Wrigley Field on Sheffield and Waveland. But that rooftop in San Diego just didn't ring true. "San Diego built rooftops, but this [in Wrigleyville] is an organic evolution," said Tom Gramatis, owner of the rooftop on 3637 North Sheffield, where people had been watching baseball since April 23, 1914, the day of the first major league game at then-Weeghman Park. "I'm a Chicago native. I grew up a Cubs fan, and at my first game at Wrigley Field in the 1970s, I remember coming and seeing people on these buildings. It's a unique thing. It doesn't have a generic feel."

No matter how hard the architects tried, they never would be able to draw up a ballpark that matched Wrigley Field's history. Babe Ruth called his shot there in the 1932 World Series; Gabby Hartnett hit his "Homer in the Gloamin'" there in 1938; Ernie Banks cranked out his 500th career home run there in 1970; Pete Rose tallied his record-tying 4,191st hit there in 1985; Kid Wood K'd 20 Astros there in 1998; and Sammy slammed his 60th home run of the season there that same year.

The ballpark moved into the future at its own lazy pace, impervious to the world around it. On August 8, 1988—about half a century behind the times—the first night game was played at Wrigley Field. It was the closest thing to a World Series atmosphere since the Cubs last had been in one in 1945. Scores of reporters milled around the field before the game, waiting to wax poetic about this matchup between the fourth-place Cubs and the fifth-place Phillies. The players, meanwhile, were more pragmatic. "I've been coming to Wrigley Field for fourteen years now, and it was the first morning I was able to sleep in," Phillies reliever Kent Tekulve said as he jostled through the pileup near home plate. "So actually, it feels pretty good coming to a night game at Wrigley Field. I wish they would have done this about fifteen years ago." Around 7 p.m., the switch was flipped and the strange new era of night baseball began.

Now Wrigley Field was crumbling. Pieces of concrete were falling from the underbelly of the upper deck—and Chicago Mayor Richard Daley was ticked off about it. In late July, Daley threatened to shut down the shrine, saying, "If one section could be dangerous, you want us to [exercise] caution on the side of the fan. Otherwise, there are going to be good lawsuits here. The trial lawyers will love it." The mayor's concerns were entirely justified, although it needed to be noted that he was a White Sox fan.

At any rate, while the Cubs were on a road trip the last week of July, workmen set out to fix the problem. Like archaeologists examining an ancient relic, they tapped the underbelly of the upper deck ever so gently with hammers, searching for patches of loose concrete. When the Cubs returned home on July 30, Wrigley Field was open for business. Netting had been installed under the suspect sections to catch any falling concrete. Wrigley Field now more closely resembled a tuna boat than a baseball shrine, but at least it was safe again. Just in case, some of the faithful at the game that afternoon wore hard hats.

By August 1, the Cubs had a safety net of their own: Garciaparra. The final game against the Phillies that afternoon promised to be a watershed moment in the storied history of Wrigley Field. Not only was Garciaparra making his Cubs debut, Maddux was going for his 300th victory. The old tuna boat was rocking and rolling.

Upon reporting for duty that morning, Garciaparra headed straight for the interview room and addressed the media. "I'm definitely nervous. It's like your first day all over again—you know, Opening Day. It's just a new environment. This is my first time ever at Wrigley Field. I've never been here, never played here, or never just stopped by or whatever. I'm excited, as well. I have the excitement because it's just a wonderful city, wonderful town. It's a wonderful organization, as well, and I'm excited to be a part of it." Garciaparra then went out on the field and viewed the greenery for the first time. He liked what he saw—and why not? He elicited an ovation from the rejuvenated faithful merely by stretching with his new teammates.

Maddux, who had been trying for days to treat this start with his customary shrug and yawn, was more than willing to cede some of the spotlight to Garciaparra. He wasn't interested in having his 300th victory commemorated with marching bands, fly-overs, or calls from the president. Simply getting him to talk about it was tough enough. In one of his rare musings on the subject, Maddux said the win only would matter in as much as it helped the Cubs get to the playoffs.

The faithful wanted the whole ball of wax in this season of great expectations. They wanted the playoffs *and* the 300th victory. For all the milestones that had occurred at Wrigley Field, no one ever had won his 300th game there. Only 21 players had reached that plateau, period. At 8:30 that morning, a good five hours before first pitch, the streets of Wrigleyville were filled with partygoers. By the time Maddux strode to the bullpen to take his warm-up tosses, the faithful were beside themselves, so much so that even the master of the shrug and the yawn was sucked into the moment. "The fans here are tremendous," Maddux said. "Even when you walk out to the 'pen, it's not normal. It's not normal to get that kind of reaction. You appreciate it so much."

But as evidenced by the netting hanging beneath the upper deck, history had a way of breaking bad at Wrigley Field. Maddux's second pitch of the game, to Philadelphia shortstop Jimmy Rollins, came to rest in the right field bleachers. The landmark day crumbled a little more six pitches later, when Bobby Abreu launched a ball into the right-center field bleachers. Maddux was still standing at the end of that first inning, but barely. The Cubs were losing 2-0, and the faithful were pensive.

In the bottom of the inning, however, hope came to the plate in the form of Garciaparra, who was losing count of all the ovations he had received thus far. There had been the stretching ovation, the batting-practice ovation, and the minute-long ovation when his name was called during pregame introductions. Now the faithful, some of whom were waving replicas of Garciaparra's Red Sox jersey (ones bearing the colors and logo of his new team hadn't been minted yet), were on their feet again.

Blurry-eyed from the life-changing events of the past 24 hours, Garciaparra felt adrift, like a man on a rudderless tuna boat. He called the whole experience "surreal." But after one pitch—one swing of the bat—this wayward ballplayer got his bearings. Did he hit a homer? A triple? A double? A single? He grounded into a double play, then shook his head repeatedly and muttered to himself upon returning to the dugout. It was official: Nomar was part of Cubdom.

This, however, wasn't the usual hack passed off on the faithful as a shortstop. It wasn't Jack the Ripper, or even Jeff Blauser or Dave Rosello. It was Nomar Garciaparra, whose maneuvers at the plate and in the field bordered on the artistic. The afternoon had started like so many others—poorly—but it wouldn't end that way.

Maddux settled into a groove, allowing just one run in his next five innings. Then he took himself out of the game, his 38-year-old body done in by the steamy August heat. The Cubs were losing 3-2, so there was no way he would be able to make history on this day. But like he had said all along, he wanted the Cubs to win more than he wanted his milestone. "I think I could've started the seventh [inning]," Maddux said. "I don't know if I could've made it out of it or not. I was pretty much done after the fifth or sixth. I would have loved to have gone out there and tried not to walk somebody, hope they hit it at somebody. But that's not right. That's not fair to the rest of the guys, to the city, whatever. It's not the way you're supposed to play the game."

Taking a cue from their spiritual leader, the Cubs began to play the game the right way in the bottom of the seventh inning. They actually played small ball, scoring runs on a double by Grudzielanek, a pinch-hit single by Macias and, of all things, a pinch-hit sacrifice fly by Barrett. Patterson then took one for the team, his body absorbing a fastball. There were two outs, Macias was on second base, and Patterson was on first, and the Cubs were leading 5-3. The small-ball stage now was set for Garciaparra, who promptly lined the inaugural base hit of his Cubs career into left field. Wendell waved, and the faithful ducked and covered, but there wasn't a fiery explosion—or even a plume of smoke. Macias slid home safely, which spurred another standing ovation for Garciaparra.

Two innings later, Garciaparra was showered with one final round of applause, the result of Chicago's 6-3 victory. Then he was back in the musty bowels of his new home, talking to the media. "The ovation I got here today, that stuff you just don't forget. That stuff stays with you. It stays with your heart, and you appreciate it every step of the way. I know there's a great tradition here. When you step on the field and see the place packed every single day and the passion the fans have, I think that's what makes it." He did, however, have one regret. "I think we were all hoping that we'd get Greg the win there."

That Wrigley Field first didn't come to pass. But as ovation followed ovation under a cloudless sky, there was a very real sense that another one might—that the Cubs would win the World Series before the old shrine finally fell to the ground, netting and all.

WRIGLEY FIELD

HOME OF

CHICAGO CUBS

HERE COMES THE WORLD
SERIES EXPRESS

TWENTY-ONE

Garciaparra was fitting right in. Forty-eight hours into his tenure with his new team, he was talking tendons. He also was mad, although not at anyone in Cubdom.

His ire was directed at the Red Sox. Nomar—or Nomah, as New Englanders called him—had been the franchise's most beloved figure since Ted Williams. Much like Slammin' Sammy in Chicago, Nomah had been synonymous with the Red Sox. But the relationship soured after the 2003 season, when the Red Sox tried to trade him and acquire shortstop Alex Rodriguez, who was younger than Garciaparra and had just won the MVP award. Garciaparra wound up staying put because Boston botched the deal, but the damage was done. Suddenly, he felt unwanted by the team that had meant everything to him.

The first part of the 2004 season was a real downer for Garciaparra. Not only was he sidelined with a strained Achilles tendon, his zest for the game seemed to be gone. There was rampant speculation that Garciaparra wouldn't re-sign with the Red Sox when his contract expired at season's end, so they made a preemptive strike. They traded him to the Cubs.

After committing the crime of the century, the team needed an alibi. The Red Sox, fighting to stay alive in the playoff race, claimed he had told them that his tendon troubles would force him to miss a large portion of the rest of the season. This, they said, left them with no alternative but to unload the shortstop.

When the news reached Garciaparra, he begged to differ. "I wanted to make sure that I would be able to go the last month of the season," he told the *Boston Globe*. "But I didn't say I'd have to miss significant time, or that there was a significant chance that I would have to go on the DL." Garciaparra was trying to move forward now. "I'm not going to rant and rave," he continued. "I'm not jabbing anybody. If they don't want me, fine. They traded me. Why can't that be enough?"

The Cubs, feeling a bit like the cat that swallowed the canary, were doing everything they could to ease Garciaparra's transition. His jersey number in Boston had been five, which belonged to Barrett in Chicago. Garciaparra wore number eight in his first game with the Cubs, but then Barrett swapped jerseys with him. It was the cordial thing to do.

The next stop for the World Series Express was Denver, where the Cubs began a three-game series against the Rockies on the night of August 3. The starter for that first game, Wood, was on the mountaintop in the Mile High City. Literally. And this time, he stayed there. Wood slipped in the first inning, allowing three runs, but quickly regained his footing. He held the Rockies scoreless through his next seven innings and was the pitcher of record in the 5-3 victory. The key hit was delivered by none other than Garciaparra, whose run-scoring single with two outs in the second inning put Chicago up 4-3.

The Cubs now were tied with San Diego in the wild-card standings.

The next evening, Zambrano was unable to function in the thin mountain air the way Wood could; the Rockies knocked him around for four runs and eight hits in six innings. But in the top of the seventh inning, balls also started flying off the bats of the jacked-up Cubs, as a three-run homer by Sosa and a run-scoring double by Walker gave them a 5-4 lead. The Rockies came right back with two runs in the bottom of the inning, but the Cubs countered with a four-run eighth that was keyed by homers from Ramirez and Walker. Chicago held off two more charges by Colorado and wound up winning the wild game 11-8.

The Cubs had a one-game lead over San Diego.

A potential sweep of the Rockies the following afternoon was in the hands of Cubdom's fallen hero, who hadn't won since June 25. "Personal statistics, wins and losses—everybody at this time of year puts them aside," said Prior. Indeed, the slate was wiped clean for one and all in this new-fangled Nomar Era. Prior picked himself up and pitched six shutout innings, which vaulted Chicago to a 5-1 victory.

The Cubs had a two-game lead over San Diego.

Although anything seemed possible now that Garciaparra was playing shortstop, the Cubs weren't going to go undefeated for the remainder of the season. Even the '27 Yankees lost a game here and there. It figured it would happen the night Clement was pitching. In the first of three games in San Francisco on August 6, the Cubs had plenty of opportunities to do in the Giants, but they left 10 men on base and scored only two runs for Clement. The Giants, on the other hand, put six runs on the board. His hopes dashed again, Clement dug out the line he had spoken so eloquently throughout the season: "It was just one of those games."

As for the team as a whole, its winning streak was over at four. But there was no reason to fret—tomorrow was another day. The sun would be shining and the birds would be chirping. Tomorrow would offer a chance to win anew. "We've had our fair share of injuries this year, and we had to battle through some stuff early in the season," Barrett said. "We've continued to be positive and continued to work hard through everything. The fact that we're winning, and we're trying to buy a spot in the playoffs, is pretty good when you consider everything."

When the moment arrived—when Maddux made history on the afternoon of August 7, 2004—it almost seemed like a footnote. The World Series Express was 2,000 miles away from Wrigley Field, in San Francisco, beyond the range of the faithful's robust vocal chords. In these parts, the featured attraction was Barry Bonds, who was on an even more historic quest than Maddux. With 687 home runs, Bonds was nearing Hank Aaron's all-time record of 755. Bonds was the most feared player in baseball, and every move he made was viewed with the utmost scrutiny. But that was just how Maddux wanted it. "When you play the Giants," he said, "the game revolves around Barry."

The deal went down just how Maddux wanted, as well: It was a total team effort. Maddux needed all the help he could get after allowing a run in the first inning and two more in the third, and his teammates were happy to oblige. In the fourth inning, the Cubs rallied with some small ball, stringing together three hits, including a two-run double by Walker. More small ball followed the next inning: Garciaparra doubled and was singled home by Ramirez, who then scored on a double by Lee. For the heck of it, the Cubs played big ball in the sixth inning, as Patterson hit a two-run homer.

Maddux had a 6-3 lead, but after giving up two straight singles to begin the bottom of the sixth inning, he could go no more. The bullpen would have to carry him to the finish line. Like a relay team passing him along like a baton—from Jan Leicester to Mercker to Remlinger to Farnsworth to Hawkins—it did just that, and Maddux was an 8-4 winner. Afterward in the clubhouse, he was given a champagne shower. "It's a sense of relief in a way," Maddux said.

"Hopefully, we can move on. I don't think anybody got too caught up with it to begin with. We just put it behind us and do what we can to get to the postseason now."

On that front, the Cubs remained two games ahead of the Padres. The World Series Express was rolling.

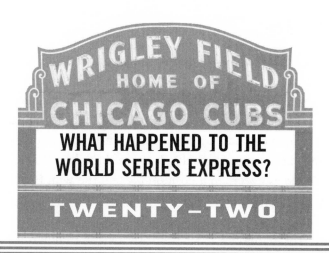

WRIGLEY FIELD
HOME OF
CHICAGO CUBS

WHAT HAPPENED TO THE WORLD SERIES EXPRESS?

TWENTY-TWO

What was the cliché? The light at the end of the tunnel was an oncoming train? Yeah, that was it. For the Cubs, the light was a lineup card, a lineup card that didn't bear Nomar Garciaparra's name. Garciaparra wasn't injured—Baker simply wanted to rest the shortstop's fragile Achilles tendon for one game—but the curse needed only the slightest opening to regain its advantage. With headlights as bright as the future had seemed just a day before, the curse sped down the tracks, straight toward the World Series Express.

Since the rubber game against San Francisco was being broadcast on ESPN's "Sunday Night Baseball," the Cubs had a national stage to showcase their time-honored brand of buffoonery. Viewers from coast to coast were able to see:

- A pop fly to Ramirez land untouched next to the third base bag. That should have been the third out of the inning, but instead the Giants scored a run on the play.
- Alou get doubled-up off first base on a fly out to right field.
- San Francisco's Pedro Feliz advance from first to third base on a routine ground ball off the bat of Bonds to Grudzielanek at second base. Grudzielanek recorded the out at first, but Feliz was able to move up two bases because a shift had been in place for Bonds, and Ramirez neglected to return from the middle infield to his post at third base after the ball was hit.

The magic returned briefly when Garciaparra came up as a pinch hitter with no outs and Martinez was on third base in the top of the eighth inning. He hit a ground ball that was gloved by third baseman Edgardo Alfonzo, Wendell waved, Martinez ran, and Alfonzo gunned the ball home to catcher A.J. Pierzynski. Martinez was dead to rights, but Pierzynski dropped the ball. *He dropped the ball.* Down only 4-3, the Cubs suddenly were in a position to steal the win. Hope had been restored. But then:

- Patterson's sacrifice bunt went up instead of down, falling into the glove of first baseman J.T. Snow. Alou and Walker followed with fly outs, and Garciaparra died relatively quietly out there on first base.
- In the bottom of the eighth inning, Farnsworth fielded a sacrifice bunt, spun around toward first base, cocked his powerful arm, and heaved the ball over Lee's head and into the night. Luckily, no one in the grandstands was injured on the play, but it did lead to two more Giants runs.

"We made a lot of mistakes," Baker deduced following the 6-3 loss. The Flubs were back.

When Chicago's 2004 schedule was released, nary a thought was given to a little series against the Padres from August 10 through 12 at Wrigley Field. Everyone figured the Cubs would have visions of Cardinals and Astros dancing in their heads, not Padres. But the wild-card race created strange bedfellows. Suddenly, there was nothing little about this series. With Chicago two games ahead of San Diego in the wild-card standings, it was epic in scope.

Said Baker, "It's almost hero time." It *was* hero time, but they were hard to find. In the first game, Chicago hit five home runs, which should have been more than enough firepower to produce a win.

These, however, were the Flubs, and all five homers were of the solo variety, the baseball equivalent of a field goal.

Then there was the conquering hero himself, Prior. He lasted only three innings—the briefest outing of his big-league career, excluding his injury-shortened start against the Brewers in July—and yielded six runs, eight hits, and five walks. When the dust settled, the Cubs were 8-6 losers and Prior had the worst earned run average on the team at 5.05. Prior had been doing a lot of pondering in this season of great expectations, but he remained puzzled by the results. "I've had probably my fair share of more games where I've struggled with control than I have in years past," he said. "But I don't have one specific answer."

The beauty of The Mad Venezuelan was that he didn't think too much. Emotion was the name of his game, and the flagging Flubs, now just a game ahead of San Diego, were in dire need of that type of lift. Zambrano gave it to them, too. He shook and shimmied, he rattled and rolled, and he pointed and postured. He also threw a stunning array of fastballs, sliders, and sinkers for eight innings in powering his team to a 5-1 win. Said Zambrano, "I was warming up in the bullpen, and everything was good, and I said, 'This is my game today.'"

Chicago's lead was two games again, and a victory in the series finale would put the World Series Express back in motion. It rolled out of the station with a run-scoring single by Ramirez in the first inning and a sacrifice fly by Clement in the second. It kept on rolling through the fifth inning, as the Cubs maintained their 2-0 lead behind the gritty work of Clement.

After that, however, two forces (excluding the curse) caused it to derail: the umpiring and the bullpen. In the top of the sixth inning—with one out, a runner on first base, and Leicester now pitching—Rich Aurilia hit a sharp grounder up the middle. Grudzielanek speared the ball and, while on his back, flipped it to Garciaparra for the force-out, but umpire Bruce Froemming blew the call. "No way," a livid Garciaparra said to Froemming. "Yes way," said the Padres, who tied the score by inning's end and then went up 3-2 in the top of the seventh.

Garciaparra gave the bullpen another lead to work with in the bottom of the seventh; his two-run homer created such pandemonium in the upper deck that the netting hanging beneath seemed to flap up and down. A hush spread across the grandstands, however, when Farnsworth lumbered to the mound to begin the eighth inning. The faithful were scared, scared of what the 6'4", 240-pounder might do with the ball. No one knew where it would go, least of all Farnsworth. The cluelessness persisted for three at-bats—a fly out sandwiched between two singles—then Baker pointed the way to the dugout. But it was too late; by the end of the inning, the score was 4-4. It remained that way all the way into the 11th inning, when San Diego's Khalil Greene hit a game-winning single.

In the clubhouse, Farnsworth was staring blankly at his locker, trying to figure out what had gone wrong this time. Or he was just staring blankly at his locker. Clement, meanwhile, quietly packed up his gear and then hightailed out of there. So did Prior. And Wood. Many of the other players were hiding out in the showers or in the trainer's room, but one was accounted for—Barrett—and he was talking. It was the cordial thing to do. Appearing even more haggard than after that hope-crushing loss to the Cardinals on July 20, he gazed up from the chair by his locker and said, "It's a tough ballgame to lose. That's a good ballclub out there. They did the little things today." Those were about the only words the catcher could muster.

Although San Diego still trailed in the standings by a game, fate was pressing up against these Flubs. Almost everyone was healthy and Garciaparra was on board, yet the World Series Express still wasn't working right. Could *anything* make it work right?

The faithful had some ideas, one of which involved tossing Sosa onto the tracks. Slammin' Sammy—the most prodigious slugger in the history of the Cubs—had become baggage, and the faithful let him know it during the extra-innings loss to San Diego:

- In the first inning, Sosa came up with one out and two men on base. After striking out swinging, he was roundly booed.
- In the third inning, he came up with one out and the bases empty. After striking out looking, he was roundly booed.
- In the sixth inning, he came up with no outs and the bases empty. After striking out swinging, he was roundly booed.
- In the seventh inning, he came up with one out and a man on base. After grounding into a force-out—yes, he put the ball in play—he was roundly booed.
- In the ninth inning, he came up with two outs and a man on base. After striking out swinging, he was roundly booed.

Following the game, Baker was asked about Slumpin' Sammy's four-K afternoon. "It's frustrating," the manager said. "Very frustrating." Sosa had even less to say. When the media descended on him as he came out of the showers, he barked, "I ain't fucking talking today." Taking him at his bark, the ink-stained wretches scattered.

It had been going on this way for nearly two weeks. In the past nine games, Sosa was batting .114 (4-for-35). Asked if he had ever seen his right fielder struggle like this, Baker said, "No, not since I've been here." Theories abounded as to why Sammy wasn't slammin', but no one had any definitive answers.

Was it the end result of that wicked beaning to the head he suffered in April 2003? Had it knocked the lights out? Ever since that fateful at-bat, Sosa had been unable to go on one of his patented hot streaks, the kind where he carried the entire offense for weeks at a time. Suspiciously, he was standing farther away from the plate, making him vulnerable to outside pitches.

Was Father Time sneaking up on him? It happened to every player, even Slammin' Sammy, gladiator *maximus*. The 35-year-old Sosa didn't seem to have the same bat speed as the 33-year-old Sosa. Pitchers now were blowing 89-mile-per-hour fastballs right by him. In the past, those balls would have landed somewhere near Lake Michigan.

Was his house large enough for Garciaparra, too? This was the most intriguing theory, one that addressed the very essence of Slammin' Sammy's psyche. Wrigley Field was his personal residence, and everyone—from friend to foe—needed to know that. Amid the wonderful greenery throughout the yard, there was a single patch of brown in right field, which looked like territory that had been marked by a dog. Slammin' Sammy didn't just stand in this spot day after day—he *owned* it. He had imposed his will on those blades of grass, changed their color with the incessant sweeping of his feet. Now, though, another big dog was roaming around.

Theories abounded, but only this much was certain: Sosa was a mess, both mentally and physically. The logical solution was to drop him down in the batting order from the marquee fourth spot, but that wasn't an option. Before the first game of the San Diego series, Baker said such a move would do more harm than good. "You just can't lose him psychologically and spiritually," he told the frothing faithful through the media messengers. "Talk is talk. Nobody here has to live with it but us. Sammy is a warrior. He is very proud. He's also sensitive. We all know that."

Following the next night's game, Baker and Sosa had a powwow— the team's desperation rubbed up against the desperation of its star attraction. No one except the two participants knew exactly what was said, but Sosa remained fourth in the batting order for the series finale against the Padres. Sosa had imposed his will on the manager, snuffing him out like a blade of grass in right field. Baker claimed the glass was half full—"Sammy's gonna bang," he said—but he wasn't fooling anyone. Selfish Sammy kept swinging and missing, and the faithful kept booing.

When the Dodgers rolled into town on the afternoon of August 13 for the first of three games, Sosa still hadn't budged from the fourth spot. The faithful booed him roundly during pregame introductions and each time he batted, but in the top of the ninth inning, they became distracted. With Los Angeles leading 2-1, Farnsworth lumbered to the mound. He faced four batters—and allowed four base runners—and was pelted with obscenities after Baker pointed him toward the dugout. The consequences of Farnsworth's brief appearance were equally obscene: six runs and an 8-1 Dodgers victory. Even worse, Chicago dropped into a tie with San Diego in the wild-card standings.

The following afternoon's game provided another distraction, but it was a good one. While Sosa scratched out a meaningless single in four at-bats from the fourth spot, Wood homered. And while Farnsworth remained planted on the bullpen bench, Wood pitched eight shutout innings. The Cubs finally heard some cheers as they left the field following the 2-0 victory. Even better, they regained a one-game lead over San Diego.

Although Sosa was his usual ineffectual self in the rubber game on the afternoon of August 15, Prior pitched respectably enough to put the Cubs in a position to win. After seven innings, they were leading 5-3. Then Farnsworth lumbered to the mound with no outs and a man on first base in the top of the eighth. He faced three batters—a hat trick consisting of a line out that was hit so hard it almost knocked over Grudzielanek, a walk, and a beaned batter—and again was pelted with every name in the book upon being directed to the dugout. As he sat there and gnawed his fingernails, the Dodgers tore off five runs. The entire team was gnawed over by the end of the ninth inning, having lost yet another game it could have won. Even worse, the Cubs dropped into a tie with San Diego *and* San Francisco in the wild-card standings.

Following the 8-5 defeat, Baker surmised that Farnsworth's problems most likely were "all mental." Now the curse was playing mind games, too. First Schizo Sammy had fallen prey and then Catatonic Kyle. Just as the Cubs were getting healthy physically, they were becoming basket cases mentally. Perhaps the schedule would provide a cure. From here on, Chicago would face only two teams, Atlanta and Florida, that were over .500. The parade of patsies began on the night of August 17 in Milwaukee. The Brewers made a nice run, but they had reverted to form in the past month and now were eight games under .500.

In the second inning of the opener, the healing seemed to begin. Sammy actually slammed, hitting a home run that gave Chicago a 1-0 lead. But his next at-bat, with two outs in the third inning, was the one that said it all. Victor Santos, who had been a thorn in the buttocks of the Cubs all season long, was on the ropes after loading the bases. A simple single by Sosa had the potential to bring in a couple of runs and knock the Milwaukee starter out of the game. Sosa worked the count to 3-2, but instead of shortening his swing on the decisive pitch, he whipped his bat around like he was trying to hit the ball back to Illinois. The ball popped into the catcher's mitt—*steeerike three!*—and hope keeled over again on the base paths.

Any momentum Chicago had established died, too. Milwaukee scored twice in the bottom of the inning, then Santos regained his magic touch. Unable to mount the slightest rally in the ensuing six innings, Chicago lost 3-1 to these hapless Brewers. Just a week earlier, the Cubs had been two games ahead in the wild-card standings. Now they were dropping fast, a game and a half behind the Giants and half a game behind the Padres. At the center of the free fall was the most prodigious slugger in the history of the Cubs. Like his house back in Chicago, Slammin' Sammy was crumbling. And he was taking the team down with him.

MOOD SWINGS

Baker's glass wasn't half full anymore. Several weren't. After the loss to Milwaukee, Baker held a rare team meeting and then went out and drained some cocktails. Baker was one of the faithful now—the Cubs had driven him to drink. When he returned to his hotel room, there were three messages from Sosa. The wobbly skipper promptly called his star attraction and was given the best news he had heard in a while: Slammin' Sammy said he was ready to drop down in the batting order.

Baker called Sosa's sudden act of altruism "a good, noble move. A good team move." Then the manager pulled out his pencil and made some moves of his own. When he finished, the top of the lineup looked markedly different: Patterson was batting first, Lee was second (from sixth), Garciaparra was third (from second), Alou was fourth (from third), and Slammin' Sammy—drum roll, please—was fifth. It was the first time Sosa was lower than fourth since 1994, to which he said. "What we need now is for everyone to get back together."

This latest incarnation of the ever-changing Cubs seemed as if it might finally do the trick. On the night of August 18 against Milwaukee, the first four batters in the lineup were a combined 9-for-21 (.429). The bullpen, however, remained stupefied, and Clement, who had a career-high 13 strikeouts and left the game after seven innings with a 5-3 lead, suffered the consequences. The eighth inning didn't begin with Farnsworth lumbering to the mound—he hadn't been anywhere near the field since the L.A. series. Instead, Remlinger had the honor of nuking a lead in this season of great expectations, allowing a score-tying homer to Russell Branyan.

The game—some would have said the season—hung in the balance through the ninth and 10th innings, then Patterson came through with a two-run, winning homer in the 11th. It was a crowning moment for Patterson, who had done a lot of growing up in the past two months. Slowly but surely, the 25-year-old was fulfilling his seemingly boundless potential. The coaching staff had been working overtime with him all season long, and things finally began clicking when he became the leadoff hitter upon the signing of Garciaparra. Now he was being more selective at the plate, hitting for average and power, stealing bases, and shining in the field with his glove and his arm.

"You have to be confident to play athletics," Patterson said, "and I'm just happy I can help this team win in other ways than just my bat—if I can steal a base, make some plays [in the field]. I was looking around, and there aren't a lot of people who can do that. I know how lucky I am, and I was blessed. I don't take anything for granted."

Everyone in the lineup seemed happy now, even Slammin' Sammy. Maybe this fifth spot wouldn't be so bad after all. In the series finale against Milwaukee, he had two hits—his first multihit game since Garciaparra's debut on August 1—including a home run. The Cubs as a whole unloaded for nine runs, saving the day for Maddux, who was roughed up for five runs in seven innings but still was the pitcher of record in the 9-6 victory. "The offense bailed everyone out today," said Baker, whose Cubs now had overtaken San Diego and were within half a game of San Francisco. The glass was half full again, and Baker didn't even feel like draining it.

The same couldn't be said of Chicago's next opponent: the Astros, whose fortunes were drying up. In the seven weeks since the teams last played each other, Houston had fired its manager and nearly dropped out of postseason contention. Injuries had forced the Astros to use a hodgepodge of pitchers, and the result was a 60-60 record. By comparison, the Cubs looked pretty good. Their roster had been equally, if not more, ravaged by injuries, yet they remained in the thick of the wild-card hunt.

"The difference is, we replaced players we expected to play with some guys who really stepped up," said Walker, who himself did that when Grudzielanek went down. "Nobody is ever going to remember when we get into the playoffs this year that we had ten guys on the DL or didn't have Kerry Wood or Mark Prior or Grudzielanek or on down the line for a lot of this year. No one is ever going to remember that because we're going to make the playoffs. But in Houston's case, they went through the same thing, and they just couldn't survive."

This three-game series at Minute Maid Park would provide the perfect opportunity for Chicago to get on a roll, and the wheels did indeed start turning in the opener on the night of August 20. Not only did the Cubs hit a season-high six home runs, they hit some with men on base. Alou, Garciaparra, and Patterson all had two-run shots in the 9-2 victory. Chicago's retooled lineup was humming, and in the nick of time. "We're closing in on September," Baker said, "and it's a good time to start playing our best baseball."

The next night, however, the curse retaliated. With Garciaparra on the bench resting his Achilles tendon, Chicago's hitters went south. Prior gamely tried to save them, but he was trailing 2-0 when he exited after seven innings. Then the Cubs did something entirely out of character: They saved themselves, scoring a run in the eighth inning and two others in the ninth to go up 3-2. More miraculously, the go-ahead run was driven in by Garciaparra's replacement, the light-hitting Martinez, on a sacrifice fly.

Winning this thing wasn't going to be easy, though. Was it ever? The bottom of the ninth began on a foreboding note when Jeff Kent singled off Hawkins. Then Macias, playing third base as a late-inning replacement for the hobbled Ramirez, pulled a Brant Brown and threw the ball away on a sacrifice bunt. Up in the radio booth, Ron Santo's hair wasn't burning, but it may as well have been. Minutes after Macias's gaffe, Jason Lane singled home the winning run for Houston. "It stings," said Baker, who no doubt felt as if phantom flames were doing a jig atop his own head.

The voice of reason was, of all people, Hawkins. He said this wasn't a crushing defeat at all—on the contrary, it was a character-builder, the type of game that exemplified the rallying spirit of these Cubbies. And sure enough, even with Nomar still on the bench, they came right back the next day, pounding the Astros 11-6 behind 14 hits. In the midst of the onslaught, Barrett walked out to the mound with his finger pointed and his chest puffed up like a blowfish after a fastball from Roy Oswalt hit the eight on the back of his jersey. He wanted to let Oswalt know that hadn't been the cordial thing to do. Maybe, just maybe, the light at the end of the tunnel was daylight.

Or unspeakable horror. When the Cubs returned to Wrigley Field to begin another series against Milwaukee, the talk didn't center on this nifty little streak they had put together, four wins in six games. It turned immediately to tendons and, a new one here, wrists. Not only was Garciaparra's Achilles tendon flaring up again, but the word also came down that he had sprained his wrist while taking batting practice before the first game of the Houston series. It was a double dose of the usual trouble. Although MRIs on August 23 didn't reveal significant damage to either body part, Nomar's prospects seemed grim. "Right now, we're looking at the present day and the very near future," the shortstop said, "and see how that goes."

Perhaps the Red Sox hadn't been the fools after all. This idea of Nomar donning the blue pinstripes had seemed too good to be true, anyway—like one of those mirages that appeared in Cubdom from time to time. For now, the Nubs would have to forge on without him. They needed direction, and when The Mad Venezuelan wasn't pointing his finger skyward that night, he pointed the way to the playoffs. Fueled by pitches that darted around like Wiffle balls, he took a no-hitter into the seventh inning. By the time the Brewers broke it up, Chicago had scored six runs, all without the benefit of a homer. The Nomar-less Cubs won 8-3 and moved into a tie for first place with San Francisco.

Fortune smiled upon the Cubs the next night, too. And it wasn't a mirage. Garciaparra had made a miraculous recovery and was back in the three spot, but the funny thing was, they didn't need him. While Garciaparra went 0-for-4, Lee hit a grand slam and Alou had a career-high six runs batted in. Clement even was credited with the win, a sure sign that the World Series Express was back on track. The wheels really were turning now. The Cubs' 13-4 victory, combined with San Francisco's loss to Florida, pushed them a game ahead in the standings.

"There are times in the year when you're expected to win and everyone feels [tight]," Walker said. "Right now, we're playing well, feeling good. That's the way to play, as loose as you can. It's just been a great little run for us. Hopefully, we can keep it going through the month of September, which we can because we're at full strength right now."

The next afternoon's game would be Chicago's last of the season against these Brewers. The Cubs hadn't played Milwaukee 74 times in the past 51 days—it only seemed that way. The teams had, in fact, met 16 times during that period, but Baker was ready to bid adieu. "I mean, you get tired of seeing the same team over and over," he said. "That's enough. We'll see them next spring."

That morning, Sosa arrived in the clubhouse at 10:18. At 10:19, his boombox still was silent. At 10:20, the players still could hear each other talk. And at 10:25 . . . and 10:35 . . . and 10:45. The minutes ticked away, but the explosion of sound never occurred. Not only had Slammin' Sammy relinquished the fourth spot in the lineup, he had turned off his boombox.

These days, the only place the Cubs were making noise was on the field. Maddux was at his best in the season finale against Milwaukee, allowing just one run in his first five innings. Chicago tied the score in the bottom of the fifth when Bako, who was batting around .180, drilled a solo home run into the right field bleachers. Was there any doubt now that the World Series Express was humming? It was the first homer of Bako's Cubs career, and he sprinted around the bases, his adrenaline pumping. "It could have been an inside-the-parker, and it wouldn't have mattered," he said of his historic blast. "Just to get it over with, it felt good." When Bako returned to the dugout, he wasn't greeted with open arms. Instead, he was given the silent treatment—not because he was hated, but because he was loved. Bako was the team mascot, the cuddly Cubs logo incarnate. "I mess with a lot of the guys a lot of the time," he said. "It was kind of expected. I knew something was going to be up."

Maddux pitched three more shutout innings, then Alou got him the lead with a solo homer in the bottom of the eighth. Even though Maddux had thrown just 84 pitches, Baker decided to start the ninth inning with Hawkins. "We thought Greg had had enough," Baker said. "Plus, that's Hawk's job." There was a moment of despair when Hawk did what anyone in the press box could have done and gave up a game-tying double to Chris Magruder. A heavyset geezer leaning against a beam in the concourse, with no one within five feet of him, shook his head repeatedly and muttered, "I can't believe it." But Patterson made things right in the bottom of the ninth by hitting a two-run homer to win it. "We have a bunch of sparkplugs on this team," Patterson said. "That's why we're doing so great. If one guy's not getting it done, we'll pick each other up."

In the clubhouse, the simple strains of country music emanated from the weight room. Someone else was rocking to heavy metal at his locker. Meanwhile, there wasn't any salsa flowing from Slammin' Sammy's boombox. It remained silent as the other styles of music had their day.

❖ ❖ ❖

Wrigley Field was everyone's house now. "In my mind, we're just starting to roll," Baker said. "We're playing good baseball, getting tremendous offensive production out of a lot of guys. And we're getting good pitching and playing good defense." It was everyone's house, but Slammin' Sammy still had a say in what went on. The Astros found that out in a hurry on the afternoon of August 26. They were in town for four games, the final series of the year between the two teams, and Sosa greeted them with a three-run homer in the third inning that turned a 2-1 deficit into a 4-2 lead.

Prior also was staking his claim to part ownership of the house. He hadn't won at Wrigley Field in nearly a year—since Game 2 of the National League Championship Series against Florida, to be exact— but when he was taken out after six innings on this afternoon, he was leading 7-2. The score was 8-3 after eight innings, then Farnsworth lumbered to the mound to begin the ninth. Was Baker out of his mind? A five-run advantage, while sizable, was by no means Farnsworth-proof. Still, Baker wanted this to be everyone's house, and although it took Farnsworth 26 pitches, he got out of the inning without surrendering the lead, or even a run.

The next afternoon, Roy Oswalt was pitching for Houston, the same Roy Oswalt who had put a fist-size welt on Barrett's back five days earlier. When Oswalt came to bat in the second inning, Barrett rose from his crouch and began jawing at him, which caused both benches to clear. Barrett wanted to remind Oswalt that he was in the Cubs' house now. The Astros, however, already had taken over the place; they had roughed up Wood and were leading 4-2.

By the sixth inning, Wood was long gone, Houston was up 8-4, and Mercker was pitching. Mercker was normally a genial sort, but these rabble-rousing Astros were getting to him. He sent another stern reminder to the villainous Oswalt, beaning him on the leg. There seemed to be no end to the policing Mercker had to do on this busy day. Fortunately, he was adept at multitasking. When he wasn't on the mound, he somehow found time to watch the game on TV and call the press box to complain that Cubs broadcasters Chip Caray and Steve Stone were being too complimentary of Oswalt.

Despite the best efforts of Mercker and his teammates, nothing could spoil Houston's house party now. In fact, the party had gotten so out of hand that Baker brought in Farnsworth to mop it up. When he lumbered to the mound to begin the ninth inning, the Astros were leading 9-6. Farnsworth cocked his arm and unloaded the ball; Lance Berkman drilled a single. Farnsworth cocked and unloaded; Mike Lamb roped a triple. Farnsworth cocked and unloaded; Jose Vizciano smoked a single. Farnsworth cocked and unloaded; Orlando Palmeiro banged a single.

As Mercker watched, he grew enraged because he thought the umpires were laughing at Farnsworth. The umps claimed they weren't, but they couldn't be blamed for wanting to join in on the fun at this Wrigley Field bash. Farnsworth cocked and unloaded; Jason Lane ripped a double. Farnsworth cocked and unloaded; Carlos Beltran blasted a home run.

This party wasn't much fun for the faithful. After Farnsworth recorded the final out of the six-run inning, they pelted him with the usual assortment of obscenities as he made his way to the dugout. Farnsworth wasn't feeling particularly joyful, either. He threw his mitt into the grandstands, then disappeared and kicked an electric fan.

Neither the sky nor concrete was falling, but something else was. Following the 15-7 defeat, a twentysomething was standing with his buddy on the corner of Clark and Addison. "It's not bad enough that they lost by eight runs," the twentysomething said, "but I just got shit on by a pigeon."

The next afternoon was pretty crappy, too. A thick cover of clouds hung over Wrigley Field, so the birds were flying low. The stuff was landing everywhere. Before the game, the Cubs announced that Farnsworth had sprained his knee while booting that electric fan and might be out for the rest of the season, prompting Baker to say, "We just have to go on out and do what we have to do." During the game, it landed all over the Mad Venezuelan. He gave up two runs in the first inning and was in even deeper shit in the second. With two outs and the bases loaded, Jeff Bagwell hit a sharp grounder down the first base line that was smothered by Lee. Zambrano covered first base, but a run scored because he dropped the throw; Zambrano whipped the ball home, but another run scored because Barrett dropped the ball; Barrett chased down the ball, but another run scored because no one was covering home plate. Soiled by that unseemly chain of events, the Cubs ended up losing 7-6.

The house was a dirty, pillaged mess—and the hits kept coming in the series finale on the afternoon of August 29. Clement became the third consecutive Chicago starter to get nailed, giving up four runs in four and one-third innings. Battered and splattered, he then hobbled to the dugout with a strained muscle in his upper back. "It kept getting tighter and tighter," Clement said, "and it was causing me to throw the ball differently."

The Cubs bravely defended their turf, narrowing Houston's lead to 5-3 after seven innings, but they came undone again in the top of the eighth. The Astros, it seemed, had saved their best for last. With no outs and the bases loaded, Remlinger threw a fastball that appeared to hit Berkman in the head. As Berkman rolled around in the batter's box, Houston's trainers hurried to his aid. Replays, however, clearly showed that the ball had missed Berkman's head and had hit his bat instead. The Cubs, as well as the umpires, had been duped. Berkman was awarded first base, which spurred a five-run inning for Houston.

As a final parting gift, Houston reliever Dan Wheeler beaned Lee on the back with two outs in the bottom of the ninth inning and the Cubs lost 10-3. This prompted Remlinger to rush out of the dugout, although the Astros didn't seem intimidated. With a scraggly goatee that was flecked with gray and a uniform that fit so loosely it looked like pajamas, the 38-year-old reliever could have passed for a panhandler who had inadvertently wandered onto the field. After the game, Remlinger called Berkman's dramatic turn in the dirt "chicken shit." It would have been an apt description, except chickens couldn't fly.

The bullpen was more of a wreck than ever, Clement's back was aching, and the wild-card standings were bunching up. The Astros had been on the brink of elimination from postseason contention upon arriving at Wrigley Field, but now they had new life; they were only four games behind. Of even more concern were the Padres and the Giants, who again were tied for first place with Chicago. Just like that, the element of doubt had fallen back onto Cubdom.

Pessimists would have said the Cubs, madmen all, were self-destructing. Baker, on the other hand, liked their gumption. "Our guys are a group of proud guys who really don't start nothing," he said, "but we don't take nothing."

Nevertheless, what they really needed to take now was a deep breath. They needed a shrug and a yawn, which was exactly what Maddux provided on the evening of August 30 in the first of three games against the lowly Expos at Montreal. There were no bean balls. No bench-clearing skirmishes. No ejections. No calls to the press box. No kicked objects. And no birds to worry about since the Expos played inside a dome.

Maddux calmly pitched seven shutout innings, and the offense calmly scored five runs. Even when Leicester allowed a two-run homer in the bottom of the ninth inning, no one's blood pressure rose. Hawkins came in and calmly recorded the final out. Life was a beach, thanks to Maddux. The veteran was, however, much more than a soothing presence. With a team-high 13 victories, he also had become the most reliable pitcher on a staff that had been haunted by injuries and other odd happenings.

The next day, it was Hendry's turn to try to settle the roster. Now that the trade deadline had passed, deals were much more difficult to consummate. A player had to clear waivers before a trade could be made, meaning he had to go unclaimed by every other team. Still, Hendry managed to pull two small rabbits out of his cell phone in acquiring outfielder Ben Grieve from Milwaukee and backup catcher Mike DeFelice from Detroit. Grieve, a former American League Rookie of the Year, had the potential to be a particularly valuable addition for the stretch run. Hollandsworth still wasn't anywhere close to being ready to return from the disabled list, so Grieve would provide some of the left-handed pop off the bench that had been missing.

Everything seemed blessedly tranquil . . . then Prior began pitching that night in Montreal. Before the fielders even could settle into their positions in the first inning, he gave up four runs. Suddenly unnerved, the Cubs proceeded to twitch their way to an 8-0 defeat. Once a savior, Prior now was one of the team's biggest problems. His earned run average in August 2003 was 0.69; in August of this year, it was 5.13. "It's a late-arriving Mark Prior," said Baker. Time was of the essence, so it seemed the Cubs needed to send out another search party. Prior's confidence was lost, as lost as his Achilles tendon had been all those months ago.

Back in Chicago, the old tuna boat had remained under siege throughout August. The city, concerned that the initial repairs weren't up to snuff, had ordered more inspections . . . and had threatened again to close the shrine to the faithful. On August 19, city building commissioner Stan Kaderbek said, "If [players] want to sign a waiver, they can go in. They certainly can play in there—they just might not have a crowd to sit there and watch."

Wrigley Field also passed those inspections, but it provided little solace for Cubs management. Feeling somewhat persecuted by the City That Works, team president Andy MacPhail wrote a letter to Kaderbek, dated August 23, that read, "The engineers completed their work in the ballpark Saturday [August 21] after demolishing significant portions of the park to review repairs, some of which were done many years ago." MacPhail concluded by writing, "As the City develops additional questions we will continue to try to address them as well. However, after three different teams of structural engineers, and the City of Chicago, have reviewed and inspected the Friendly Confines and found the ballpark is safe and should be open, any further doubt about our maintenance of the park to date is unjustified."

Mayor Daley was infuriated by MacPhail's letter and responded the next day. The mayor, born and bred on the South Side, didn't say to MacPhail and the Cubs, "You suck." As a local dignitary—as the leader of the third-largest city in America—he had to maintain a certain level of decorum. So he said, "Get a team." The White Sox, incidentally, were slumping badly and had fallen out of postseason contention.

The Cubs simply wanted to focus on baseball, which was difficult enough. They were battling other forces that were far more powerful than the mayor. Barrett, a relative newcomer to Cubdom, didn't believe in the curse, but he didn't discount it, either. "The thing is, it's hard for anyone coming into the Chicago area, who hasn't lived here as long as most of the Cubs fans have, to try to understand what this curse is all about," the catcher said. "For me personally, after seeing what happened at the beginning of the year, it's sort of curious and interesting to try to figure it out."

Only the curse knew what riddles the end of the year would bring. The season to this point had been a cascade of confusion—from mysterious injuries to fiery train wrecks to periodic bouts of dementia to low-flying birds to a crumbling shrine and star attraction. It seemed as if the Cubs were 12 games under .500, yet they were 12 games over. Tied with San Francisco for first place in the wild-card standings, they still were in a position to make everyone's wildest dreams come true. With 30 games to go, the playoffs appeared so close and, at the same time, so maddeningly out of reach.

September

IN THE EYE OF THE STORM

TWENTY-FOUR

As circuses went, few were better than Ringling Bros. and Barnum & Bailey. The outfit had spent more than a century scouring the planet for attractions, and with overwhelming success. There had been the Quiros high-wire troupe; Sara, the beautiful and brave tamer of tigers; the flying Tabares family; an ever-changing array of colorful clowns; and Michu, the 2'9" Hungarian dynamo. "The Greatest Show on Earth," as it was billed, provided a thrill a minute, filling stadiums nationwide.

Suddenly, though, Ringling Bros. and Barnum & Bailey was facing some stiff competition for the circus dollar. The 2004 Chicago Cubs had their own collection of misfits, lunatics, and daredevils—and they, too, were packing stadiums everywhere. Since April, people had been showing up en masse to see the exploits of Slammin' Sammy, The Mad Venezuelan, Howlin' Hawkins, Homeless Mike Remlinger, Sweaty Joe, Wavin' Wendell, Pissin' Moises, Magic Dust Baker, Can't-Buy-Me-a-Win Clement, Catatonic Kyle, Mini Mark Prior, and the rest of the gang.

In Denver, the grandstands had been a pulsating mass of blue. In San Diego, too. And Milwaukee. And San Francisco. And Houston. Wherever. The Cubs had averaged about 38,000 people per road game in 2004, more than any team except the Yankees. America loved a winner, which explained the drawing power of the Yankees.

America also got a kick out of the perennial loser clumsily trying to become a winner, which explained the drawing power of the Cubs.

Garciaparra, one of the newest additions to the traveling show, hadn't been around long enough to contemplate such deep philosophical matters. He simply was enjoying the ride. "It's a great feeling," the shortstop said of the sellouts at visiting stadiums. "It says a lot. It's a pretty special feeling when you get the support like that. We do appreciate all the effort our fans make to go see us no matter where we're at."

The Cubs, however, were feeling kind of lonely at Montreal's Olympic Stadium. Not even the few fans of the home team spent much time there. Harry Caray used to call it a mausoleum. Another wise man once said the city of Montreal would like baseball a lot more if it were played with a hockey puck. Attendance at Expos games had dwindled to such ridiculously low levels that the franchise would be moving to Washington, D.C., in 2005.

In the meantime, the Cubs had to play one more game there. On the night of September 1, before 5,837 people and 40,663 empty seats, they were trying their damnedest to beat the Expos and keep pace with San Francisco in the wild-card race. It wasn't going well. Wood was untouchable, but so was Montreal starter Tony Armas Jr. Chicago's hitters popped up ball after ball, their grunts of frustration reverberating off the empty seats and through the mausoleum.

After 10 innings of listlessness on both sides, Chicago took a 1-0 lead on, fittingly, a wild pitch that scored Garciaparra. The Cubs even plated an insurance run on a single by Grudzielanek, which they wound up needing because Hawkins allowed a run in the bottom of the 11th inning. Not that the good folks in Montreal noticed. The stadium was even more desolate by then, and the rest of the city was fixated on that night's action in hockey's World Cup.

Call it the quiet before the storm. Following the win over the Expos, the Cubs were scheduled to fly directly to Miami for a series against the Marlins, which would begin September 3. There wouldn't be any thoughts of hockey pucks during these three games. Played before full houses, they would feature a whirlwind of compelling story lines, including:

- *Revenge.* The Cubs hadn't played the Marlins since October 15, 2003, the night glory turned to gloom.
- *The playoffs.* Chicago was back in first place in the wild-card standings, a game ahead of San Francisco. But with Florida lurking just three games behind and riding a six-game winning streak, this series would go a long way in determining the postseason picture.
- *Slammin' Sammy.* No story about the Cubs would be complete without somehow involving the team's star attraction. South Florida was sprinkled with people from Sosa's native Dominican Republic, and they all seemingly wanted to catch a glimpse of their island country's most famous export.

Still, something was lacking—the freakish type of riddle that had defined this season of great expectations. So at the 11th hour, another plot twist developed:

- *A hurricane.* As those grunts of frustration echoed through the mausoleum, the quiet before the storm really did become the quiet before the storm. Hurricane Frances was charging across the Atlantic and seemed headed for South Florida. This riddle was particularly difficult to solve. "Most [computer] models show the hurricane going to Palm Beach County, which obviously is subject to change," said Cubs president Andy MacPhail. "They're not going to know for a while. There is no hurricane watch yet. There will be no verdict on Friday's game [on September 3] now."

The World Series Express was at a standstill. Instead of going to Miami, the Cubs went back to Chicago to await word on these crucial games. On September 2, the next night's opener was officially cancelled, but no one was ready to pull the plug on the rest of the series. Rescheduling all the games would adversely effect the fortunes of both teams, and, of course, the South Floridians really wanted to see Slammin' Sammy.

On September 3, as the Cubs staged an impromptu workout at Wrigley Field and Baker whiled away the rest of his time by watching the Weather Channel, the next night's game also was scrapped. Still, hope remained that there would be baseball—a doubleheader, perhaps—on the final day of the series. "We were practicing, we were working out, we were training," recalled Garciaparra of the weather-imposed hiatus. "We were on call because we didn't know if we were going to have to fly out at any given moment. So we were waiting—we were just getting ready. It's strange because, like I said, you're on call waiting to hear that you have to pack up and jump on a plane, so you really don't know."

The Cubs and the Marlins were the only ones who didn't know. Everyone else had a pretty firm grasp of the situation. The highways in Florida were clogged with cars driving north out of harm's way, not south in anticipation of the much-trumpeted arrival of Slammin' Sammy and the rest of the circus from Chicago. On September 4, as the Cubs practiced again at Wrigley Field and Hurricane Frances ripped into South Florida, the obvious occurred: The remainder of the series was called off.

After Hurricane Frances passed, the picture wasn't pretty, in either storm-ravaged South Florida or curse-ravaged Cubdom. This was the first time since 1938 that a hurricane had wiped out games for the Cubs. To make up the lost dates against the Marlins, the Cubs would have to play 29 games in the final 28 days of the season, including two doubleheaders. Nevertheless, they maintained a stoic front, bravely saying they'd somehow find a way to navigate this latest stretch of adversity.

When the season resumed on the afternoon of September 6, against the Expos at Wrigley Field, the Cubs seemed revitalized by their four-day layoff. Barrett, Grudzielanek, Ramirez, and Lee homered with the aid of a stiff wind that was blowing out. The Mad Venezuelan provided thrills aplenty, and Chicago won 9-1 to stay ahead of San Francisco by half a game.

Of course, there still were some of the usual signs of impending doom. Slammin' Sammy was conspicuously absent from the lineup because of bursitis in his hip, so Ben Grieve played in his place. Five innings into his debut in the blue pinstripes, Grieve ran face-first into the brick outfield wall while going after a fly ball. Grieve made the catch—it was a spectacular circus catch, too—but he also sliced open his eyelid and had to leave the game to get stitches at Northwestern Memorial Hospital. Welcome to Chicago, Ben.

There were more signs of impending doom the next evening: (1) Clement's back still was sore, (2) the bullpen was not revitalized by the four-day layoff, and (3) the wind had switched directions and was blowing straight in at about 20 miles per hour. The Cubs survived Clement's back spasms. Although he left the game in the third inning, they were in front 3-2 entering the top of the seventh. The Cubs even survived the bullpen. Although Remlinger walked in two runs and Montreal took a 5-3 lead, they tied the score in the bottom of the seventh.

They could not, however, survive the late-summer gales, which had turned otherwise cozy Wrigley Field into the most spacious ballpark in America. After tying the score, the Cubs proceeded to swat towering fly balls into the crafty wind, like a lumbering heavyweight fighter whose only punch was a powerful right hook. "The game changes [with the wind], but your swing can't change," Baker reasoned. "Your swing is your swing. The swing that you have probably took you your whole life to get. It's hard enough to hit that sucker, more or less to try to hit it low or hit it high. The best thing to try to do is just hit it. We have some guys that have enough trouble hitting sometimes, more or less change the trajectory of the hit."

While the Cubs hit towering fly balls and left a bunch of runners on base, the Astros, reinvigorated by their August house party at Wrigley Field, won their 11th straight game. "The Astros were picked to be in the hunt from the beginning," Baker said. "It doesn't matter when you do it—it matters *that* you do it. They're playing good ball. It can't go on forever." While the Cubs hit more towering fly balls and left a bunch more runners on base, the Marlins won their eighth straight game. Said Baker, "The Marlins are playing good baseball."

By the top of the 12th inning, the one-punch Cubs seemingly had left the entire population of Rhode Island on base. The Expos hadn't done any better, but then they tried something radical, something sly, something positively brilliant: They sidestepped the wind and began hitting *ground balls*, enough of them to break the deadlock and go up 7-5. Chicago hit more fly balls in the bottom of the inning—one of which actually left the park, courtesy of Patterson—and lost 7-6.

The Giants also lost, but of more concern were those Astros and Marlins, who now were within half a game and two games, respectively, of the Cubs. Nevertheless, Baker was as happy as ever when he arrived at the ballpark the next afternoon for that evening's finale against the Expos. His glass was over-the-top full. "Our streak is coming, too," he said with a knowing smile.

Baker's boys seemed to be buying it. This didn't look like a team that had lost a heartbreaker the night before and had the Giants, Astros, Marlins, Padres, and the curse nipping at its Achilles' heels. Barrett's left ankle was taped, but he still managed to hobble from locker to locker and give his teammates peppy pats on the back. Several other players were engrossed in a game of cards at a nearby table. Sosa was feeling particularly cheerful. His name was on the lineup card for the first time since the hurricane struck, and he was ready to start slammin'. "He said he's one hundred-percent," Baker said. "I asked him three times." Slammin' Sammy's boombox was cranking out the melodies again, including the wedding favorite "Celebrate" and a variety of other love songs.

As the players trickled onto the field for stretching, Sosa followed Garciaparra up the dugout steps and playfully poked the shortstop in the back. Garciaparra spun around and returned the poke, then the two exchanged a laugh and gave each other peppy pats on the back.

Baker made the rounds during stretching, joking and laughing with his boys every step of the way. He happened upon a cluster of his prized pitchers near home plate—Prior, Zambrano, Wood, Hawkins, and Rusch—and stopped for a guffaw or two. Prior was wearing batting gloves; it was 65 degrees on the field, but it felt a good two degrees cooler than that. Alou, meanwhile, was taking time out of his brutally hectic pregame schedule of hanging out to sign some autographs by the dugout.

Ryan Dempster was providing the comic relief. Dempster was a right-handed fireballer who blew out his elbow while pitching for the Reds in 2003. The Cubs took a flyer on him the following January, and he spent the ensuing seven months rehabilitating his arm. Now he was in the big leagues again, working out of the bullpen and solidifying his status as the class clown, particularly on this evening. Dempster, who was decidedly white in complexion, made everyone smile by parading around the dugout with a black Afro wig under his Cubs cap. Later, Sosa grabbed the wig off the bat rack in the dugout, pointed at it, and laughed heartily. Amid the high jinks, no one even seemed to care that a frightful wind was blowing in again.

Were these happy-go-lucky Cubbies in a delusional state? Gosh, no. There was good reason for the optimism: Montreal's starting pitcher that night was Scott Downs, who had a 7.75 earned run average and had given up 17 runs in his past 15.1 innings. Downs once was a resident of Cubdom, but his stay was so brief that few of the faithful even remembered him. The left-hander came up to the big leagues with the Cubs, making the first start of his career in April 2000.

A few hours before that game, Cubs first baseman Mark Grace ambled up to Downs and inquired, "You pitching today, Downs?"

The rookie nodded tentatively.

"Don't fuck it up."

As Grace wandered off, the rookie nodded tentatively again.

Downs heeded Grace's words, going seven innings and earning the win. Then the road got rocky, and the Cubs unloaded him on Montreal that July. Shortly thereafter, he blew out his arm. Downs managed to return from that injury, but he still was struggling to find his stuff.

He found it against the Cubbies. Not only did he find it, he threw like he was the reincarnation of Warren Spahn. Downs/Spahn delivered just 19 pitches in the first two innings, flummoxing the lumbering Cubs with his combinations of floaters.

Fortunately, Maddux also was on his game and held the Expos at bay. In the top of the third inning, however, Montreal's Maicer Izturis led off by hitting a seemingly routine fly ball to right field. Slammin' Sammy sprinted in to catch it, then turned on a dime and sprinted back out. In the press box, where any type of human emotion was viewed with disfavor, the ink-stained wretches couldn't help it. They burst out laughing as the ball sailed over Slammin' Sammy's head and rolled to the ivy.

The faithful weren't as amused, mostly because the Expos wound up taking a 1-0 lead as a result of the routine fly-ball-turned-double. On the upper-deck patio, another of those heavyset geezers was shaking his head in disgust while talking to his friend. "You know what's the worst thing about that play by Sammy?" muttered the geezer, cradling a beer cup with fingers that were as plump as sausages. "It was called a hit. The pitcher gets blamed for that shit."

Downs/Spahn breezed through his half of the inning; Maddux followed suit. Downs/Spahn breezed through the next inning; Maddux followed suit. Downs/Spahn kept breezing; Maddux kept following suit. In the seventh inning, the Cubs actually did something: Lee drew a walk. One pitch later, however, Garciaparra grounded into a double play and the inning ended.

Maddux tried to follow suit in the top of the eighth, but errors by Lee and Bako helped key a five-run rally by Montreal. "Things didn't go well," Baker concluded. Still, somewhere in the depths of the grandstands, hope lived. As Chicago came to bat in the bottom of the ninth trailing 6-0, a lone, cracking voice could be heard: "Let's go, Cubbies!" Seventeen pitches later, Scott Downs completed the first, and probably the last, shutout of his major league career.

In the home clubhouse, no one was smiling and laughing any-more. Actually, no one was there. The players were hiding out in the trainer's room . . . or the weight room . . . or the equipment room . . . or the broom closet . . . or above the ceiling tiles. It was anyone's guess. A block down Clark Street, a giant billboard on the side of a building advertised the upcoming movie *Resident Evil: Apocalypse*. Those words aptly described the post-loss mood. So much for the happy-go-lucky approach. Darkness had enveloped Cubdom yet again.

The faithful were in another full-blown panic. Not only had the Cubs fallen half a game behind Houston and San Francisco, but the red-hot Marlins were coming to town for a four-game series begin-ning September 10. The phone lines at WSCR were sizzling with angst:

- Brad in Valparaiso, Indiana, was ready to barf on Alou, who was doubled up on a routine fly ball for the umpteenth time of the season during the finale against Montreal: "First of all, Moises Alou makes me sick. I don't understand what is going through this guy's head when a ball is hit in the air. I've umpired Little League baseball for six years, and I don't think I've seen some-body get caught off base as many times as he has this season. I don't get it at all. It just makes me want to throw something at the TV."
- Chip in nobody-knew-where was ready to be medicated: "This is the bummer of all bummers. I mean, Scott Downs pitching a complete-game shutout epitomizes the despair Cubs fans like myself have suffered throughout our lives. He joined a list of hundreds of ex-Cubs who have bitten the hand that once fed them. The most minimal and least famous Cubs of all time have

at some point turned the knife in our backs. I'm beginning to think there is something to this curse."

• Chris on the North Side was ready to move to the South Side: "I just wanted to say, I don't think the Cubs are going to make it this year. It's been such an embarrassing year. I went to six Cubs games, and they lost all of them."

When the players came out of hiding, they weren't particularly pleased, either. "We have to find a way," said Lee. "There are no excuses for getting shut down, no matter which way the wind is blowing. There are four or five teams in [the wild-card race]. Every game's big, so we have to find a way to win as many as possible. The Astros turned it around big time; Florida's playing great. You've got to get hot to win this thing. You can't play .500 baseball because one of those teams is going to stay hot. We have to find a way to get on a roll."

It wouldn't be easy—not against these Marlins, who now had won nine in a row. There would be two games on the first day of the series, one of which was a makeup from that lost weekend in Miami. The first sign of impending doom was obvious: Chicago's starting pitchers for the doubleheader were Wood and then Prior, the same tandem that lost to the Marlins at Wrigley Field in the deciding games of the National League Championship Series. Florida's starter for the opener was Carl Pavano, who left four tickets at the gate for Bartman in hopes of getting a karmic lift. Bartman was a no-show—he still was underground—but the Marlins didn't need him. Their opponent was perfectly capable of jinxing itself.

The next sign of impending doom appeared in the sixth inning: Sosa and Patterson lost a fly ball in the sun. By the time they found it—the sneaky little devil had been hiding between them, like a snake in the grass—two base runners were safe at home and Florida's lead was extended to 5-0. Ron Santo, his hair ablaze, responded to the play in his customary manner from up in the radio booth: He ranted inaudibly. The radio listeners didn't know what had happened, but they *knew*. All told, the Cubs committed three errors, ran themselves out of a couple of scoring opportunities, and lost 7-0.

Baker felt embarrassed by what he witnessed, saying it was a "total breakdown." Impending doom had turned to flat-out doom. Worse yet, there was another game to play that day. . . .

THE RESURRECTION

TWENTY-FIVE

There was a place where the Cubs supposedly were blessed. St. Raymond De Penafort was nestled in the sleepy middle-class suburb of Mount Prospect, about 20 miles northwest of Wrigley Field. At first glance, it was like many other houses of worship, adorned with crucifixes galore, stained glass, and depictions of Jesus in various stages of suffering. But a closer inspection revealed something that set it apart: On those days when the Cubs won, a "W" flag flew out front. The office of the parish's pastor, Bernard Pietrzak, was even more suspicious: Several copies of *Vine Line*, the official publication of the Cubs, were spread across a table.

This holy man had spent most of his 48 years in the material world following the Cubs, and he wanted them to win as much as anyone did. He also was as confused as anyone. Father Bernie dismissed this notion of a curse, saying in a baritone voice, "I find that so ridiculous." But when asked to explain the goings-on of the past century, he shook his head and muttered like the rest of the faithful. "I can't tell you," he said. "Winning's about timing, and somehow the timing never seems to be there. I can't understand it."

Father Bernie grew up on the South Side, where his family, rugged individuals all, had established a Cubs outpost. Surrounded by White Sox fans, he was persecuted for his beliefs. "You're born into it," Father Bernie said of his devotion to the Cubbies. "All of my friends growing up were Sox fans, so I got so much verbal abuse." But the tongue lashings only strengthened his faith.

Now he was in a position to pass that faith on to the parishioners at St. Raymond. Like any good evangelist, he started with the young ones. Father Bernie regularly did a mock radio broadcast over the parish school's PA system, in which he played Cubs-themed music, discussed the upcoming series, and provided historical tidbits about the shrine (the one on Clark and Addison, not in Rome).

One year he gave Cubs T-shirts to all of the kindergarten graduates, although this loving gesture sparked a controversy within the parish. Apparently, there were some lost souls who didn't want their children wearing Cubs T-shirts. "Given the location, you would think 90 percent of this parish would be Cubs fans," he said, "but we have a lot of Sox fans."

Father Bernie was undeterred. His job was to lead his flock into the shaft of light, and he was determined to do it. "In a very unique way, the Cubs spirit is a very Catholic spirit," he said, his voice growing louder and firmer. "Death brings about resurrection. In every dying, there's a rising. And we've experienced that mystery of faith over and over again with the Cubs. Just a taste of victory kind of heals all the wounds of death in the past."

The Cubs, unfortunately, were in the downward part of the cycle. Their pulse was becoming fainter by the hour. If it had been possible to take all of the mangled body parts from the 2004 Cubs—all of the bum ligaments, tendons, and bones—and roll them into a single person, that person would have been Nomar Garciaparra. Now his groin was aggravated, adding to his sprained wrist, inflamed Achilles tendon, and whatever else was ailing him. Once again, the shortstop's immediate future was in doubt.

"This has been the worst year of injuries I've had as a manager," said Baker, who'd been at it since 1993. "Just as soon as you get whole, another part breaks down. That's why I don't really appreciate a lot of people getting on this team about different tedious, small things. Simply because of the amount of injuries we've had, we've had to overcome a lot. When it starts, they ask you what you want out of the year. You say, 'Good health,' and everyone laughs because good health is something that we take for granted. But it's something real. We've done it short most of the year. After a while, you keep getting bad news, and you sort of accept it. You know what I'm saying?"

The Cubs were praying that maybe, just maybe, Neifi Perez could rise up in Garciaparra's place. Perez, a light-hitting infielder, was released by the Giants on August 13. Six days later, Hendry pulled the 31-year-old journeyman out of his cell phone and then stashed him in the minor leagues until the major league rosters were expanded on September 1. Perez was about all the Cubs had left to throw at this curse.

Miraculously, their prayers were answered. As the late-afternoon shadows spread across Wrigley Field on September 10, Perez helped bring the team back from the dead. Batting in the two spot, he went 4-for-4 as Chicago pounded the Marlins 11-2. But Perez wasn't the only hero. Prior did something that had become excruciatingly difficult for him: He conquered. In eight innings—his longest outing of the season—he allowed just two runs.

When the complicated calculations from the day were completed, the Cubs still were kicking. Somehow, some way, they had gained half a game in the standings and were tied with the Giants for first place. The Astros, meanwhile, had dropped a game behind. "We did what we had to do," Prior said. "The second game, we played a really good baseball game."

To ensure the Cubs played another really good baseball game the following afternoon, Baker dropped Strugglin' Sammy another notch toward oblivion, into the sixth spot in the batting order. "This is the stretch run right here," Baker said, "so we all have to do whatever we can down this stretch here to get into the playoffs. It's what's best for us now as a unit." Sosa didn't object. In fact, he had a score-tying single in the eighth inning, just before Lee broke the game open with a three-run double. Not even The Human Bandage, Garciaparra, could bring down the Cubs. His aggravated groin forced him out of the game in the fifth inning, but Perez rose up in his place and sparked that pivotal rally in the eighth with a leadoff single.

Following the come-from-behind, 5-2 victory, the sky suddenly seemed to be the limit for these ascendant Cubbies. "When you're playing well," Baker said, "no one can stop you." Then the sky fell again—on Perez, on Rusch, and on everyone else who had the misfortune of being at the crumbling shrine. In the final game of the series on the afternoon of September 12, Perez wasn't able to rise above a deathly offense that managed just six hits; Rusch's run of good fortune as a spot starter ended, as he failed to make it past the fourth inning; and the Cubs were buried by the Marlins 11-1 and lost their hold on first place.

Meanwhile, the latest news on Garciaparra was ominously familiar: The Cubs were in the dark as to when he'd be back in the lineup. Said Baker, "I really don't know. He doesn't know. The doctors don't know. It's all a guess." Cubdom again was experiencing the mystery of faith—faith that somehow, some way, things would turn out OK.

And maybe, just maybe, they would. The Cubs' next opponent was Pittsburgh, which was 11 games under .500. Furthermore, Chicago's hottest pitcher, Maddux, would be on the mound in the opener on the evening of September 13 at Wrigley Field. Lo and behold, the Cubs rose. Maddux pitched seven shutout innings, and the Cubs clubbed three home runs en route to a 7-2 victory. Perez had one of the homers, but the biggest came from Slammin' Sammy. It was his 30th homer of the season, marking the 10th consecutive time he had reached that plateau. The milestones kept coming for Sosa, but his team remained half a game behind the Giants.

There was a theory that the pressure of this season of great expectations was getting to the Cubs. If that was true, it wasn't evident before the next night's game. Had the players been any more relaxed, they would have been dead. Ramirez, Barrett, Zambrano, and Hawkins were at their lockers chatting on cell phones, Walker was working on a crossword puzzle, and Alou was sorting a wad of money from his billfold. As Walker was leaving the clubhouse to stretch and take batting practice, someone asked him about the recent Usher concert, which the second baseman had attended. "Oh, it was outstanding," Walker said. "Good show."

Perhaps the Cubs were in fact dead. Pittsburgh starter Josh Fogg entered the game with a 5.03 earned run average, but on this night he threw like he was the reincarnation of Christy Mathewson, mercilessly rolling over the blue-clad corpses as his team took a 2-0 lead after seven innings. To the Cubs' credit, they finally had mastered the black art of hitting ground balls. They tapped 11 of the things during those initial seven innings, although they apparently didn't realize the wind had changed directions and now was blowing *out*.

Then in the bottom of the eighth inning, with Barrett on first base, Patterson did something radical, something sly, something positively brilliant: He hit a *fly ball* into the crafty wind, which carried all the way into the basket in left field and tied the score. "I really didn't think it was going out," Patterson said. "I hit it and just got under it. But I guess I got it up in that jet stream, and it kept going." After that, the Cubs tapped more ground balls—10, to be exact. But in the bottom of the 12th inning, with the score still 2-2, Patterson did something radical, something sly, something positively brilliant: He hit another fly ball. This one traveled over the center field wall and ended the game. Patterson, a soft-spoken young man, had this to say about his game-winner: "It feels good, obviously."

Chicago's starter that night, Clement, was feeling pretty good, too. He failed to get the win—that would have been way too much to ask for—but he did beat those pesky back problems into submission. After nearly being knocked out of the game in his first two innings, he was close to perfect in his final four. "I think I just settled down and wasn't worried about how I was going to feel," he said. "It was real encouraging."

That same night, the Cardinals, now roughly a gazillion games ahead in the N.L. Central, finally lost. It figured Houston was the team that beat them. San Francisco won, too. So did Florida. "I just think we need to get on a roll," said Wellemeyer, who was the pitcher of record in the extra-innings victory over Pittsburgh. "Yeah, we won today, but shut it down and focus on tomorrow. I think tonight was huge. It's huge for that game, but the big thing is to go out tomorrow and do the same thing."

If the Cubs hoped to keep doing the same thing, they would need their star attraction, he of the .257 batting average and the 119 strikeouts in 413 at-bats. Baker, he of the half-full glass, reassured the faithful that Slammin' Sammy was on his way. "He's swinging better," he said. "I've seen too many guys get written off and then come back. The guy loves to play, that's the number one thing. I remember when I talked to him years ago, when I was on the other side, I asked him, 'Why do you play so hard?' He told me he was trying to make the team. This time, he told me he'd do anything to help us get to the postseason and win—so he can shine, so *we* can shine. I can see it coming."

Maybe Sosa saw it coming, as well. He had been Smilin' Sammy during the Pittsburgh series. Before that extra-innings game, he stood by his locker, with the salsa turned low, and entertained some reporters who wanted to know his thoughts on his hitting 30 home runs for 10 straight seasons. Smilin' proclaimed with conviction that individual milestones didn't matter anymore—only the World Series did. "We're in a situation where we need to concentrate and win some games," he said. "No question, [the milestone] is something I'm proud of, but this is not the right moment to celebrate."

After batting practice that day, a kid in a wheelchair was brought onto the field. Sosa stopped and chatted with the kid, even patted him on the shoulder and took a picture with him. The kid didn't stand up and walk following his encounter with Saint Sammy, but he was happy just the same.

During the series finale against Pittsburgh on the afternoon of September 15, *everyone* in the Friendly Confines was brimming with hope and joy. The boos that had rained down on Sosa for more than a month suddenly turned to cheers when his homer in the first inning helped key a four-run rally. And the old tuna boat swayed back and forth when he hit a grand slam in the eighth inning to seal the 13-5 victory. The jubilant faithful demanded a curtain call, and Sosa, never one to shun a cheer, gave it to them. Slammin' Sammy had risen again. So had the Cubs, who were riding a three-game winning streak.

Having blown nearly every deadline in this season of great expectations, the Cubs finally had gotten serious about playing baseball. As usual, though, the trail ahead would be unforgiving. The Cubs were about to play 12 road games in 11 days, including a makeup doubleheader against the Marlins in Miami.

The first stop was Cincinnati, where the Reds had fallen on hard times since their promising start to the season. They were 67-78 and had lost six of their past 10 games. This leg of the journey should have been a cakewalk. It wasn't. Wood created all sorts of problems for Chicago in the opener on the night of September 16, letting a 3-1 lead evaporate into a 4-3 deficit after six innings. Luckily, the Cubbies were saved by Ramirez, who belted three home runs, including one in the top of seventh that gave them a 5-4 lead. Said Ramirez, who drove in all five of the runs against Cincinnati and was leading the team with 97 RBI: "If it's not me, it's going to be someone else."

Even the bullpen, a hodgepodge of nut jobs and ne'er-do-wells for most of the season, was getting its act together. Mercker and then Hawkins made Chicago's lead hold up, something that was starting to happen with surprising regularity. In its past 14 innings, the bullpen had allowed just two runs. "We've had some setbacks, and we have to step it up," Wellemeyer said of himself and his fellow relievers. "I think we all believe in ourselves enough to where we can go out there and shut them down. It's not going to be a problem for us."

Despite Chicago's four-game winning streak, the Giants wouldn't budge. They still were half a game ahead.

The Cubs kept pushing. The next night, someone else played the hero: Lee, who had a homer and five runs batted in as Chicago blew out the Reds 12-4. "Like [September 16] was Aramis's day, today was D-Lee's day," Baker said. "There are a lot of heroes on a daily basis."

Nevertheless, the Giants wouldn't budge.

The Cubs kept pushing. "There's a cliché that you take it one day at a time, but it's really so true," said Garciaparra, who still was taking it one day at a time from an examination table in the trainer's room. "That's all we can do. You talk about high expectations—I think we have them on ourselves. Your goal is to win a World Series when you step on the field from day one in April. I don't know if expectations can get any higher than that. So we keep it on ourselves."

The players may have been dealing OK with the pressure of this stretch run, but Santo wasn't. The morning after Chicago's latest victory over Cincinnati, he accidentally took the wrong medicine for his battle-scarred heart. Had it not been for his built-in defibrillator, he probably would have suffered another heart attack. Although Santo's ticker still was ticking following the scary episode, he wasn't in the radio booth for that night's game. Instead, he was recuperating.

It was a good thing he wasn't there, as his defibrillator may not even have saved him then. Alou did all he could to play the hero, hitting a home run in the first inning to give the Cubs a 1-0 lead and a two-run homer in the sixth to put them up 3-1. Later in the sixth, Lee scored on a wild pitch to extend the advantage to 4-1. Chicago was rising, especially since the Giants had just dropped a 5-1 decision to the Padres. Then Maddux, a pillar of stability throughout the second half of the season, crumbled. In the bottom of the sixth, the Reds toppled him and his team by scoring five runs.

The Cubs, however, dusted themselves off and got back up in the eighth inning. After Sosa homered to cut Cincinnati's lead to 6-5,

Grudzielanek was on second base and Goodwin was on first with just one out. Grieve, in action again following his bout with Wrigley Field's outfield wall, grounded a single up the middle and into center field, prompting Wendell to wave. With the final score of the Giants-Padres game shining brightly on the outfield scoreboard behind him, Wily Mo Pena scooped up the ball and fired a perfect strike home. Grudzielanek tried to slide around the tag and sweep his hand across the plate, but he was out by the width of a finger. That distance, while ever so slight, was enough to keep the Cubs separated from their October dreams.

They lost 6-5, so San Francisco remained planted in first place.

The series finale on the afternoon of September 19 should have been a cakewalk. It wasn't. Never mind that Cincinnati's starter, Paul Wilson, had an earned run average of 4.85. Never mind that Wilson hadn't won a game since July 8. Against Chicago, he threw like he was the reincarnation of Walter Johnson. The Cubs were stumbling all over themselves, although Patterson preferred to view it from a different vantage point. "You look at our lineup, and we don't have one weak spot," he said. "If we're not getting runs or hitting the ball, that should tell you something. It's probably the pitcher who did a good job."

Wilson/Johnson was doing such a good job that Cincinnati led 1-0 going into the eighth inning. The Cubs needed a hero again, and Alou played the part to perfection. After Chicago eked out a run against Wilson/Johnson in the eighth, Alou hit a two-run double off Danny Graves in the final inning to pave the way for a dramatic 5-1 victory.

The Cubs were pushing, but with only 15 games to play, the Giants still wouldn't budge.

September 20 was supposed to have been a day of rest for the Cubs. Instead, they jumped on a plane and flew to Florida to play two against the Marlins. This schedule was brutal, but the Cubbies kept pushing. As far as Baker was concerned, sleep was overrated, any-way. "That's part of the game—that's how it is," he said. "I didn't sleep much when I was playing." Besides, Chicago was catching Florida at an opportune moment. The Marlins had faltered in the past week and now were almost out of the race, four and a half games behind San Francisco.

Florida's starting pitcher for the first game was Carl Pavano. This time, he didn't leave any tickets at the gate for Bartman, but he probably should have. Chicago pounded him for four runs in the first two innings, then Prior, the conqueror once more, took over. In seven and two-thirds innings, he yielded only one run and five hits. Said Baker, "This was one of his best performances of the season." The timing couldn't have been better. Chicago now was tied with the Giants, who were idle that day.

With another win against Florida, first place would belong solely to the Cubs. There was, however, an itsy-bitsy problem: Clement was pitching. The Cubs responded like they normally did to the sight of the Abraham Lincoln-goateed one on the hill, scattering five hits and two runs. Not that the Abraham Lincoln-goateed one helped himself much. He didn't even make it out of the third inning, and the Marlins won 5-2.

The Giants were back in the spot they had occupied seemingly for eons: first place, by half a game.

The Cubs promptly boarded yet another plane and, at about midnight, arrived in Pittsburgh, where they would play three games against the Pirates in as many days. Chicago kept pushing in the opener on the night of September 21 . . . well, sort of. In the top of the fourth inning, with the Cubs trailing 1-0 and Ramirez on second, Sosa hit a laser beam into right field. As the ball flew, Slammin' hopped and watched. But that ball never reached the seats—instead, it bounced off the top of the wall. Even though Ramirez scored, Sosa was tagged out at second because he had wasted too much time hopping, effectively killing the rally. (The homer that wasn't spurred a heated debate among the faithful over whether Sammy should be hopping this time of year. After giving the matter some thought, Baker later decreed that Sammy could keep hopping.)

Things turned out OK, anyway. For once, the baseball gods seemed to be in the corner of the Cubs. The team wasn't even undone by Hawkins, who blew its 4-3 lead over Pittsburgh in the bottom of the ninth inning by allowing the tying run to score. Patterson crossed the plate on a wild pitch in the top of the 10th, then Dempster did what Hawkins, or anyone in the press box, couldn't do: He nailed down the win. "Hawk has bailed us out many times," said Baker. "We bailed him out tonight."

The Giants, however, still wouldn't budge.

The Cubs kept pushing, but they were growing weary. In the bottom of the eighth inning the next night, they were clinging to a 1-0 lead and Pittsburgh had the bases loaded with two outs. When Ty Wigginton hit a ball into the right-center field gap, a sinking liner that had the potential to clear the bases, Chicago seemed just about ready to fall to its knees. But the baseball gods still were in the corner of the Cubs. Like a shimmering, heavenly streak of blue in the dark night, Sprintin' Sammy Sosa shot out of nowhere, dove, and speared the ball with his outstretched glove. The road-worn players in Chicago's dugout roared to life when Sammy made the catch. "The guys jumped for joy, including myself, as if we won the World Series," Baker said. "That was a big play." Remlinger then found a temporary home in the closer's role, retiring the Pirates in order in the ninth to preserve the 1-0 victory.

The celebration was short-lived, though. Those evil-doing Giants still wouldn't budge.

The Cubs kept pushing. They left nothing to chance—nothing to the whims of the fickle baseball gods—in the final game of the series on the afternoon of September 23. A four-run second inning enabled Maddux to coast to a 6-3 win. The day delivered more history to Maddux, who now had won at least 15 games for a record 17 consecutive seasons. But like his 300th career victory back in August, it was a mere footnote in this season of great expectations. That night, San Francisco fell to Houston 7-3. The Giants finally had budged, and the Cubs were half a game ahead in the race to October.

The Promised Land, once so hopelessly far away, was in plain view.

WRIGLEY FIELD
HOME OF
CHICAGO CUBS

THE FINAL PUSH

TWENTY-SIX

Gladys Nunley had a perfect last name. The woman must have been something close to a saint, having put up with the Cubs for nearly all of her 81 years on this planet. That was more pain and suffering than any person should have had to endure, but Gladys Nunley didn't see it that way. "I just love baseball," she said. Specifically, the Cubs.

As was the case with so many of the faithful, this twisted love of the Cubbies cursed—er, coursed—through her veins. "Well, I was the only son my father ever had," she said with a laugh. Good old Dad told her he would take her to her first Cubs game as soon as she learned to score. She became fluent in the intricate language of baseball by listening to the games on the radio, and by the age of four, in 1927, she was ready to go to Wrigley Field.

Seventy-seven years later, she still was there on most days. Aisle 26, Row 5, Seats 103 and 104—near the on-deck circle on the first base side—was her home away from home, a 40-minute bus ride away from her official residence in Chicago. Nunley stood a slight 4'8" and needed a walker to get around the ballpark, but she sure struck a vibrant pose. In fact, she was nearly impossible to miss, dressed from head to toe in various shades of blue, starting with six Cubs-themed earrings and ending with a pair of homemade Cubs-themed shoes.

Nunley was such a fixture that Wrigley Field didn't seem quite right when she was absent. One Sunday in the late 1970s, friends were visiting her from the West Coast, so she gave them her usual seats and sat somewhere else. When she returned home after the game, there was a message on her answering machine from Chicago's starting pitcher that day, Lynn McGlothen. "Where the hell were you today?" he said. "I missed you."

Believe it or not, Nunley once saw the Cubs play in a World Series. "I did see a World Series game in 1938, but I really didn't appreciate the magnitude of it at the time," she said, her voice tinged with regret. She could be forgiven for underestimating the moment. Gladys Nunley was a lot of things, but she wasn't clairvoyant. How could she possibly have known what the ensuing decades would bring?

In 1984, she was sure she would get another crack at that elusive World Series. She saw the Cubs beat the Padres in the first two games of the National League Championship Series at Wrigley Field, then flew to San Diego to watch the clincher. The clincher never happened. "I was totally devastated," she said, her voice still tinged with anguish.

The 2003 season seemed as if it would make up for everything, but that didn't quite work out, either. "My intentions were to have my hip replaced as soon as the season was over," she said, "but when they blew it, I was so crushed I couldn't even do it. I didn't see a doctor until I couldn't walk anymore." Somehow, some way, she got herself to the 2004 home opener, then had her hip replaced five days later. By early summer, she was back in the Friendly Confines.

Gladys Nunley didn't simply put up with the Cubs—she lived for them. In 1981, she and 11 fellow believers founded The Wild Bunch. They'd meet up at a nearby bar after the games and discuss all things Cubs. The group quickly swelled in size and set up shop at Bernie's, a tavern located about a block from Wrigley Field. The Wild Bunch even included players such as Jerry Morales, Willie Hernandez, and Hector Cruz, who would stop by after games to share a few beers and discuss all things Cubs. Nearly everyone was in attendance for Nunley's 60th birthday party in 1983; Fergie Jenkins, Chicago's 6'5" Hall of Fame-bound pitcher, joked that she wasn't tall enough to blow out the candles on her cake. By 2004, the Wild Bunch was 3,000 strong, with members throughout the country, and had a newsletter, preseason and postseason parties, and a couple of gatherings each year at away games.

Of the original dozen, only Nunley remained. The rest either had "retired" or moved on to that big patch of blue in the sky. Nunley knew she would be joining them sooner rather than later, as it was becoming increasingly difficult to keep coming back to Wrigley Field. "Now I'm walking around with bandages and braces," she said, "but I still get to every game I can." She was planning to have both of her knees replaced at the conclusion of the 2004 season—"I scheduled my surgery for November 8, when baseball season will be over," she said—and after that, who knew? The summers were running out for Gladys Nunley, but she would be hopeful to the very end. "I'm not going to quit loving the Cubs, even if they never win." After a long, contemplative pause, she added, "Of course, I'd like to see them win."

She knew better than almost anyone that winning wasn't going to be easy. Yes, the Cubs were surging—having won seven of their first nine games on this road trip to wrest first place from the Giants—but it never was over until it was over. And even then, it wasn't over.

On the evening of September 24, the Cubs were in decrepit Shea Stadium to begin a three-game series against the Mets. Although the Mets were among baseball's most horrendous teams, no one with any type of memory was feeling particularly good about this last leg of the road trip. *New York, New York.* Those words made the faithful shudder. The black cat had danced in Shea Stadium 35 years earlier, turning a championship season into a funeral march. This was unholy ground, and regardless of how well the Cubs were playing right now, they were vulnerable. The team's hellish September schedule was starting to take a toll. Barrett was gaunt, Lee's right wrist was bandaged, and nobody was swinging the bat with much vigor.

"It's late in the season," said Lee, who mustered only two hits in the three games at Pittsburgh. "Guys are worn down. You're not going to be fresh like the beginning of the year, but it's just one of those things where we have to fight through it. You rely a lot on adrenaline at this point in the season."

In the opener at Shea Stadium, the Cubs also would be relying on chance, mostly because Kris Benson was pitching against them. There was the bad Kris Benson, the one who gave up six runs in six innings on September 19 against Pittsburgh and looked like the reincarnation of Paul Reuschel. And the good Kris Benson, the one who threw a complete-game shutout against Atlanta on September 14 and looked like the reincarnation of Don Drysdale. Which Kris Benson would show up on this night? The good one, obviously. Through the first six innings, he held the Nubs scoreless. Rusch, however, was equal to the task. He was pitching in place of Clement—whose touchy back and spooky inability to win had caused him to be dumped from the starting rotation—and gave up only one run during the same span.

The Nubs finally got to Benson in the top of the seventh when Ramirez hit a solo homer to tie the score, but then there was a sighting in the bottom of the inning. Although it wasn't a black cat, the faithful got chills just the same. Sweet mother of doom—Farnsworth was lumbering in from the bullpen. Since his epic confrontation with that electric fan, Farnsworth had been on the comeback trail, pitching some simulated games to work his knee back into game shape. Farnsworth didn't maim himself or anyone else in those outings, so Baker eased him back into action against Florida on September 20 and Pittsburgh on September 23. Those, however, hadn't been pressure situations.

This was. Farnsworth now was clean-shaven, and his shaggy hairdo had been replaced by a neatly cut, conservative style. On the surface, he looked like a new man; beneath it, he was undeniably Catatonic Kyle. After striking out the leadoff hitter, Farnsworth allowed a single and a walk—certain doom was a pitch or two away. But maybe, just maybe, the baseball gods still were in the corner of the Cubs. Somehow, some way, Farnsworth retired the next two batters, and Chicago won in the 10th inning on a bloop single by Lee that brought home Grudzielanek. "Honestly," said Lee, "I don't think it matters how we win. I mean, 1-0, 2-1, 10-1—as long as we win, that's all we care about." Indeed, as wobbly as this victory at Shea Stadium was, it stretched Chicago's lead to a game and a half over the Giants, who lost to Los Angeles later that night.

All the while, though, demons were swirling. They were everywhere the next afternoon, even though Chicago was leading 3-0 after eight and a half innings. Consider:

- *Slammin' Sammy Sosa.* After rising briefly, he had plunged back down into the crapper. Swinging as if he were trying to hit the ball from Queens into a different borough, he whiffed four times in his first four at-bats and left eight men on base. If Sosa had come through in even one of those run-scoring situations, the game would have been well out of reach heading into the bottom of the ninth inning.
- *Howlin' Hawkins.* The demons were in a frenzy during New York's last at-bats (two runners were on base), but they still were being kept at bay (there were two outs and Victor Diaz, a rookie with just one career home run, was down to his final strike against Hawkins). Diaz had grown up in Chicago and was a huge Cubs fan. Of course, Bartman also had been a huge Cubs fan. Hawkins did what anyone in the press box or nearby Flushing Cemetery could have done, serving up a fastball to Diaz—to this huge Cubs fan with one career home run who was down to his final strike—that was driven over the right field wall and tied the score.
- *Mighty Mark Prior.* Prior did everything he had been expected to do on this autumn day. He conquered the Mets—crushed them like toy soldiers—by allowing no runs in seven and two-thirds innings. Ultimately, though, he was unable to save the Cubs from themselves.

In the top of the 10th, Suckin' Sammy finally made contact with the ball, but it was a grounder to the shortstop that resulted in an inning-ending double play. Sosa was lifted from the game after that feeble at-bat—about 10 innings too late—replaced by a September call-up named Calvin Murray. Could Calvin Murray miraculously rise up in place of Suckin' Sammy? He never got the chance. Another anonymous figure, New York's Craig Brazell, beat him to it, hitting a home run in the bottom of the 11th inning to end the game. It was, fatefully and fittingly and frighteningly, the first homer of Brazell's career. After Brazell's shot flew over the right field wall, Baker threw down a towel in the dugout. For the record, he wasn't smiling. Later, Baker muttered, "That was real tough because we were one strike away from winning the game."

This wasn't The Goat Game. Or The Durham Game. Or The Bartman Game. Or even The Black Cat Game. But it was close, too close for comfort. The demons were loose, dancing invisibly on the cursed turf of Shea Stadium.

San Francisco was pressing up against Chicago, too. As the Cubs collapsed in Queens, the Giants defeated the Dodgers to close to within half a game. The Cubs had to find a way to beat back their destiny, but in the series finale on the afternoon of September 26, they played like they were spooked, like they had seen a ghost. Wood gave up three runs in the first inning, and the Cubs never recovered. Behind an ever-spiraling offense that had only three hits, they lost 3-2. Then they ran for their lives, ran out of this haunted house in Queens as fast they could.

Ah, but there still was a flicker of hope. The Giants also lost that day. Somehow, some way, the Cubs remained in first place.

These were dark times, but the 2004 Cubs had one thing going for them: They were used to spectacular failure. They had crashed and burned at every turn in this season of great expectations, yet they always had risen again. Baker, whose glass was more chipped than ever but still was half full, was sure they'd rise once more, especially since their final seven games of the season would be played in the Friendly Confines.

"We're still here in a position to go to the playoffs and the World Series," he said. "This is what you live for—this is what guys play this game for. I know everybody talks about how big the money is, but these are guys who are playing to win and want the [World Series] ring. Everything else follows after that. To me, this is the position you're supposed to be in right now. It's the position I *expect* to be in." Baker was experiencing the mystery of faith. "It's all about faith, basically, when you fall back," he said. "You have to have faith and confidence that some kind of way it's going to work out."

And by god, maybe it would. On the night of September 27, in the first of four games against the Reds, the Cubs came alive and scored 12 runs, nearly double their output from the entire series against the Mets. The catalyst was Garciaparra, who had returned from the trainer's table five days earlier. He did his best impression of Neifi Perez, going 3-for-3 with two doubles and three runs. The Mad Venezuelan, meanwhile, spent the evening pumping his fist after punching out Cincinnati's overmatched batters. When Zambrano left the game in the seventh inning, he tipped his cap to the fanatical faithful, who reciprocated by merrily raising their beer cups above their heads. "I prepared before this season to be strong at the end," said Zambrano, who was 4-0 with a 1.01 earned run average in September and now had a team-leading 16 wins. "It's better to finish strong." Chicago's 12-5 victory was tough to stomach for the Giants, who didn't play that day. They now were a full game behind in the standings.

There was a soft-marker board inside the entrance of the Cubs' clubhouse that listed the times for various pregame chores, such as stretching and batting practice. Before the second game against the Reds on the evening of September 28, the words NEXT SIX DAYS, PULL IT ALL TOGETHER were scrawled on it in thick black ink. These 2004 Cubbies weren't wilting. On the contrary, they suddenly were glowing. As Lee was at his locker dressing for that night's battle, he was smiling from ear to ear. "We're just having fun," he said. "This has been cool, man. Being right here in the playoff hunt, this is what it's all about. So hopefully, we can bring a World Series to the fans of Chicago."

Santo, on the other hand, was not glowing. Although he had made it back to the radio booth, there was no guarantee he would last long. Chatting with a couple of reporters in the media center before that night's game, he said, "The way things are going, it's going to come down to the last day, and then my defibrillator will go off."

Perhaps Santo had noticed that the wind had switched directions again and was whipping in at about 20 miles per hour. Baker certainly was aware of this foreboding development. "I feel at the mercy of the wind all the time in Chicago," the manager said. "There's nothing you can do about the wind. Your stroke is your stroke. We've already been over this about two weeks ago. You just go out there and play your game. That's all you can do."

The players weren't scared. During batting practice, Ramirez was swinging at ball after ball with all his might. Finally, one landed in the basket in left field. "Yeah, I got it," he said, walking away from the batting cage with a proud smile on his face.

Later in batting practice, Ramirez hit another shot into the teeth of the wind. He stood and watched as it cleared the wall, his smile turning from prideful to menacing.

"It [the wind] don't matter," Grudzielanek shouted to Ramirez. "You come to hit any day of the week. Any day of the week."

As it turned out, that big, bad wind wasn't so big and bad after all. Fly balls did indeed leave the ballpark; three did. The problem was, they came off the bats of Cincinnati's players—with Chicago's pillar of stability on the mound, no less. The Cubs' hitters, in contrast, were powerless against the forces of nature. And against Josh Hancock, who entered the game with a 5.50 earned run average but pitched like he was the reincarnation of Dizzy Dean. Greg Maddux, future Hall-of-Famer, was outdueled by Josh Hancock, future nobody.

It was a staggering turn of events for these glowing Cubs. "I didn't pitch good," Maddux said following the 8-3 loss. He looked every bit of 38 years old as he addressed the media, the circles under his eyes shaped like potholes. "I made a couple of mistakes, and they were all home runs. We've just got to play the game right. If you do that, you usually come out on top."

The Cardinals, who already had clinched the N.L. Central title, actually lost that night. It figured Houston was the team that beat them. The Astros now were within half a game of first place, while the Giants, who also won, were tied with Chicago. The demons were closing in fast. "The heat was on way before tonight," a shirtless and haggard Walker said as he stood by his locker. "It's going to come down to the last day probably. You just keep battling. The reality of it is, you can't try any harder, you can't think any different—you've just got to keep going out and playing. Really, a lot of it just comes down to luck."

That was what the faithful were afraid of. A wicked wind continued to blow in when the Cubs strapped it on the next afternoon, and the team's hopes and dreams were pinned to a journeyman, Rusch. This wasn't how things had been drawn up back in February. Really, though, where would these 2004 Cubs have been without Rusch? When Prior and then Wood went down, he rose in their places. When the relievers disintegrated, he rose in the bullpen, even earning a couple of saves. Now he was going for the biggest save of all—he was being asked to save this season of great expectations.

Rusch couldn't have done the job any better. He made just one mistake in his six and two-thirds innings—giving up a solo homer to Adam Dunn in the top of the second—but quickly atoned for it. In the bottom of the third, he hit a homer of his own to tie the score 1-1. Although Chicago's "real" hitters remained beaten and battered by this wind storm, Alou managed a sacrifice fly in the seventh inning to put his team up 2-1. That was the score when Hawkins stepped onto the mound to begin the bottom of the ninth inning. It still was the score when, with two outs and a man on third base, Austin Kearns was down to his final strike. The score changed, however, when Hawkins did what anyone in the press box or a leper colony could have done, allowing a soul-piercing, score-tying double to Kearns.

After Kearns, the newest face of this diabolical curse, hit a home run in the top of the 12th inning to give the Reds a 4-2 lead, there wasn't a sound from Santo in the radio booth. Had his defibrillator malfunctioned? Had the Cubs finally done him in? Not this time. A long sigh spread across the radio waves and through Cubdom, followed by these somber words: "Boy, I tell you, this is tough. This is real tough to take."

It got even tougher. The Cubs narrowed Cincinnati's lead to 4-3 in the bottom of the inning—as if only to set up the frantic faithful for another painful fall—then Lee whiffed with the tying run on first base to end the game. That evening, the Astros completed a sweep of the Cardinals—as if only to pile on the pain, it was the first time St. Louis had been swept since June—to move half a game ahead of the Cubs.

Ah, but there still was the slightest flicker of hope. Later that night, the Giants lost to San Diego, so they remained tied with Chicago. All was not lost yet. Said Baker, "We either keep fighting or roll over and die."

Mighty Mark Prior kept fighting. He came to conquer the Reds and the multiplying demons on the afternoon of September 30, pitching like he never had pitched before. In his first six innings, he struck out 13 batters and allowed just two hits. This was a day of redemption for Slammin' Sammy, too. When it mattered most, he came through, hitting a home run in the bottom of the sixth inning—a majestic fly ball that landed on Waveland Avenue—to give the Cubs a 1-0 lead. Although Prior surrendered a score-tying, solo home run in the top of the seventh to the curse—er, Kearns—he was perfect in his final two innings and finished with a career-tying-best 16 strikeouts.

Surely the Cubs would break this 1-1 deadlock. Surely they would find a way this time against Cincinnati, which had the worst pitching staff in the National League. Surely they would overcome the forces of nature, which suddenly had delivered a kinder, gentler wind.

Surely the baseball gods hadn't deserted them altogether. Surely *this* wouldn't happen:

- In the bottom of the 11th inning, with two outs and the bases loaded, Barrett struck out swinging.
- In the top of the 12th inning, with two outs and a man on third, Cincinnati's Javier Valentin doubled to bring home the go-ahead run.
- In the bottom of the 12th inning, with two outs and the tying run on second base and the winning run on first, Alou hit a sickly fly ball to center field that never had a chance.

Surely what happened—this latest unfathomable collapse in a century that had been dotted with them—didn't really happen. "It just hasn't worked out," a bitterly disappointed Prior said afterward, confirming that it did happen. "I don't have any great philosophical quote about it. We just lost."

With three days remaining in the season, the Cubs trailed both Houston (which had been idle) and San Francisco (which had won) by a game. Only a miracle could save them now. And in the star-crossed universe of Cubdom, miracles were in short supply.

October

WRIGLEY FIELD
HOME OF
CHICAGO CUBS

THE PASSION OF THE CUBS

TWENTY-SEVEN

There was a theory that if the Cubs ever won the World Series, it would upset the delicate balance of the cosmos and bring the apocalypse. Following a fiery explosion, the thinking went, the world would be cast into everlasting darkness. Dogs would sleep with cats, Cubs fans would get along with White Sox fans—stuff like that.

The faithful were willing to take their chances. They experienced the apocalypse every year, and a championship would have to bring something better than that empty feeling. Sometimes the end arrived early. Sometimes it arrived late. But it *always* arrived.

In 2004 it came late, very late—but it came just the same, in the form of the team's most breathtaking fold since 1969. First, though, a final circus act had to be played out before the whole shithouse went up in flames:

There had been a lot of mini Bartmans in this season of great failure—the string of mysterious injuries, the appearance on the cover of *Sports Illustrated*, the crumbling shrine, the hurricane, the crafty wind at Clark and Addison, the fateful swing through Shea Stadium—but no single symbol of doom. The Cubs needed to find a scapegoat—with the emphasis on goat—and quick. So they turned to Steve Stone, the longtime broadcaster of Cubs games for WGN-TV.

Stone was among the most respected broadcasters in Chicago because of his astute knowledge of baseball and his uncanny ability to predict what would happen in a game. In 2004, however, his analysis touched a nerve with the fragile Cubbies. Alou pissed and moaned about it; Baker didn't smile about it; and, of course, Mercker called the press box to complain about it.

These Cubs, and others, thought the broadcaster should be focusing on the positive, particularly since he was a representative of WGN-TV. The superstation was the property of the Tribune Company, which also owned the team and seemingly everything else in Chicago. But what was Stone supposed to do? Pat the boys on the back after they left 57 runners on base in yet another one-run loss? Say "Nice try" after Pissin' Moises was doubled up on a routine fly ball for the 32nd time in a two-week span? Laud Catatonic Kyle's composure after he booted an electric fan? Stone simply pointed out what the faithful saw with their own eyes, in as objective a manner as possible for someone who had to follow these Flubs on a daily basis.

After the unfathomable collapse against the Reds on September 30, the situation boiled over like a pot of poisonous brew. Stone was a guest that evening on a sports-talk show on WGN-Radio (which, of course, was owned by the Tribune Company), and he echoed the sentiments of the faithful. Among other things, Stone said: "You want the truth? You can't handle the truth. Let me tell you something, guys: The truth of this situation is an extremely talented bunch of guys who want to look at all directions except where they should really look, and kind of make excuses for what happened."

The next morning, instead of focusing on the first of three games against Atlanta at Wrigley Field—their final chance to save this season of great expectations—the Cubs were obsessed with Stone. Baker, Hendry, and team president Andy MacPhail had a powwow with Stone to discuss matters, after which Hendry said Stone had crossed the line and made things personal.

No one was buying it. In 2004, anyway, the Cubs themselves were the goats. Not Bartman. And certainly not Steve Stone. The Cubs cursed themselves. Victory had been there for the taking—the World Series had been well within reach—and they were the ones who let it slip away.

Maddux, at least, was brave enough to look in the mirror and fix his eyes on the unsettling reflection of a mangy beast. "We had our opportunities, but we didn't take advantage of them," he said. "It's one thing to get beat, but I don't really feel like we got beat. I'm embarrassed. You just feel like it was ours to take."

On the afternoon of October 1, with the lurid Stone affair boiling over, the Flubs took the field against Atlanta. The Braves had nothing to play for, having already clinched the N.L. East title. Although Mike Hampton had a torn knee ligament, they wheeled him out to the mound, anyway—just to see how fit he would be for the playoffs. Hampton was gimpy, particularly after falling while fielding a grounder early in the game, but that didn't stop him from mowing down the one-punch Cubs. Chicago couldn't do a thing against Hampton or a wind that continued to blow in, scoring one run in the pitcher's six innings of rehab work.

Meanwhile, Cubs "ace" Kerry Wood got nowhere near the mountaintop, unless a trash heap counted. He was kicked around for five runs in seven innings, even surrendering a homer to the one-legged Hampton. In the eighth inning, with Chicago losing 5-1, the faithful in the bleachers began throwing their empty beer cups onto the field—lots of them. Once the garbage was picked up, the Flubs did what they always had done best: They mounted a late rally that fell just short. Chicago scored three runs in the bottom of the ninth to cut Atlanta's lead to 5-4, but with two outs and the tying run on first base, Lee grounded out.

The Cubs now were two games behind Houston and San Francisco, both of which won that day. With two games left in the season, they would need more than a miracle. Nothing short of a complete overhaul of the heavens would suffice. Mathematically, the Cubs weren't dead—but in reality, they already had been loaded into a hearse and were on their way to the morgue. On the afternoon of October 2, The Mad Venezuelan got shelled, Catatonic Kyle punched a water cooler after another hair-raising relief appearance, and Atlanta, which used the game to limber up eight different pitchers for the playoffs, won 8-6.

The 2004 Cubs were officially dead.

"It's unexplainable, really," said Walker.

It always was.

The temperature was in the mid-60s on October 3, the last day of the season—quite pleasant for this time of year. Contrary to what *Sports Illustrated* predicted all those months ago, hell had not frozen over.

There was, however, a distinct chill in the Cubs' clubhouse that final morning. ESPN's NFL pregame show was playing on the televisions, and the words NEXT SIX DAYS, PULL IT ALL TOGETHER had been erased from the soft-marker board. The weight room was empty; there was no further reason to bulk up. The trainer's room was mostly empty, too; there was no further reason to heal up.

Ramirez wandered in about three hours before first pitch, sporting a leather jacket and haunted eyes. He was in no hurry to change into his uniform. Instead, he sat and stared despondently into his locker, as if he barely had the will to make the transformation from a civilian to a ballplayer one last time. Eventually, the leather jacket came off and the uniform went on.

Barrett hobbled down the clubhouse stairs, his pale face partially obscured by sunglasses. He had spent the season taking a pounding behind the plate—and had done so with aw-shucks charm—but for what? For *this*? He pulled off his sunglasses and said to two young acquaintances near his locker, "Tell the Braves to go fuck themselves." Michael Barrett wasn't feeling cordial anymore. Eventually, though, his uniform went on.

The players continued to drift into the clubhouse and cobble themselves together. Although they weren't going to the playoffs, they still had a job to do. Clement was cleanly shaven now, the Abraham Lincoln-goatee fad having gone the way of the Hula Hoop, but he was in uniform and ready to face the brokenhearted faithful. So was Prior.

And Wood. And Zambrano. And Farnsworth. And Hawkins. And Lee. And Alou. And Patterson. And the rest of the circus.

Garciaparra, his uniform on, sat in the dugout and reflected on it all. "We're disappointed," said the shortstop, who had gone from a savior to a casualty within two months and would become a free agent at the end of the day. "My goal every year is to try to win the World Series. We're not going to be able to go out and do that this year." Nevertheless, Garciaparra was ready to face the faithful. "My Cubs experience would be [classified as] unbelievable," he said. "Just to be welcomed the way I was. I love Wrigley Field, I love the city, and I love the fans."

Everyone was ready to face the faithful—everyone except the star attraction. His mitt was in his locker, and his boombox, though silent, was nearby. But Slammin' Sammy himself was nowhere to be found. Although Sosa was afflicted by an unnamed injury and wasn't scheduled to play that day, he was expected to be in uniform alongside his teammates. When asked about the whereabouts of his right fielder, Baker said, "Sammy's just ailing physically. I assume [he's here]. That's your job."

Apparently, Slammin' Sammy, the face of the franchise, didn't want his job anymore. He did appear at around noon, but he never put on his uniform and wound up leaving the ballpark at 1:35, just after the start of the game. "I'm tired of being blamed by Dusty Baker for all the failures of this club," said Sosa, he of the $16 million annual salary and the .253 batting average, to the *Chicago Sun-Times*. "I resent the inference that I'm not prepared. I live my life every minute, every day to prepare for combat." Not on this day. Sulkin' Sammy Sosa had deserted the team, *his* team. Maybe for the last time. His act of cowardice, this latest distraction, raised rampant speculation that the Cubs would do everything they could to get rid of him in the off-season, even if it meant eating some of the tens of millions of dollars they still owed him.

In that final game, the team—*his* team—faced the faithful without him. And it did just fine. The wind finally had changed directions and was gusting straight out, and Jason Dubois, a highly touted prospect starting in place of the AWOL Sulkin' Sammy, responded by slamming a two-run triple off the right field wall in the bottom of the first inning. In his next at-bat, Dubois hit a majestic home run, the first of his big-league career. "In my mind," Dubois said, "I have a good opportunity to be a starting outfielder here, but that's not up to me."

Following the traditional singing of "Take Me Out to the Ballgame" midway through the seventh inning, the crowd chanted "Stoney . . . Stoney," then gave the beleaguered broadcaster a standing ovation. A couple of innings later, after winning 10-8, the team itself received a standing ovation from the forgiving faithful. As a show of gratitude, the players did more than tip their caps—they tossed them into the grandstands like Frisbees.

And then the 2004 Chicago Cubs were gone.

While the players began packing their gear in the clubhouse, the Astros began celebrating. Houston had just beaten Colorado—its seventh consecutive victory—to capture the wild-card title by a game over the Giants. The contrast did not escape the Cubs. Walker had signed with Chicago in the off-season for the once-in-a-lifetime opportunity to help finally conquer this curse. Now the Astros—the very team he had pronounced dead back in August—were popping bottles of champagne, and he was standing next to neatly stacked boxes at his locker.

"It's been tough because we expected to make the playoffs up until three or four days ago, and it didn't happen," the second baseman said. "It's not that we didn't try, or that we had too much pressure—we just played, and it didn't work out. We felt great about this year, and look what happened. You can take from this year what you can take from it, which is: Expectations only carry you so far."

The morning of that final game in the season of great expectations, people were piled up by Wrigley Field's main entrance, anxiously waiting for the gates to open. Some of the usual faithful were absent, having sworn off the Cubs once and for all. But they'd return. They always returned. A record 3,170,172 fans had streamed through the old tuna boat's turnstiles in 2004, and future seasons would bring more of the same.

Mark Baumgartner, a 32-year-old accountant from Canada, was occupying a seat after the gates opened. This was his first visit ever. "My hometown in Canada had the [WGN] superstation, so I've been a fan for twenty years," he said in the measured tone of one who counted money for a living. "The fans have kind of shaken the Tribune Company into supporting the team, so I think perennially, we'll be closer every year now. For a long time in the 1980s and '90s, the Trib was just happy to maybe turn a profit. Now they seem to have put some money behind the team. I think the future is good."

Marion Kincade, age 73, was at Wrigley Field, too. He had made the pilgrimage from central Indiana. A Cubs fan ever since he was "old enough to know anything," he had a leathery face and a country drawl that dripped with nostalgia. "I started listening to them on the radio—we didn't have TV then. Bill Nicholson was my favorite. They'll win it someday, hopefully in my lifetime."

Six-year-old Steven Lussnig barely filled up half of his choice box seat. He was chewing on a soft pretzel while trying to absorb the whirl of pregame activity. If—when!—the Cubs finally won a World Series, what would it mean to this wide-eyed boy in the blue cap? "They would be the coolest team in the whole world."

They already were. Actually, the Cubs were more than a ball team. Much more. They were a symbol—a symbol of eternal hope in the face of constant, blistering defeat. The 2004 edition of the Cubs had turned out to be bums, crazies, and stooges, but maybe the next one would be different.

Dusty Baker's glass was half full. He already had beaten prostate cancer, in 2001. Someday he'd get this curse, too. "There are a few guys who have expressed interest in playing for the Cubs," the manager said with a sly smile. "They'd like to play here or play for me."

Ron Santo was predicting 95 victories for 2005.

Gladys Nunley was confident her brand-new knees would take her back to Wrigley Field.

Father Bernie would continue to fly his "W" flag in front of St. Raymond De Penafort on those days when the Cubbies rose.

Sports Illustrated's Larry Burke couldn't guarantee that he'd spare the Cubs from the cover of the magazine's 2005 baseball preview, but he figured some other team would be the pick.

Hope was hatching. Not the usual blind, misguided hope—but legitimate hope. Prior and Wood, the two anchors of the team, would be healthy in 2005. "That's why I'm so faithful about next year," Baker said, his smile growing wider. "You mean to tell me Wood's going to go 8-9 again and Prior's going to be 6-4? We all learned a lot this year."

Maddux would be around again to show those two young studs, as well as Zambrano, more about the right way to play the game. Ramirez would be entering the prime of his career, a scary thought for pitchers throughout the National League. Patterson would be a year older and a year wiser. Lee would keep hitting and fielding. Sweaty Joe would spend the winter working toward yet another comeback. And Hendry would be dialing his cell phone like a man on a mission, tinkering with his World Series brew.

Hope lived. Angel Guzman, a right-handed starter, was the team's prized prospect. He was so smooth and controlled on the mound, it was hard to believe he was only 22 years old. Pitching for the Cubs' Double-A affiliate in Tennessee in 2003, he posted a 2.81 earned run average and struck out 87 batters in 89.2 innings. Guzman, of course, had experienced some shoulder problems since then, but he was on the comeback trail. He was bound for Chicago, possibly by 2005. *Angel Guzman.* The name said it all. He could come down from the heavens and carry the faithful to The Promised Land on an angel's wings.

Maybe, just maybe, Wood and Prior and Maddux and The Mad Venezuelan and Ramirez and Patterson and Lee and Sweaty Joe and

Hendry's cell phone and Angel Guzman—or any combination thereof—would be enough to win that ever-elusive World Series title. Until it happened, until hell froze over, at least the beer at Wrigley Field would be cold.

APPENDIX 1
2004 Day-by-Day Results

APRIL

Date	Team	Result	Score	Winner	Loser
4/5	at Cincinnati	W	7-4	Wood	Lidle
4/7	at Cincinnati	L	3-1	Wilson	Maddux
4/8	at Cincinnati	L	5-3	Acevedo	Clement
4/9	at Atlanta	W	2-1	Mercker	Cunnane
4/10	at Atlanta	L	5-2	Alfonseca	Pratt
4/11	at Atlanta	W	10-2	Wood	Ortiz
4/12	vs. Pittsburgh	L	13-2	Benson	Maddux
4/14	vs. Pittsburgh	W	8-3	Clement	Vogelsong
4/15	vs. Pittsburgh	W	10-5	Zambrano	Fogg
4/16	vs. Cincinnati	W	11-10	Borowski	Graves
4/17	vs. Cincinnati	L	3-2	Wagner	Wood
4/18	vs. Cincinnati	L	11-10	Jones	Borowski
4/19	vs. Cincinnati	W	8-1	Clement	Haynes
4/20	at Pittsburgh	W	9-1	Zambrano	Vogelsong
4/21	at Pittsburgh	W	12-1	Mitre	Fogg
4/23	vs. N.Y. Mets	W	3-1	Maddux	Seo
4/24	vs. N.Y. Mets	W	3-0	Wood	Yates
4/25	vs. N.Y. Mets	W	4-1	Clement	Leiter
4/26	at Arizona	L	9-0	Johnson	Zambrano
4/27	at Arizona	L	10-1	Webb	Mitre
4/28	at Arizona	W	4-3	Hawkins	Mantei
4/30	at St. Louis	L	4-3	Kline	Farnsworth

April record: 13-9

MAY

Date	Team	Result	Score	Winner	Loser
5/1	at St. Louis	W	4-2	Clement	Suppan
5/2	at St. Louis	L	1-0	Isringhausen	Farnsworth
5/3	at St. Louis	W	7-3	Maddux	Marquis
5/4	vs. Arizona	L	6-3	Sparks	Mitre
5/5	vs. Arizona	L	2-0	Daigle	Wood
5/6	vs. Arizona	W	11-3	Clement	Dessens
5/7	vs. Colorado	W	11-0	Zambrano	Estes
5/8	vs. Colorado	L	4-3	Jennings	Maddux
5/9	vs. Colorado	W	5-4	Rusch	Fassero
5/11	at Los Angeles	L	7-3	Weaver	Wood
5/12	at Los Angeles	L	4-0	Alvarez	Clement
5/13	at Los Angeles	W	7-3	Zambrano	Nomo
5/14	at San Diego	W	6-1	Maddux	Valdez
5/15	at San Diego	W	7-5	Mitre	Eaton
5/16	at San Diego	W	4-2	Beltran	Wells
5/18	vs. San Francisco	L	1-0	Schmidt	Clement
5/19	vs. San Francisco	W	4-3	Borowski	Brower
5/20	vs. San Francisco	L	5-3	Herges	Borowski
5/21	vs. St. Louis	L	7-6	Carpenter	Mitre
5/22	vs. St. Louis	W	7-1	Rusch	Williams
5/23	vs. St. Louis	W	4-3	Clement	Morris
5/25	at Houston	L	5-0	Oswalt	Zambrano
5/26	at Houston	L	7-3	Lidge	Maddux
5/28	at Pittsburgh	L	9-5	Torres	Borowski
5/28	at Pittsburgh	L	5-4	Gonzalez	Beltran
5/29	at Pittsburgh	L	10-7	Fogg	Mitre
5/30	at Pittsburgh	W	12-1	Zambrano	Grabow
5/31	vs. Houston	W	3-1	Maddux	Oswalt

May record: 14-14
Season record: 27-23

JUNE

Date	Team	Result	Score	Winner	Loser
6/1	vs. Houston	L	5-3	Miceli	Farnsworth
6/2	vs. Houston	L	5-1	Clemens	Clement

Date	Team	Result	Score	Winner	Loser
6/4	vs. Pittsburgh	L	2-1	Torres	Borowski
6/5	vs. Pittsburgh	W	6-1	Zambrano	Benson
6/6	vs. Pittsburgh	W	4-1	Maddux	Vogelsong
6/7	vs. St. Louis	L	4-3	Carpenter	Rusch
6/8	vs. St. Louis	W	7-3	Clement	Williams
6/9	vs. St. Louis	L	12-4	Morris	Prior
6/10	vs. St. Louis	W	12-3	Zambrano	Haren
6/11	at Anaheim	L	3-2	Lackey	Maddux
6/12	at Anaheim	W	10-5	Rusch	Colon
6/13	at Anaheim	W	6-5	Leicester	Hensley
6/14	at Houston	W	7-2	Prior	Clemens
6/15	at Houston	W	4-2	Farnsworth	Dotel
6/16	at Houston	W	4-1	Maddux	Redding
6/17	at Houston	W	5-4	Rusch	Oswalt
6/18	vs. Oakland	L	2-1	Redman	Clement
6/19	vs. Oakland	W	4-3	Farnsworth	Bradford
6/20	vs. Oakland	W	5-3	Zambrano	Zito
6/22	at St. Louis	W	5-4	Farnsworth	Isringhausen
6/23	at St. Louis	L	10-9	Kline	Remlinger
6/24	at St. Louis	L	4-0	Carpenter	Clement
6/25	at White Sox	W	7-4	Prior	Garland
6/26	at White Sox	L	6-3	Diaz	Zambrano
6/27	at White Sox	L	9-4	Loaiza	Maddux
6/29	vs. Houston	W	7-5	Beltran	Weathers
6/30	vs. Houston	L	3-2	Lidge	Hawkins

June record: 15-12
Season record: 42-35

JULY

Date	Team	Result	Score	Winner	Loser
7/1	vs. Houston	W	5-4	Leicester	Lidge
7/2	vs. White Sox	W	6-2	Zambrano	Loaiza
7/3	vs. White Sox	W	4-2	Maddux	Diaz
7/4	vs. White Sox	W	2-1	Hawkins	Takatsu
7/5	at Milwaukee	L	1-0	Sheets	Clement

Date	Team	Result	Score	Winner	Loser
7/6	at Milwaukee	L	4-2	Santos	Prior
7/7	at Milwaukee	L	4-0	Davis	Zambrano
7/9	at St. Louis	L	6-1	Marquis	Maddux
7/10	at St. Louis	L	5-2	Suppan	Clement
7/11	at St. Louis	W	8-4	Wood	Carpenter
7/15	vs. Milwaukee	W	4-1	Rusch	Davis
7/16	vs. Milwaukee	L	3-2	Santos	Clement
7/17	vs. Milwaukee	W	5-0	Maddux	Sheets
7/18	vs. Milwaukee	L	4-2	Capuano	Beltran
7/19	vs. St. Louis	L	5-4	Carpenter	Zambrano
7/20	vs. St. Louis	L	11-8	King	Hawkins
7/21	vs. Cincinnati	W	5-4	Wellemeyer	Van Poppel
7/22	vs. Cincinnati	W	13-2	Maddux	Lidle
7/23	at Philadelphia	W	5-1	Wood	Myers
7/24	at Philadelphia	L	4-3	Abbott	Zambrano
7/25	at Philadelphia	L	3-2	Madson	Hawkins
7/26	at Milwaukee	W	3-1	Clement	Santos
7/27	at Milwaukee	W	7-1	Maddux	Sheets
7/28	at Milwaukee	L	6-3	Capuano	Wood
7/29	at Milwaukee	W	4-0	Zambrano	Hendrickson
7/30	vs. Philadelphia	W	10-7	Leicester	Cormier
7/31	vs. Philadelphia	L	4-3	Millwood	Clement

July record: 14-13

Season record: 56-48

AUGUST

Date	Team	Result	Score	Winner	Loser
8/1	vs. Philadelphia	W	6-3	Mercker	Wolf
8/3	at Colorado	W	5-3	Wood	Fassero
8/4	at Colorado	W	11-8	Farnsworth	Chacon
8/5	at Colorado	W	5-1	Prior	Jennings
8/6	at San Francisco	L	6-2	Schmidt	Clement
8/7	at San Francisco	W	8-4	Maddux	Hennessey
8/8	at San Francisco	L	6-3	Lowry	Wood
8/10	vs. San Diego	L	8-6	Eaton	Prior

Date	Team	Result	Score	Winner	Loser
8/11	vs. San Diego	W	5-1	Zambrano	Hitchcock
8/12	vs. San Diego	L	5-4	Stone	Dempster
8/13	vs. Los Angeles	L	8-1	Perez	Maddux
8/14	vs. Los Angeles	W	2-0	Wood	Ishii
8/15	vs. Los Angeles	L	8-5	Sanchez	Farnsworth
8/17	at Milwaukee	L	3-1	Santos	Zambrano
8/18	at Milwaukee	W	7-5	Mercker	Phelps
8/19	at Milwaukee	W	9-6	Maddux	Capuano
8/20	at Houston	W	9-2	Rusch	Munro
8/21	at Houston	L	4-3	Lidge	Hawkins
8/22	at Houston	W	11-6	Leicester	Oswalt
8/23	vs. Milwaukee	W	8-3	Zambrano	Sheets
8/24	vs. Milwaukee	W	13-4	Clement	Capuano
8/25	vs. Milwaukee	W	4-2	Hawkins	Vizcaino
8/26	vs. Houston	W	8-3	Prior	Backe
8/27	vs. Houston	L	15-7	Oswalt	Wood
8/28	vs. Houston	L	7-6	Clemens	Zambrano
8/29	vs. Houston	L	10-3	Hernandez	Clement
8/30	at Montreal	W	5-2	Maddux	Biddle
8/31	at Montreal	L	8-0	Hernandez	Prior

August record: 16-12
Season record: 72-60

SEPTEMBER

Date	Team	Result	Score	Winner	Loser
9/1	at Montreal	W	2-1	Hawkins	Vargas
9/6	vs. Montreal	W	9-1	Zambrano	Armas
9/7	vs. Montreal	L	7-6	Cordero	Wellemeyer
9/8	vs. Montreal	L	6-0	Downs	Maddux
9/10	vs. Florida	L	7-0	Pavano	Wood
9/10	vs. Florida	W	11-2	Prior	Kensing
9/11	vs. Florida	W	5-2	Dempster	Mota
9/12	vs. Florida	L	11-1	Burnett	Rusch
9/13	vs. Pittsburgh	W	7-2	Maddux	Brooks
9/14	vs. Pittsburgh	W	3-2	Wellemeyer	Meadows

Date	Team	Result	Score	Winner	Loser
9/15	vs. Pittsburgh	W	13-5	Wuertz	Perez
9/16	at Cincinnati	W	5-4	Wood	Wagner
9/17	at Cincinnati	W	12-4	Zambrano	Hudson
9/18	at Cincinnati	L	6-5	Harang	Maddux
9/19	at Cincinnati	W	5-1	Leicester	Graves
9/20	at Florida	W	5-1	Prior	Pavano
9/20	at Florida	L	5-2	Weathers	Clement
9/21	at Pittsburgh	W	5-4	Hawkins	Torres
9/22	at Pittsburgh	W	1-0	Zambrano	Perez
9/23	at Pittsburgh	W	6-3	Maddux	Figueroa
9/24	at N.Y. Mets	W	2-1	Remlinger	Looper
9/25	at N.Y. Mets	L	4-3	Seo	Mercker
9/26	at N.Y. Mets	L	3-2	Leiter	Wood
9/27	vs. Cincinnati	W	12-5	Zambrano	Claussen
9/28	vs. Cincinnati	L	8-3	Hancock	Maddux
9/29	vs. Cincinnati	L	4-3	Riedling	Leicester
9/30	vs. Cincinnati	L	2-1	Padilla	Remlinger

September record: 16-11
Season record: 88-71

OCTOBER

Date	Team	Result	Score	Winner	Loser
10/1	vs. Atlanta	L	5-4	Hampton	Wood
10/2	vs. Atlanta	L	8-6	Gryboski	Farnsworth
10/3	vs. Atlanta	W	10-8	Maddux	Byrd

October record: 1-2
Final record: 89-73

APPENDIX 2: Individual Statistics

BATTING

Player	BA	AB	R	H	2B	3B	HR	RBI	BB	SO	SB	E
Aramis Ramirez	.318	547	99	174	32	1	36	103	49	62	0	10
Todd Hollandsworth	.318	148	28	47	6	2	8	22	17	26	1	1
Mark Grudzielanek	.307	257	32	79	12	1	6	23	15	32	1	5
Nomar Garciaparra	.297	165	28	49	14	0	4	20	16	14	2	3
Moises Alou	.293	601	106	176	36	3	39	106	68	80	3	8
Michael Barrett	.287	456	55	131	32	6	16	65	33	64	1	6
Derrek Lee	.278	605	90	168	39	1	32	98	68	128	12	6
Todd Walker	.274	372	60	102	19	4	15	50	43	52	0	7
Jose Macias	.268	194	23	52	6	3	3	22	5	38	4	1
Corey Patterson	.266	631	91	168	33	6	24	72	45	168	32	1
Ben Grieve	.260	250	30	65	17	0	8	35	39	70	0	4
Neifi Perez	.255	381	40	97	17	1	4	39	24	41	1	8
Sammy Sosa	.253	478	69	121	21	0	35	80	56	133	0	4
Ramon Martinez	.246	260	22	64	15	1	3	30	26	40	1	9
Jason Dubois	.217	23	2	5	0	1	1	5	1	7	0	0
Paul Bako	.203	138	13	28	8	0	1	10	15	29	1	4
Tom Goodwin	.200	105	11	21	8	0	0	3	8	22	5	0
Calvin Murray	.200	5	2	1	0	0	0	1	1	0	0	0
Mike DiFelice	.000	3	0	0	0	0	0	0	0	1	0	0

PITCHING

Player	W	L	ERA	G	GS	SV	IP	H	R	ER	HR	BB	SO
Kent Mercker	3	1	2.55	71	0	0	53.0	39	15	15	4	27	51
LaTroy Hawkins	5	4	2.63	77	0	25	82.0	72	27	24	10	14	69
Carlos Zambrano	16	8	2.75	31	31	0	209.2	174	73	64	14	81	188
Mike Remlinger	1	2	3.44	48	0	2	36.2	33	16	14	3	16	35
Glendon Rusch	6	2	3.47	32	16	2	129.2	127	54	50	10	33	90
Matt Clement	9	13	3.68	30	30	0	181.0	155	79	74	23	77	190
Kerry Wood	8	9	3.72	22	22	0	140.1	127	62	58	16	51	144
Jon Leicester	5	1	3.89	32	0	0	41.2	40	20	18	7	15	35
Ryan Dempster	1	1	3.92	23	0	2	20.2	16	9	9	1	13	18
Greg Maddux	16	11	4.02	33	33	0	212.2	218	103	95	35	33	151
Mark Prior	6	4	4.02	21	21	0	118.2	112	53	53	14	48	139
Michael Wuertz	1	0	4.34	31	0	1	29.0	22	14	14	4	17	30
Kyle Farnsworth	4	5	4.73	72	0	0	66.2	67	39	35	10	33	78
Todd Wellemeyer	2	1	5.92	20	0	0	24.1	27	16	16	1	20	30
Sergio Mitre	2	4	6.62	12	9	0	51.2	71	38	38	6	20	37
Joe Borowski	2	4	8.02	22	0	0	21.1	27	19	19	3	15	17
Andy Pratt	0	1	21.60	4	0	0	1.2	0	4	4	0	7	1